Y0-BRY-561

INTERNATIONAL ECONOMIC REFORM

Collected Papers of Emile Despres

INTERNATIONAL ECONOMIC REFORM

COLLECTED PAPERS OF EMILE DESPRES

Edited by GERALD M. MEIER

New York
OXFORD UNIVERSITY PRESS
London 1973 Toronto

Library of Congress Catalogue Card Number: 72-88067
Printed in the United States of America

Editor's Foreword

Few, if any, economists can have exercised so much influence on their profession while remaining so unpublicized as has Emile Despres. He has been offering master lessons in international economics since the 1930's. This collection of his papers, most of which have been hitherto unpublished, reveals some of his insights over a period that spans more than three decades of extensive change, both in the world of economic thought and in economic affairs. In assessing these developments, Despres has shown not only supreme analytic powers as an academic economist but also remarkable intuition and judgment as one of the most acute policy advisors of his generation.

Despres's influence on policy began early when he went directly in 1930 from his undergraduate studies at Harvard to the Federal Reserve Bank of New York. During those years of world deflation, the Bank was to play an important role in international management. Despres immediately became a strong advocate of expansionary policies. He has remained so—always transforming the conventional or timid policy into a more imaginative or bolder recommendation. His writings in this volume on international trade, development, and monetary reform reflect these qualities as well as an exceptionally high level of analysis. This has also been characteristic of his successive activities at the Federal Reserve

System, Office of Strategic Services, State Department, Agency for International Development, and on visiting missions to less developed countries.

Although he has written relatively little under his own name, he has inspired many others to major advances in economic thought. For the professional economist, official policy-maker, and student alike, he has always had unlimited time to explore a theoretical point or policy issue. Many articles and books owe their genesis to their authors' discussions with Despres. Many public policy measures have been shaped by an official decision-maker's discussion with him. This influence was appropriately acknowledged in the citation upon his receipt of an honorary degree from Williams College:

> Recognized throughout your profession as perhaps the most original and insightful non-writing economist, you have warmed and refreshed us all as an observer of the human scene and proved in a world overwhelmed by print that a brilliant analyst and probing teacher need neither publish nor perish.

Although his influence has not had to depend on his pen, I have nonetheless thought it desirable to let a wider audience now have the benefit of some of Despres's written international economics commentary. I have therefore overborne his reticence and have happily persuaded him to collect his papers in international economics. This collection constitutes not only a unique commentary on international economic affairs since the 1930's, but also—what is even more significant—some incisive reflections on the larger questions of international political economy that still remain unresolved.

The first two papers, written before World War II, raise questions in connection with Britain's and Germany's foreign exchange policies that must yet be settled if there is to be progress toward international equilibrium. Quickly grasping the significance of Keynesian analysis, Despres was among the first to stress the problems of reconciling a country's policy of internal expansion with its external foreign exchange position. The paper on Germany's exchange control mechanism is especially notable for constituting what was probably the first recognition of the macro-economic significance of German trade and exchange controls under conditions of unemployment. It clearly shows an early appreciation of how Keynes's *General Theory* can apply to an open economy: Despres emphasizes that the German trade and exchange controls suppressed what was later to be termed the "foreign leakage" and thereby were devices that permitted Germany to pursue a fiscal policy for internal expansion without encountering the balance-of-payments deficits that would otherwise have frustrated such expansion. Despres also reconciles the macro-economic function of these external controls with classical theory regarding the effects of such controls on real income by indicating wherein their effects would differ under conditions of full employment. Furthermore, he anticipates a great deal of subsequent international monetary history in demonstrating how and why this method of stimulating employment without running into balance-of-payments difficulties was a more desirable policy for Germany than the conventional alternative of devaluation.

The other papers in Part I, written after the war, underscore the promising opportunity and urgent need for commercial arrangements that would achieve a genuine liberalization of trade and some modifications of international financial and monetary arrangements. The opportunity and need still remain.

As a pioneer among development advisors, Despres was also early in his warnings about some development problems that many economists are only now recognizing. The papers in Part II emphasize that the process of development in low-income countries sets up tendencies toward greater inequality; that there has been excessive concentration on the urban industrial sector; that price distortions weaken the development process; and that unemployment can remain a developing country's major problem in spite of capital accumulation and an increase in national output.

Despres's advocacy of the more ambitious policy is again well illustrated by his interpretation of the Pakistan Draft Development Plan (Paper 8) where a discussion of the basic resources available for development is unerringly directed to an analysis of how much of its development expenditure the government may finance by borrowing from the banking system without risking inflation. Observing that saving performed by the private sector is held mainly in the form of monetary assets, Despres concludes that the amount which the government can borrow from the banking system without causing inflation is not determined by conventional monetary rules of thumb but is determined by, and equal to, the excess of the private sector's saving over its direct investment. If the government does not borrow more than this amount, it need not fear that resulting increases in the money supply will be excessive. It should, however, adapt its borrowing instruments as much as possible to the demand of the market for financial assets.

Similarly unconventional and forthright are the recommendations to the Malaysian Planning Unit (Paper 11) advocating a vigorous use of foreign borrowing on the ground that it is necessary to avoid not only a decline in the rate of growth but also a deterioration in the balance-of-payments position, and insisting that "vigorous growth generates its own financing."

Perhaps of greatest immediate interest are the papers on international monetary reform in Part III. In the context of international monetary events following President Nixon's declarations of August 15, 1971, Despres's earlier proposals for demonetization of gold and the establishment of a world dollar standard are now of added significance. As an early interpreter of the key-currency approach to postwar international monetary arrangements and a persistent advocate of the demonetization of gold, he has again been ahead of his time and has had to wait for subsequent events to bear him out. It is, for example, noteworthy that he recommended as long ago as April 1963 the establishment of the two-tier gold market (Paper 13), five years before that policy was in fact adopted. Further, throughout the papers in Part III, Despres foresaw the unique role of the dollar as an international currency, and he forecast the dangers that a contained international monetary crisis would create for a system of liberal trade and international capital movements. As in his earlier papers, so too in his later papers he strongly opposes the forces of international restriction and retardation. These papers indicate that his have been not only essays in persuasion, but also in prophecy.

In editing this volume, I have had invaluable encouragement from Moses Abramovitz, Kermit Gordon, Charles P. Kindleberger, and Paul A. Samuelson. I am especially indebted to Walter S. Salant, who has been extraordinarily generous with his time and assistance.

Above all, I am gratified that Emile Despres has allowed this collection to be printed. It has been a privilege to work on his papers. I am pleased that many more, as readers, may now also be stimulated by his thoughts.

Stanford, Cal. G. M. M.
July 1972

Author's Preface

There is a heavy emphasis on policy in the selections in this volume. I might offer some retrospective comment on this.

I always had a morbid interest in witnessing the process of policy decision-making. Fairly early in my career I had the opportunity to gratify this interest. In the summer of 1931, when employed at the Federal Reserve Bank of New York, I was given the task of familiarizing myself with the short-term capital movement figures which the Reserve Bank had been collecting on a highly fragmentary basis from some of the New York banks. When the spreading international crisis overwhelmed sterling and resulted in British suspension of gold payments on September 21, 1931, the run against London was followed by a severe run against New York. I had the good fortune to accompany Randolph Burgess, who was Deputy Governor of the Reserve Bank, to Basle, where he was being sent to hear what the Central Bank heads would say at their monthly meeting at the Bank for International Settlements. Shortly after we set sail, Burgess received from New York a cable which I painfully decoded. It said that at the next Thursday meeting of the Board of Governors of the Federal Reserve System, it was likely that the decision would be taken to increase the discount rate, and Burgess was asked if he wished to express any views on this matter. Burgess asked my opinion, which I offered with passionate vigor. The underlying United States balance of payments was heavily in surplus. The gold outflow from the United States was due wholly to the flight of foreign balances from New York. Any attempt to beat the problem by intensifying deflation was likely to produce the most disastrous consequences for the United States, and its international consequences also would be rather frightening. Burgess agreed and instructed me to draft a cable along these lines to New York.

In due course a reply was received. I again laboriously deciphered it. The message reported that Burgess's views had been carefully considered at the Board meeting, and the Board expressed their thanks. They had decided to postpone their decision for twenty-four hours and meet again the following day. When the Board again met, they decided to go ahead with the increase in the discount rate. Our sole accomplishment was to delay by all of one day what was perhaps the most disastrous policy decision of the Great Depression! This initiation into policy formation always seemed to me like the story of my life.

A vigorous expansion policy by the Federal Reserve might have wholly averted the subsequent financial collapse and the breakdown of the institutional fabric in the United States. Perhaps, in retrospect, the devaluation of the dollar which finally ensued can be defended; something like this kind of nonsense was essential to get reflation at home under way. But when the United States did devalue, the important international effect was to reverse our meager remaining capital exports and induce capital inflows. As the United States balance on current account continued in surplus, our devaluation only intensified the world deflation.

One consequence of the failure in financial statesmanship by American authorities in this period was the collapse of the German external debt structure. American policy worked directly to choke off private credit to Germany and, indirectly, to increase substantially the real burden of her reparations through the deflation of world prices. Under normal financial conditions, Germany's large reparations burden would have been viable. Germany could still have been saved in late 1931 by an easy money policy in New York. For lack of this kind of support Germany eventually had no alternative but to repudiate her foreign debts—as the National

Socialists had been insisting all along. More immediately, when American creditors withdrew their support of the German financial structure, both a fiscal crisis and a substantial further increase in unemployment developed in the first half of 1932. These events contributed decisively to the decline of Germany's last hopes for parliamentary democracy.

We should have learned our lesson better. It is hard to overestimate the abiding gold-hunger of American officials. It was this fetish, perhaps more than anything else, which led the United States to reject Keynes's plan for the establishment of an International Clearing Union and to accept instead the White plan as a basis for the International Monetary Fund.

By contending (even if half-teasingly) that the surplus country is to blame for another country's deficit, Keynes's proposal for automatic overdrafts was calculated to maximize the antagonism of the United States. But even though it was not proposed in a diplomatic fashion, Keynes's plan did offer the possibilities for negotiating a superior international monetary system than that which was ultimately imposed on the world at Bretton Woods. The attitude at the time may have been that something is better than nothing, and Secretary of the Treasury Henry Morgenthau and Harry White may have had to be indulged. It is, however, ironical that if the American Treasury had been more receptive at Bretton Woods—if Keynes's proposal had been allowed to form a basis for more discussion—there need not have been the series of postwar international monetary crises, the trade and capital controls of recent years, and the dollar démarche of August 15, 1971.

A special word might be said about the selections in Part I relating to Europe's early post–World War II balance-of-payments problem. The fashionable doctrine at the time was that Europe faced a chronic dollar shortage. This view was widely retailed through a number of Organization for European Economic Cooperation publications. It is interesting to note that their argument followed precisely Chapter II of Keynes's *Economic Consequences of the Peace*. It will be recalled that this chapter simply asserted that the factors supporting Europe's prewar prosperity—high overseas investment income, handsome shipping receipts, favorable terms of trade against primary producers—had suffered tragic reversals during the war. Keynes became very nostalgic about the "1913 equilibrium," but argued that, like Humpty Dumpty, it could never be put together again. After World War II, his slavish imitators repeated the same argument. The methodology was simple: pick a prewar year—say, 1938—and extrapolate the worst. (The irony here is that 1938 was such a horrible year for the European economy that no one could be very nostalgic about *it*!) Understandably then, these observers regarded the prospects for Europe's regaining economic independence from the United States as very dim.

Pitted against this pessimistic view was the theory underlying the European reconstruction effort—essentially the same theory which had been proposed under the Young Plan in 1930 for extracting reparations from Germany. Capital exports to Germany would raise production dramatically. This would enable Germany to increase its export earnings and permit large reparations to be paid. Clearly the German experience under the Young Plan had not been very impressive. But that did not mean that there had been anything wrong with the theory. Capital export techniques for raising German productivity had never been tried!

Needless to say, the Marshall Plan did work. Perhaps too well! We are now relatively poorly prepared psychologically to accept the present problem of the dollar glut experienced by other industrial countries.

Anxiety over the gold stock and the United States balance-of-payments "deficit" intensified during the 1960's. Arthur Schlesinger, Jr., recounts that:

> The balance of payments remained a constant worry to [President John F.] Kennedy. Of all the problems he faced as President, one had the impression that he felt least at home with this one. He used to tell his advisers that the two things which scared him most were nuclear war and the payments deficit. Once he half-humorously derided the notion that nuclear weapons were essential to international prestige. "What really matters," he said, "is the strength of the currency. It is this, not the *force de frappe*, which makes France a factor. Britain has nuclear weapons, but the pound is weak, so everyone pushes it around. Why are people so nice to Spain today? Not because Spain has nuclear weapons, but because of all those lovely gold reserves." He had acquired somewhere, perhaps from his father, the belief that a nation was only as strong as the value of its currency; and he feared that, if he pushed

things too far, "loss of confidence" would descend and there would be a run on gold.[1]

As can be noted in Part III of this volume, my own papers during this period proposed gold demonetization and recognition of the unique functions of the dollar in world trade and capital markets. Much earlier, in the 1920's, Dennis Robertson had recognized the potential of the dollar standard. In discussing the value of money and the value of gold under the gold standard, Robertson observed that

> The world's demand for gold includes the demand of the particular country we are considering; and if that country be very large and rich and powerful, the value of gold is not something which she must take as given and settled by forces outside her control, but something which up to a point at least she can affect at will. It is open to such a country to maintain what is in effect an arbitrary standard, and to make the value of gold conform to the value of her money instead of making the value of her money conform to the value of gold. . . . [I]t would be misleading to say that in America the value of money is being kept equal to the value of a defined weight of gold: but it is true even there that the value of money and the value of a defined weight of gold are being kept equal to one another. We are not therefore forced into the inconveniently paradoxical statement that America is not on a gold standard. Nevertheless it is arguable that a truer impression of the state of the world's monetary affairs would be given by saying that America is on an arbitrary standard, while the rest of the world has climbed back painfully on to a dollar standard.[2]

I still believe that when I wrote the papers that now appear at the end of this volume, it was correct to urge demonetization of gold along the lines I proposed. I have left these papers in their original form—for the interest they may have as an interpretation of international monetary events prior to the imposition of the two-tier gold market in March 1968 and the formal suspension of the dollar's convertibility into gold on August 15, 1971.

In light of recent monetary developments, it now appears that

1. Arthur M. Schlesinger, Jr., *A Thousand Days* (Houghton Mifflin, 1965), pp. 654-55.

2. D. H. Robertson, *Money,* Cambridge Economic Handbook, 1928 edition, reprinted in 1948, Pitman Publishing Co., pp. 80-81.

John Williams was really right in emphasizing a key-currency approach to the postwar international monetary arrangements.[3] His proposal for a key-currency dollar area and sterling area, with mutual overdraft lines to moderate a floating dollar-pound rate, may still be considered as the best proposal available today. This proposal differs little in principle from my suggestion at the end of the Brookings study of the United States balance of payments that one possible solution for the international monetary problem might be reached through fixed exchange rates within the European Common Market and the dollar bloc and flexible rates between them.[4] Now that the United Kingdom is joining the European Economic Community it would be possible to make London the real capital market for the Common Market, and have a stable rate among the Common Market members, with each member's currency pegged against sterling, and then some flexibility in the rate between the dollar bloc and the Common Market. Such an arrangement may now restore international monetary order and provide a more permissive environment for international economic expansion. And if all these papers have any moral, it is that expansionary policies are to be favored whenever appropriate.

My lifelong aversion to writing for print must have made the task of editing this volume particularly onerous. Although I accept full blame for its inherent shortcomings, G. M. Meier deserves large credit for conceiving order out of chaos and producing essays from notes and fragments. Walter Salant offered valuable suggestions on selections to be included and other editorial advice. Moses Abramovitz performed the painstaking task of reading early manuscripts. Lorie Tarshis previously urged publication of the international monetary papers. Part of this Introduction originated in a draft composed by David Dod; I also apprecite the assistance of Patricia DeCoster. To them all, and especially Jerry Meier, I am immeasurably grateful.

Stanford, Cal. E. D.
July 1972

3. J. H. Williams, *Postwar Monetary Plans and Other Essays* (A. A. Knopf, 1944), Part I.

4. Walter S. Salant et al., *The United States Balance of Payments in 1968* (Brookings Institution, 1963), p. 259. It is true that, at the time, this idea was offered as an alternative to an increase in reserves; but the two are not mutually exclusive.

Contents

I INTERNATIONAL TRADE

1 *Britain's Foreign Exchange Policy* 3
2 *Germany's Exchange Control Mechanism* 13
3 *American Aid and Western European Recovery* 28
4 *Western Europe's Long-Term Balance-of-Payments Problem* 39
5 *The Mechanism for Adjustment in International Payments—the Lessons of Postwar Experience* 45
6 *The Significance of the European Common Market to the American Economy* 60

II INTERNATIONAL DEVELOPMENT

7 *Dimensions and Dilemmas of Economic Development* 89
8 *Determining the Size of a Development Plan: Pakistan* 99
9 *Price Distortions and Development Planning: Pakistan* 133
10 *The Welfare State and Development Expenditure: Pakistan* 146

11 *Financing Development: Malaysia* 154
12 *Inflation and Development: Brazil* 184

III *INTERNATIONAL MONETARY REFORM*

13 *Capital Movements, Gold, and Balance of Payments* 209
14 *A Proposal for Strengthening the Dollar* 213
15 *Toward the Demonetization of Gold* 236
16 *International Financial Intermediation* 257
17 *The Dollar and World Liquidity: a Minority View* 266
18 *Gold–Where To From Here?* 279

Index 289

I *INTERNATIONAL TRADE*

1 *Britain's Foreign Exchange Policy*[1]

The British authorities seem disposed to adhere rather rigidly to fairly well-defined guiding principles governing the technique of exchange rate management. The most notable features of their operating methods are a thoroughgoing empiricism and a resolute avoidance of commitments. The background of influences of which these methods are the outgrowth is more difficult for an American visitor to understand than are the operating practices themselves. These practices, in fact, are quite simple, almost incredibly simple, and the feeling of perplexity which is likely

1. From a Report on European Economic Conditions, written in 1938 for the Federal Reserve Bank of New York, based on a trip through Western European countries with L. Werner Knoke, a vice-president of the Federal Reserve Bank of New York. The purpose of this trip was to visit the major central banks of Western Europe and report on monetary affairs. The Report was written by Despres, who was at that time the Chief of the Foreign Information Division of the Federal Reserve Bank of New York.

During the prewar period under review in this Report, the British Exchange Equalization Account attempted to keep the dollar-sterling rate fairly stable. At the same time, the "gold-bloc" countries—notably France, Switzerland, Belgium, the Netherlands—had agreed at the London Economic Conference in July 1933 to stay on gold at existing parities. The gold-bloc countries attempted to maintain their exchange parities during the depression years but were subject to increasing exchange pressures, ultimately experiencing devaluations in 1936. Throughout the period, Nazi Germany maintained and increased exchange controls and restrictions over capital movements and trade.—Ed.

to be experienced in discussing technical problems of exchange management with the operating officials in London is due less to subtleties in the British operating technique than to a difficulty in understanding why the simple operating rules are almost literally followed. Before proceeding to a discussion of operating methods, it seems desirable to review the factors in the background which lie behind British foreign exchange policy.

In our judgment the principal factors to be kept firmly in mind in seeking to understand and interpret British foreign exchange policy are: (1) the present strong public preference for managed currency; (2) the precariousness, according to the view in responsible British quarters, of the whole structure of international currency relationships; and (3) the potential vulnerability of the British balance-of-payments position. Of these three factors, the second was continually emphasized in discussions at the Bank of England, the first was referred to on several occasions but was not stressed, and there was considerable reluctance to discuss the third.

With respect to the first factor, one official of the Bank of England said that outside the City virtually no one in England favors a return to a regime of fixed exchange parities, even as a remote and distant objective. Memories of the chronic depression or semi-depression during the postwar gold standard period and of the marked recovery which followed the suspension of gold payments are largely responsible for the prevailing popular attitude. It was suggested that public opinion on this score will change "only after the public has lost its faith in human ability permanently to manage a currency." At the Bank of England, a return to some modified form of an international gold standard is apparently looked forward to as a distant hope, but the assumption by the British of any commitments, however tentative, with respect to the range of possible fluctuation in the gold value of sterling is regarded as very nearly out of the question within the foreseeable future.

With respect to the second factor, the structure of monetary relationships is held to be so precarious and delicately poised that any significant departure from existing arrangements, in whatever direction, might have highly unfortunate and unpredictable consequences.

1. The end of French difficulties is not yet in sight, and it was said in London that England would have no alternative but to accept further franc devaluation, if this step were decided upon. The effect on other currencies and on the Tripartite Agreement itself of further changes in the status of the franc cannot be foretold. It is thought at the Bank of England, and, we later gathered, at the Dutch and Swiss banks of issue, though not at the National Bank of Belgium, that the psychological links between the Belgian and French currencies are so close that the Belgians could scarcely withstand the flight of capital which would be likely to follow a further change in the French currency.

2. Despite the stability of the American dollar price of gold over a period of four and a half years, the officials of the Bank of England concerned with exchange rate management regard the American monetary objectives, and consequently the status of the dollar, as far from settled. The violence of our economic fluctuations, the apparent turbulence of the American political scene, and the fact that, in their view, our basic monetary and financial ideas are in a state of fluidity provide the basis for the attitude held in these quarters regarding the dollar.

3. The war danger is of importance in this connection, both because of its influence on private capital flows and gold hoarding and because the possibility of war is actively taken into account in official circles in its bearing on all aspects of public policy, including monetary and exchange policy. For example, it was apparent that a good deal of thought had been given to the question as to what American gold and exchange policy would be in the event of a European war.

4. It was held that the type of monetary standard which can operate effectively at a particular time is determined in part by the prevailing psychological background, and it is regarded as quite impossible under existing world condi-

tions to establish the type of faith which would be necessary for the successful functioning of a more ordered and uniform international monetary system. Under the old gold standard, it was pointed out, established exchange parities were taken for granted as almost immutable, with the result that the market itself performed most of the job of maintaining rates within the gold points, gold being shipped only in small amounts and as a last resort. Under present conditions, on the other hand, gold movements are called upon to play a much larger role in the settlement of international balances, since much less assistance is received from the market. In this connection, it is significant that attempts to hide the Equilization Account's operations from the market have been entirely abandoned in the hope that the market, after observing and becoming familiar with the Account's manner of operations, will be able to anticipate the Account's moves and will itself assume some part of the task of ironing out fluctuations. It was said, however, that the exchange dealers in London continue, by and large, to be reluctant to share in this function and hold rather rigidly to even, or almost even, positions in exchange. One of the merits of the Tripartite Agreement, it was suggested, was that it furnished a useful mechanism for effecting gold transfers without the necessity for extensive preliminary cooperation and collaboration between countries in the formulation of exchange rate policy. In other words, a machinery for gold transfers had been established among the participating countries, but it left individual countries wide latitude in the formation of their own national policies with respect to the foreign exchanges. This, it was held, was essential in view of the widely divergent views among the participating countries regarding monetary and exchange policy.

5. Some feeling of uncertainty regarding the maintenance in the future of the present high monetary value of gold itself should probably be listed as one of the elements lying behind the British view that the structure of currency relationships is highly precarious. While the gold scare of 1937

has definitely descended into the background for the present,[2] there is some feeling that this problem may recur in the event of war, or a restoration of prosperity in one or more major countries.

Only veiled references were made by the people with whom we spoke to the third factor mentioned above, England's relatively exposed and potentially vulnerable balance-of-payments position, but in our judgment this factor should not be left out of account in seeking to interpret British exchange policy. Owing to the failure during the postwar gold standard period of the traditional method of correcting a weak balance-of-payments position through deflationary credit policy and to the effects of this policy in accentuating internal economic strain, this method of combatting exchange weakness has become almost completely discredited in England. Moreover, in adopting protectionism and imposing controls on foreign investment, Great Britain has, in effect, "shot her bolt" in applying measures which operate directly to strengthen the balance of payments. It is true, of course, that further measures which would impinge directly upon the balance of payments could be applied, but the application of such measures on an extensive scale would probably be considered only in an emergency, if at all. In view of these considerations the British authorities can hardly fail to be aware of the question as to how a balance-of-payments deficit, if it became really chronic, could be corrected otherwise than through exchange depreciation. We do not wish to suggest that the present deficit in the British balance of payments is clearly of this type. Indeed, its present size is due in considerable part to the rapid business decline in the United States, which through its effects on basic commodity markets and on the purchasing power of outlying countries has resulted in a contraction in demand for British

2. During the spring of 1937, rumors persisted that the United States might lower the dollar price of gold, and it was expected that other countries might follow suit. During this "gold scare" the demand for dollars increased and the amount of gold held in London on private account declined considerably. Later in the year, with the slump in business activity in the United States, there was a fear that the dollar might be devalued as an anti-recession measure, and the "gold scare" then reversed itself into a "dollar scare."—Ed.

goods, reduced shipping receipts, and smaller income from overseas investments. Since British business, and consequently her volume of imports, have been well sustained, these losses have been only partly counterbalanced by the lower cost of imported goods. Moreover, the inability of raw-material-producing countries to contract their imports promptly in keeping with the lower prices of the exports has caused these countries to draw upon their accumulated London balances to cover their balance-of-payments deficits, and this largely temporary factor has probably been a more substantial source of commercial pressure against sterling than the balance of payments of Great Britain itself. Nevertheless, British reluctance to assume commitments regarding exchange rate policy probably reflects in part a feeling of doubt regarding Great Britain's ability to make a sustained defense of any particular rate or range of rates, if such a defense should be called for.

The preceding observations may be broadly summarized by saying that the operating officials at the Bank of England consider a purely empirical exchange rate policy which avoids definite commitments of any sort to be essential because under present-day conditions market forces may become irresistibly strong, the future seems highly uncertain, and the British public is still firmly convinced of the merits of a flexible monetary standard. Consequently, as was repeatedly emphasized, the basic operating rule governing exchange rate management is that it is always unwise to fight strongly against a market tendency and that the proper objective of official intervention should be merely to cushion the market. It should be underscored that this represents for the British not a vague statement of general objectives prepared for public consumption but an actual operating rule. Officials at the Bank of England think that the French have made a major technical blunder in seeking at various times to maintain particular rates or ranges of rates, and they said, putting the matter perhaps too strongly, that in their own operations they never had in mind an exchange rate or a gold price, and that they always bend before a storm. (Incidentally, it is questionable whether it was open to the French authorities to imitate the British practice in view of the French public's strong distaste for freely fluctuating currencies and the obligations assumed by France under the Tripartite Agreement.)[3]

The implications of this rule may be traced in their application to day-to-day operations. For example, it was said that the setting of gold prices or exchange rates at which the Bank would stand ready to deal with the market, even though such prices or rates might be varied from day to day, would involve too great a commitment. The gold prices at which the Bank deals with continental European central banks are subject to change during the day, and Bank officials feel that they are going quite far in fixing buying and selling prices good overnight for dealings with the American Stabilization Fund.

During recent years the Equalization Account's operations in the bullion market have exceeded in magnitude its exchange dealings, and it may broadly be said that the exchange value of sterling has been largely controlled through the London gold price rather than the other way around. Nevertheless, we gathered that the officials at the Bank of England tend frequently to view their bullion operations almost as if the bullion market were in a separate watertight compartment divorced from the exchange market, and that in gauging their operations they seem to focus their attention rather narrowly on the supply and demand situation in the bullion market itself.

The empiricism of British exchange policy is clearly brought out in the methods by which the tendency of the market is determined. Efforts are, of course, made to determine through market contacts and observation the character of the forces at work, and some slight attempt is made to distinguish superficial and

3. In a joint announcement of the devaluation of the French franc on September 25, 1936, the governments of France, Britain, and the United States also promised to avoid competitive exchange depreciation among their currencies, declared their governments in favor of relaxing trade and exchange controls, and asked other countries to join in similar pledges. This so-called Tripartite Monetary Agreement was also adopted in late 1936 by Belgium, Holland, and Switzerland. Policy commitments supplementary to the original Agreement involved cooperation among the British, French, and American exchange funds and provided for convertibility of the franc, pound, and dollar at fixed prices prevailing from day to day.

See also Despres's suggestions in 1959 that the Tripartite Monetary Agreement be revived in new form between the European Common Market countries, Britain, and the United States (Paper 6., p. 75 below).—Ed.

transitory influences from those which are more durable and persistent. In view of the complexity of present-day market conditions, however, chief reliance seems to be placed on a series of charts depicting past movements of exchange rates, both absolutely and in relation to the changing London gold price. By an examination of movements in these charts over the recent part, it is thought possible to estimate whether the prevailing tendency of sterling is strong or weak. The technique here seems essentially comparable to the various chart-reading methods of forecasting stock prices. Without inquiring into the general validity of such techniques from the standpoint of an ordinary market operator, it may be questioned whether the method is an appropriate one for a controlling authority, since the past movements shown on the charts are very largely influenced by the direction and scale of the control's own past operations.

Regarding the present position of sterling, the view taken by the operating officials at the Bank was that the prevailing tendency was definitely toward weakness. As noted earlier, it was said that the Account has been intervening more vigorously to check the downward movement than a rigid application of its customary operating rules would permit. The officials at the Bank have been inclined to ascribe the pound's weakness very largely to war fears, and when we left London they had only begun to admit that economic factors were also having some influence on the sterling market. The view was generally held in Continental centers that purely commercial factors were playing an important part in the weakness of sterling, and it was our impression that the expectation that the pound would weaken for purely commercial reasons had fully as much as war fears to do with the shifting of liquid funds out of sterling into gold and dollars. It is not our intention to suggest that war fears have not been a significant factor—but it appears to us that the bearish attitude toward sterling over recent months has rested in considerable part on an appraisal of the commercial factors at work.

The combined balance-of-payments position of Great Britain and the sterling area countries has undoubtedly shown deterioration during the past year. Exports, shipping receipts, and income from overseas investments have undergone contraction, and although lower prices have meant some saving in the cost of imports, the armament program and the fact that British prosperity generally has been relatively well maintained have prevented any substantial curtailment in volume of goods imported. A considerable decline in invisible receipts has consequently been accompanied by an increase in the passive balance on merchandise account.

Changes during the past year in the international accounts of those raw-material-producing countries which hold their international reserves in London have probably been a more important source of commercial pressure against sterling than have the developments in the balance of commercial and income payments of Great Britain proper. These countries, faced with sharp declines in the prices of their principal export products, found it difficult to effect quickly a corresponding contraction of their imports, and they were forced to draw extensively on their sterling reserves to cover the deficits on their own international accounts. Such countries as Argentina, Australia, and India made large inroads on their accumulated London balances. The current deficit in the combined international accounts of Great Britain and the sterling area has been the principal counterpart, from a world standpoint, of the United States' large export surplus.

Apart from the unpredictable changes in the intensity of war fears, the prospects for an early cessation of pressure against sterling appear remote. The sterling market is, in a technical sense, becoming progressively less able to absorb heavy commercial demands for dollars. Until recently, the large balance due the United States on merchandise account was settled by drawing upon accumulated foreign balances in New York. These balances represented, in effect, the floating supply of dollars which became rather readily available to the exchange for current settlements in response to a relatively small firming of dollar exchange. The rapid drawing-down of this floating supply may well mean that the settlement of commercial accounts will tend to be effected more largely through gold movements in the future.

Taking a longer view, there are grounds for believing that the commercial pressure against sterling may itself subside. In the first place, the deficit in the international accounts of the countries which maintain their reserves in sterling is due to the lagging nature of the process by which imports are curtailed in response to a sharp decline in the prices of raw materials exports. These countries cannot persist, however, in covering balance-of-payments deficits by drawing on international reserves, and they have already made considerable progress in adjusting their imports to the lower prices of their exports. In the second place, a substantial recovery in the United States, through its effects on raw commodity prices, and on the export volumes of outlying countries, would increase the international receipts of these countries, thereby enabling them to replenish their depleted sterling reserves. Moreover, recovery in the United States, through its effects on purchasing power throughout the world, should increase the general demand for British exports. Finally, a continuing gradual decline in British business activity would doubtless be accompanied by a slow contraction in import volumes. During the past year the combined effect of a sharp business decline in the United States and relatively well sustained prosperity in England has been to intensify greatly the commercial pressure against sterling; correspondingly, substantial recovery in the United States accompanied by a slow further recession in England would serve to relieve this pressure. If we make substantial progress towards recovery in the first half of 1938 while trade in England continues to recede slowly, an abatement of commercial pressure against sterling might reasonably be expected; whether this abatement of commercial pressure would be in some measure offset by a renewed movement of investment funds from London to New York for the purchase of American securities cannot be foretold.

As is well known, one of the conspicuous features of the London market in recent months has been the heavy private demand for gold. Though a large part of this movement into gold has been linked to additional transfers of funds from foreign centers, a considerable portion of the movement into gold, particularly during recent months, has represented a switching of funds out of previously acquired sterling balances and investments. It is only the second type of movement which has contributed to the pressure against sterling.

2 *Germany's Exchange Control Mechanism*[1]

Germany's elaborate machinery of exchange control was the outgrowth of the banking and credit moratorium of 1931 and of the efforts, begun in 1932 and intensified after Hitler's achievement of power in 1933, to reconcile a program of restoring employment through internal expansion financed by public borrowing with the facts of Germany's international economic position. That special measures were necessary is at once apparent when one recalls that Germany undertook to combat unemployment through internal expansion at a time when her ability to import was drastically limited owing to the virtual exhaustion of her international reserves, her poor credit standing, and her depressed export markets. It was the urgency of the unemployment problem, and the consequent necessity of seeking an expansion of internal activity in spite of the limitations imposed by Germany's international position, which led to the progressive elaboration of control over the whole range of both external transactions and internal economic life. Germany's present coherent system of controlled economy, though now maintained consciously and deliberately for the fulfillment of specifically National Socialist objectives, developed almost accidentally as the result of a series of measures designed primarily to meet particular economic embarrassments. The sys-

1. Note 1 to Paper 1 is also applicable to this paper.—Ed.

tem was the outgrowth of the banking and credit moratorium and of the subsequent efforts to restore employment in the face of the limitations imposed by Germany's international position.

A systematic account, or even a comprehensive summary, of the mechanism through which control is exercised over Germany's international transactions would lie outside the scope of these notes. Since the broad outlines of the system are generally known, all that will be attempted here is to summarize the particular facts and impressions gathered as the result of conversations with German officials. Information regarding exchange control was obtained through conversations with officials of the Reichsbank's foreign exchange department and with the heads of some of the special agencies which form part of the general exchange control machinery, such as the Conversion Office, the Clearing Office, and the Gold Discount Bank.

Some hint of the elaborateness of the administrative machinery required for exchange control is revealed in the fact that the Reichsbank's exchange department employs in its Berlin office several thousand workers and an even larger number in its branches outside Berlin. This represents but a small part of the whole machinery of exchange control. There are, in addition, twenty-six supervisory offices for imports, one for each major category of goods, which have charge of the granting of permits to individual importers and supervise the negotiation of compensation and barter arrangements. A clearing office maintains the records which are required for the functioning of Germany's numerous clearing agreements with foreign countries. It was said that about half of Germany's external trade passes through clearing accounts. The largest clearing is done with Holland, Italy ranking second and Switzerland third. A conversion office has been established to issue funding securities to foreign holders of German bonds against the receipt of interest payments in reichsmarks from the debtors, and to act as the depository of blocked reichsmarks resulting from repayments of principal. Special agreements with respect to long-term debt service have been entered into by the conversion office with twelve foreign countries, the most important agreements being with Holland and Switzerland. The Gold Discount Bank pays subsidies to exporters and collects the special taxes for this purpose. The number of border officials has been greatly increased, since in addition to the customs officers, special officials are required to inspect outgoing shipments in order to detect possible undervaluation of exports, and an additional staff of inspectors is required to enforce the rigid restrictions governing the taking of currency across the border. Finally, both the regular police and the secret police seek to detect violations of the exchange regulations.

The principal tasks of the exchange control machinery consist in the mobilization of exchange resulting from exports and its allocation among the various categories of imports. With respect to the first task, exporters are required to file a declaration with the Reichsbank prior to each shipment of merchandise, giving all relevant details including terms of sale and expected date and form of payment. A duplicate of this declaration is attached to the goods; after examination by border officials the duplicate is transmitted by them to the Reichsbank. Exporters are obliged to deliver all exchange within three days after receipt to the Reichsbank or to another bank authorized to act as its agent, and these declarations enable the Reichsbank to see that this regulation is observed. Exporters receive only the official rate for foreign currencies, but manufacturers in most industries are periodically paid a subsidy on their total foreign business. The official exchange rates are established each day at one o'clock by a representative of the Reichsbank at the Berlin Bourse. No exchange business is done at the Bourse, and the announcement of the official rates on the Bourse merely provides a means of informing the banks of the rates at which exchange may be furnished to holders of import permits. In his business with importers the exchange dealer adds his own commission to the official quotations. The Reichsbank buys forward exchange from a few large concerns doing an extensive export business, such as the I. G. Farbenindustrie, when the need for providing hedging facilities of this sort can be demonstrated, but with this exception there are no forward transactions in Germany. Term bills in foreign currencies are purchased by the Reichsbank from exporters at spot rates less discount based upon the central bank discount rate of the country on which the bill is drawn. The exporter who is trading with a country whose currency is under severe pressure thus secures relatively favorable terms from the Reichsbank on his time drafts, but this, it was said, was essential to enable the German exporter to compete effectively in such markets.

The task of allocating exchange among the various categories of imports is supervised by a committee composed of representatives of the various ministries. Authority in this field is of great importance in determining the direction of German economic activity. Prior to Schacht's resignation as Minister of Economics, he exercised authority over the allocation of exchange for imports, and, in fact, over the whole field of both foreign trade and internal finance; but we were repeatedly told, both in Berlin and elsewhere, that Dr. Schacht had now largely withdrawn from participation in the formulation of policies and was now merely the technical head of the Reichsbank.

Reports are also furnished by the twenty-six supervisory offices for imports with respect to such matters as stocks, imports, and domestic consumption of imported goods, and on the basis of this and other information the committee allocates the available exchange "in accordance with National Socialist objectives." In its decisions the committee is obliged, of course, to observe the requirements of the clearing and payments agreements to which Germany is a party. These agreements, besides specifying the proportion of the proceeds of German exports which shall be expended by Germany for the purchase of goods and services from the importing country, frequently contain numerous requirements governing expenditure on particular goods and services. For example, the payments agreement with Great Britain calls for certain purchases of British textiles and clothing, the one with France requires purchases of French wines, and the clearing agreement with Switzerland sets aside a small sum for German travel in Switzerland.

This committee, together with the Ministry of Economics, has general supervision over the special compensation arrangements entered into by German importers of raw materials with certain exporting countries, under which the importer makes payment in compensation marks which may be used only for the purchase by the exporting country of certain specified types of German goods.

Regret was expressed by officials at the Reichsbank at the fact that these compensation marks were dealt in at substantial discounts in foreign markets in which German importers have compensation arrangements, but they denied that the existence of this discount amounted, in effect, to dumping of exports. It is entirely understandable that the existence of wide discounts on compensation marks was a source of regret, since such discounts serve, in effect, to raise the cost to Germany of her imports. The Reichsbank has sought to make arrangements with foreign central banks to prevent the development of excessive discounts on compensation marks, but has been successful only in Argentina. Its difficulties in handling this problem were substantial, it was said, because the Ministry of Economics sometimes puts through arrangements which are economically unsound, such as the one which provides for Uruguayan wool purchases at a considerably higher cost than that for comparable New Zealand grades.

After the decisions of the committee supervising the allocation of exchange have been made, the various supervisory officials are advised concerning the total value of import permits they may issue. These offices, in turn, grant import permits to the individual firms under their jurisdiction in conformity with their total authorizations.

On the basis of the above description, it would appear that expenditure on imports is very rigidly tied to receipts from exports. While this is approximately the case, there is, nevertheless, a considerably larger measure of day-to-day elasticity than would at first appear. First, in addition to its published gold and exchange reserves of about 75 million reichsmarks, the Reichsbank holds a varying amount of gold, usually, it was said, in the neighborhood of 100 million reichsmarks, which is included in the published statement among miscellaneous assets and which was described as a hedge against import permits issued. The former gold holdings of the Austrian National Bank are now the property of the German government, and are included among the Reichsbank's assets. Second, through the compensation arrangements entered into with many foreign suppliers of raw materials, it is possible for German imports to run ahead of exports, the outstanding amount of compensation marks representing, in effect, an extension of credit to Germany by the exporting countries. We are unable to learn the amount of compensation marks which had been paid to foreign exporters and not yet expended for the purchase of German goods, but it was suggested that the figure was not insignificant. Similarly, Germany, by permitting her debit balance on clearing account to grow, can increase imports from countries with which she has clearing agreements without correspondingly increasing her exports. By accumulating a debit balance on clearing account of 600 million reichsmarks during 1933 and 1934, before the machinery of foreign trade control had reached its present state of refinement, Germany was able to obtain needed imports despite her small reserves of gold and foreign exchange, poor credit standing, and limited export markets. Following the substitution of import permits for exchange permits and the inauguration of an export subsidy scheme under the so-called New Plan inaugurated in September 1934, the growth in clearing debt was halted, and it was said that the net debit balance on clearing account had been reduced by the end of 1937 to 200 million reichsmarks, equivalent to only 40 per cent of one month's exports. The extensive network of clearing agreements continues, however, to provide Germany with a potential source of foreign credit which could presumably be drawn upon if necessary for the acquisition of imports, and, in practice, variations of considerable magnitude are continually occurring in the net balances in Germany's clearing accounts with individual foreign countries.

It is frequently stated that what Germany has gained through exchange restrictions, clearing and compensation arrangements, and export subsidies might have been more readily obtained simply through devaluation of the reichsmark. This view overlooks a number of important considerations.

First, as regards restriction of capital movements, devaluation would not have obviated the need for checking the withdrawal of foreign short-term credits nor for prohibiting the flight of domestic capital. Some sort of standstill arrangement was indispensable after the 1931 crisis, and restrictions on domestic capital exports have had to be maintained, in view of National Socialist policies, not only to prevent the flight of Jewish capital but also because outlets for the investment of current savings within Germany are virtually confined to Reich securities and government-sponsored undertakings.

Second, as regards rationing of exchange for imports, it is frequently held that this was essential only because of the overvaluation of the reichsmark (at the official rate), and that if devaluation had been undertaken the allocation of exchange for imports might have been permitted to take place through the natural play of market forces. The available external purchasing power would automatically have gone to pay for those goods which were in heaviest market demand; the controlled allotment of exchange for imports, and the progressive extension of price control and rationing methods throughout the whole economy, would consequently have become superfluous. For example, very high prices for clothing made from imported wool or cotton would have stimulated an increased domestic production of synthetic fibers without special government planning. Similarly, very high prices for meats and dairy products would have made it necessary for ordinary consumers drastically to curtail their total expenditure on these articles and to concentrate their expenditures on the cheaper foods, thus making it advantageous for German farmers to shift from the raising of fodder and livestock to the production of bread grains and potatoes.

In our judgment, however, it is most doubtful that devaluation without an extension of direct government control over the whole range of Germany's economic life would have produced the same final results as did the measures which were actually adopted. From the very beginning of the program of internal expansion, Germany faced a bottleneck with respect to imports. The government was eager that a given amount of public expenditure should have the largest possible effect in increasing employment rather than in raising prices, and it was dangerous from this standpoint to permit market forces to have free play. The import bottleneck has been made even narrower by reason of the fact that a large part of the available external purchasing power has been allocated for raw materials required by the armament program and, more recently, the Four Year Plan. It is doubtful that such large amounts of imported raw materials could have been obtained for the uses of the State without rationing methods and merely by competitive bidding in the market. The diverting of external purchasing power to the uses of the State certainly could not have occurred on anything like the present scale without an enormous rise in the prices of imported goods and a very large devaluation of the reichsmark. Devaluation of around 40 per cent to restore the old relationship with the dollar and sterling would clearly have been far from sufficient.

Finally, the methods adopted by Germany—export subsidies, and clearing and compensation agreements—have, in our judgment, done more to increase her ability to import than would have been possible through devaluation. It is frequently alleged that export subsidies are merely the equivalent of devaluation in their effect on exports. This is in a sense true, but it is important to recognize that whereas devaluation operates more or less uniformly over the whole field of exports, the subsidy device can be separately adjusted for each category of merchandise. Manufacturers of cameras and optical instruments receive no subsidy whatever because of Germany's pre-eminence in this field and because it is felt that the increased volume of export sales which would result if these products were offered abroad at a lower price would not be sufficient to compensate for the price reduction. On the other hand, very large export subsidies are paid to producers of certain goods which meet strong foreign competition, such as industrial machinery and automobiles. The flexibility of the export subsidy scheme consequently enables Germany to obtain a larger advantage from her exports, in terms of command over imports, than would be possible through devaluation.

The aspect of Germany's system of foreign trade control which has received greatest attention in governmental and foreign trade circles in this country is her elaborate network of payment, clearing, and compensation arrangements. These arrangements may be classified broadly into two groups. The first group consists of the clearing and payment agreements which have been imposed on Germany by other countries, such as Great Britain, France, Holland, and Switzerland. These countries, which have usually had an import balance in their trade with Germany, have made use of this fact to protect their own export markets and to secure more favorable treatment for their nationals who hold German securities. As a result of these clearing and payment agreements, Germany has been obliged to increase her debt service payments and to purchase more goods from these countries than she would otherwise have done. The clearing and payment agreements in this group, imposed by other countries, have clearly been a handicap to Germany, though the handicap has been no more than a partial offset to the advantages derived from debt default.

The second group of bilateral arrangements consists of the clearing and compensation agreements undertaken at Germany's initiative with many raw-material-producing countries in Eastern Europe, Latin America, and elsewhere. All the arrangements in this group, despite variations in detail, produce the same general result, which is to earmark specifically for expenditure on German products the proceeds accruing to foreign sellers of raw materials to Germany. Raw-material-producing countries have been ready, in view of the depressed world markets for their products, to sell their surplus output to Germany even if they could use the proceeds only for purchasing German goods. Through these special measures Germany was able to circumvent the exchange restrictions in raw-material-producing countries, and in many countries quotas and tariffs were either reduced for German goods or increased for the goods of competing countries in order to facilitate the utilization of the blocked reichsmarks resulting from sales to Germany. In this way the demand for German exports has been partly divorced from the general level of purchasing power in foreign countries and has become more largely dependent upon the specific purchasing power derived from sales of raw materials and foods to Germany. During periods of depressed, or semi-depressed, world conditions these arrangements strengthened the demand for German exports, and enabled Germany to obtain an increased volume of imports at particularly favorable terms. By linking the market for her exports as closely as possible to her own purchases of imported goods, Germany has partially insulated the foreign demand for her goods from the effects of depressed world conditions. In the conditions actually prevailing in world markets she has undoubtedly gained much more in this way, in terms of ability to import, than she has lost through diversion of trade into "uneconomic" channels. These losses, illustrated by the case cited earlier of purchases of Uruguayan wool in preference to the cheaper New Zealand product, have been far from negligible, however, and under conditions of sustained world prosperity, when there would be little advantage for Germany in seeking to insulate her export markets from general world conditions, the losses through diversion of trade into uneconomic channels would be extremely large. This is particularly the case in view of Germany's former great dependence on multilateral balancing of trade.

It is possible, in fact, that sustained world prosperity would lead to a considerable reduction in the scope of these bilateral arrangements. Raw material countries, finding a large and growing demand for their products in unrestricted currency markets, would not continue to accept blocked reichsmarks in payment for their goods except at terms increasingly unfavorable to Germany. If, as a result of sustained world prosperity, clearing and compensation arrangements should become unpopular with raw-material-producing countries and ineffective for Germany, this would be likely to have significant consequences in the political as well as the economic sphere, since these arrangements have occupied a central position in the extension of German hegemony over Eastern Europe and the strengthening of her influence in other outlying countries.

It is frequently claimed that external forces no longer exert any significant influence on German economic life. In our judgment, this view cannot be supported, since Germany's dependence on foreign trade, though smaller than formerly, is still substantial. The way in which Germany's economic life is affected by external conditions has been vastly altered, however, during the past five or six years. During the period from 1924 to 1932 employment and income in Germany were primarily governed by two external influences: the foreign demand for German goods and the willingness of foreign countries to lend to Germany. Employment responded sensitively to changes in either one of these factors, and the alternations of prosperity and depression were predominantly outside Germany's control.

As a result of the transformations of the past five years, the level of employment and national money income in Germany are predominantly determined by government spending and have become almost entirely independent of external influences. The claim that the German economy as now organized is virtually free from the danger of slack business activity and unemployment seemed to us well founded. A more real danger is that the pressure upon living standards resulting from the diversion of human and material resources to the uses favored by the State and the party may eventually proceed to an intolerable point.

It is with respect to their bearing upon German living standards rather than upon employment that external economic influences are of importance to Germany. Unlike most other industrial countries, Germany does not seek increased exports as a means of providing employment or money income, but only as a means of securing increased imports. From this standpoint world prosperity would be seriously detrimental rather than helpful to Germany. In the first place, the development of prosperous world conditions would raise the prices of raw materials, which Germany imports, relative to the prices of manufactured goods, which she exports. In the second place, Germany's system of clearing and compensation agreements, which serves during periods of depressed world conditions to broaden the market for German exports and, consequently, to increase her ability to import, would result, under conditions of world prosperity, in an uneconomic diversion of trade probably even more costly to Germany than to other countries. For both reasons, Germany would be faced with the painful necessity of either curtailing imports or employing a larger proportion of her resources on the production of goods for export, or both. Since Germany's productive resources are fully and intensively employed, either alternative would present acute difficulties. The process of adjustment to prosperous world conditions would involve a further lowering of living standards or a substantial curtailment of government undertakings. The adaptation of Germany's economic organization to depressed world conditions has reached a high degree of refinement, but the consequence of this adaptation is that world prosperity would create serious difficulties for Germany.

Reference has previously been made to the size of administrative machinery required for the enforcement of the exchange control measures. We sought to gain some idea of the degree to which the regulations are effectively enforced, particularly with respect to the prohibition of private capital export. Our general impression was that although capital export is doubtless taking place continually, either by taking advantage of minute loopholes in the regulations or through their violation, the amount involved is probably quite small when viewed in the perspective of the German balance of payments as a whole.

Divergent views were expressed regarding the long-run workability of the control machinery. Most of the Reichsbank officials, who were trained in the doctrines of orthodox economic liberalism and who still retain serious doubts regarding the effectiveness of a controlled economy in general, said that the system of exchange control, as indeed the whole system of control over Germany's economic life, was quite unworkable in the long run, although they saw no possibility of returning to a freer system until fundamental changes occurred both in external economic conditions and in Germany's internal politics. Others whose economic and political philosophy was more completely in accord with that of the present regime regarded the present system of controlled economy as entirely workable for an indefinite period. Our own guess was that the workability of both the exchange control machinery in particular and the whole machinery of economic control in general depended essentially upon public morale, and that the machinery now functions with a considerable degree of effectiveness because the dominant groups in Germany heartily support all or most of the essential objectives of the regime. The chief reasons for the apparently widespread popular support seemed to be (1) the restoration of full employment and (2) the popularity of Hitler's achievements in foreign policy.

It was said by people whose own attitude was at best lukewarm that suppressed dissatisfaction with the regime is more prevalent among well-to-do classes than among industrial and agricultural workers. The well-to-do classes, while retaining their property, have lost much of their economic power, since at least as regards the control of large enterprises, all major policy decisions are made by the State or the party, and these groups have had to bear the restriction of dividend payments, increasing taxation of corporate earnings, and a rather pronounced scarcity of luxury and semi-luxury goods and services.

Although it was acknowledged that working-class living standards were somewhat below pre-depression levels, it was frequently suggested that so long as these groups retain their enthusiasm for the objectives which necessitate these material sacrifices, the distance they will go in making sacrifices is probably considerable. The reduction in working-class living standards in comparison with pre-depression years has occurred primarily in food and clothing. With respect to foods, the consumption of meats and dairy products has been substantially reduced while consumption of cheaper foods—potatoes and other starches—has increased. The use of synthetic fibers on an extensive scale is generally admitted to have reduced the durability of clothing, although in appearance and warmth the newer garments are said to compare favorably with those made entirely of cotton or wool. Moreover, it was frequently stated that the adoption of new technological improvements had considerably increased the durability of rayon and its variants. It was frequently pointed out that the reduction of workers' living standards in the sphere of food and clothing has been partly compensated by gains in other directions, such as cheap radios (capable of receiving only the programs of German stations) and cheap vacations. While the bulk of the public investment expenditure has been on projects which have made little or no contribution to living standards (armaments, Four Year Plan, stadia for political rallies, roads), many promises are made for the future—automobiles, rebuilding of cities, better housing, and electricity development, all under State sponsorship. Although these projects seem to depend for their fulfillment on a curtailment of outlays under the armament program, it is by no means inconceivable, barring the danger of war, that they will gradually be achieved. Most important of all, however, is the fact that for the dominant groups of the population the deficiencies of the material diet have been compensated by an abundant and apparently satisfying emotional diet. It is largely for this reason that we were inclined to conclude that the workability of the present system depends primarily upon the state of popular morale, and that, so long as the enthusiasm of the people for the objectives of the regime is maintained, the degree to which they will accept material hardships is considerable.

Dr. Schacht and other Reichsbank officials do not seem entirely to have given up hope of an eventual return to a freer economic organization. In outlining his ideas of how the world could work out of its present difficulties, Schacht suggested the following programs: (1) cancellation of all government debts; (2) conversion of all private debts to a lower interest basis; (3) general return to a gold standard; and (4) a binding commitment among countries to have recourse to economic sanctions if, for reasons of economic advantage, one or more countries subsequently break away from the gold standard. He was puzzled as to what would happen if some such program is not developed, and complained about United States commercial policies in Brazil, which he said were a perfect example of the bilateral practices which he had introduced and which he heartily rejected.

In appraising the prospects of a relaxation of foreign exchange and foreign trade control, it is important to keep in mind the conditions out of which the present system arose and the purposes it is designed to serve. As noted earlier, the financial crisis of 1931 greatly curtailed Germany's ability to import, and the problem became even more acute after the deflationary internal policy of the depression years was replaced by a policy of internal expansion, the need for special measures to enlarge imports tending to become intensified as German internal recovery outran world recovery. The development of the system of controlled economy was the outgrowth of these conditions. The present regime has sought increasingly to govern the country's economic activities in the light of specifically National Socialist objectives, and this has further accentuated the scarcity of imports. Imports of consumption goods, notably foodstuffs and textile fibers, have been held down as much as practicable in order to leave the greatest possible amount of exchange available for the importation of raw materials required for the armament program, the Four Year Plan, and similar projects. The system of foreign exchange and foreign trade control is thus an important part of the machinery by which German productive resources are guided into channels selected by the State and the party, and it is for this reason that a substantial modification of the present system in the sphere of exchange and foreign trade control seemed to us strongly improbable except as the outgrowth of a weakening of public morale and of basic changes in guiding political and social objectives. As mentioned earlier, the development of prosperous world conditions might lead to a restriction in the scope of clearing and compensation arrangements.

3 *American Aid and Western European Recovery*[1]

Western Europe's current transactions with the outside world in goods and services yielded a deficit of $5.6 billion in 1948; with the United States alone the deficit on current account was $3.6 billion. These deficits were made possible by American aid. The problem of closing, or greatly reducing, this gap as American aid to Western Europe is progressively tapered off over the next three years is rapidly becoming the central problem of international economic relations.

To consider Western Europe as an economic unit, and to speak of its balance-of-payments problem as a single problem, is an over-simplification. The causes of balance-of-payments difficulties, and the measures appropriate for meeting them, differ considerably

1. Written in September 1949 for the Council on Foreign Relations Study Group on Aid to Europe. This group was formed by the Council in 1948, with Dwight D. Eisenhower as Chairman. Other members were: Hamilton Fish Armstrong, Hanson W. Baldwin, Allen W. Dulles, Edward Mead Earle, George S. Franklin, Jr., Graeme K. Howard, Walter H. Mallory, Stacy May, Isidor I. Rabi, Jacob Viner, John H. Williams, and Henry M. Wriston. A small technical staff assembled the basic material for the discussions of this group. Despres was a member of this technical staff. Other staff members were: Percy W. Bidwell, McGeorge Bundy, William Diebold, Jr., Brig. Gen. Arthur S. Nevins, and Ragnar Nurkse.

Sections of this paper appeared in Howard S. Ellis, *The Economics of Freedom: the Progress and Future of Aid to Europe,* published for the Council on Foreign Relations by Harper & Brothers, 1950, pp. 42-50.—Ed.

from country to country. Britain's problem, for example, is not the same as that of France, and both are different from Italy's. Moreover, to treat Western Europe as an economic unit is to ignore the problem of trade and payments within Western Europe. Nevertheless, as a starting point this approach is legitimate and useful. Western Europe's balance-of-payments problem is, in its basic character, a single problem. The complications of trade and payments within Western Europe and the balance-of-payments difficulties of particular countries can be adequately understood only when they are fitted into a general framework embracing Western Europe as a whole.

The balance-of-payments problem is not simply one of narrowing the present gap. It is merely a truism—since Western Europe's reserves of gold and dollars are limited—that a reduction of the balance-of-payments deficit will, in some fashion, follow automatically, as American aid is tapered off. The problem is, rather, to narrow the gap without incurring an excessive loss of real income.

The problem, then, is essentially one of real income. It derives its importance from the crucial contribution of external trade to real income in Western Europe. The special significance of external trade is due to Western Europe's rather meager endowment of land and natural resources in relation to population. Despite this handicap, a relatively high real income was made possible in the past by importation of food and raw materials from the outside world in exchange for exports of manufactured goods, shipping and other services, and earnings of European capital invested abroad. In this way Western Europe secured relatively ample supplies of primary products at moderate cost. World War II not only impaired Western Europe's physical capacity to supply goods and services to the outside world but also disrupted overseas markets, sources of supply, and sources of investment income. The first handicap is temporary and is being rapidly overcome; the second, however, creates difficulties of a much more persistent sort.

In 1948, little more than 60 per cent of Western Europe's imports was covered by exports and invisible income, the remainder being financed by American aid. As American aid under the European Recovery Program (ERP) is gradually tapered off over the next three years, this percentage must somehow be substantially increased. It would not be accurate to say that this figure must be brought up to precisely 100 per cent. The figure may not have to be quite as high as this; on the other hand, it may have to be somewhat higher. In a favorable economic and political climate private American investment in Europe or repatriation of private French and other European flight capital might provide a flow of funds partly replacing ERP aid. Moreover, Italy might qualify for further American aid under a "Point Four" program, and our special commitments in Germany may well continue beyond 1952. To the extent that funds flow to Western Europe from these sources, the size of Western Europe's adjustment problem will be reduced. On the other hand, a part of the proceeds of Europe's exports will be applied to repayment of accumulated external debt and perhaps also to new investment in colonies and other non-European areas. Although one can hardly guess on which side the balance will lie, it seems safe to estimate that the net flow of capital in or out will not be large, probably less than $1 billion. This means that an improvement of about $4 to $6 billion in the balance of payments on current account is called for between 1948 and 1952, or a narrowing of the gap at an average rate of $1 to $1.5 billion per year.

What will be the effect of this process of adjustment on the momentum of Western European recovery? The official American doctrine underlying the European Recovery Program is that, with American aid, it should be possible sufficiently to increase Western Europe's productivity so that the gains from this source will overshadow and absorb the burden of external adjustment as our aid is tapered off. Statements of Western European governments, on the other hand, have become more and more explicit in asserting that Western Europe's dollar shortage is chronic and deeply imbedded in the structure of world trade. Translated into terms of real income, this means that, in their view, the costs of the adjustment process, in the years ahead, will overshadow gains in productivity in individual industries.

The total supply of goods and services available to Western Europe is estimated at $145 billion in the year 1948-49, of which Western Europe's gross national product accounts for $140 billion and net imports of goods and services from the outside world for the remainder. Thus, the external deficit has recently been providing only 4 per cent of the goods and services available to Western Europe, the remaining 96 per cent coming from Europe's own production.

Clearly, however, these percentages provide no indication of the key role of American aid in expanding Western Europe's real income, nor of the consequences for real income of a cessation of American aid. If the cessation of aid were abrupt and unforeseen, the effect on real income would, of course, be exceedingly severe. A large expansion in exports cannot be brought about overnight, nor can the domestic production of primary products be suddenly increased. The burden of adjustment, under these circumstances, would chiefly be borne by reducing imports, with resulting severe curtailment of available supplies of foods and raw materials. Even if one disregards the possibility of acute political and social disturbance, a sudden loss of primary products would have a greatly multiplied effect in reducing real income, as the result of food shortages and industrial shutdowns and unemployment caused by lack of raw materials.

The adjustment which Western Europe must make as ERP tapers off is not of this type, however. ERP is providing sufficient time so that adaptation can be progressively made without acute disruption and unemployment. But ERP not only provides time for shifting resources and readapting production; it also contributes to the raising of productivity by making possible a high rate of capital formation in Western Europe. If directed into appropriate fields this new investment should facilitate the structural readjustments in industry and agriculture which are needed to meet the balance-of-payments problem.

It is to be expected that the process of adjustment will be characterized by balance-of-payments crises. It is also to be expected that the process will generate some friction and ill-will both between the United States and Western Europe and among the Western European countries themselves. The significant question, however, is whether and to what extent the gradual tapering off of American aid will obstruct the progress of Western Europe's recovery.

If a satisfactory upward trend of real income can be maintained in the face of diminishing outside aid, the basic objective of ERP, which is to restore the economic foundation for strong and stable democratic governments in Western Europe, will be fulfilled. In that event, balance-of-payments crises need not be viewed with too much concern; indeed, such crises are often essential to create the atmosphere of urgency which is needed for carrying out radical adjustments. Moreover, the diplomatic task of keeping animosities within bounds, so that necessary military, political, and economic cooperation is not endangered, should not be too difficult.

If, on the other hand, the burden of external adjustment seriously obstructs Western Europe's material progress, the objectives of ERP are not likely to be realized. A mood of hopelessness regarding the prospects for improvement in living standards and intense social and political conflict over the distribution of the burden may well lead to economic and political breakdown.

Nor could continuation of American aid on a permanent or semi-permanent basis provide a satisfactory means of averting this danger. Our willingness to grant aid without exercising control over the domestic policies of recipient governments rests upon the assumption that this aid is being used to enable these countries to become self-supporting. Even with this assumption, it is becoming more difficult each year to resist Congressional demands for pervasive controls over the domestic policies of recipient governments. It would be impossible to resist these demands if the Administration should propose that American aid be prolonged beyond 1952. Since outside control is intolerable to Western European countries, American attempts to exercise such control would play strongly into the hands of extremist political groups. When the political dangers of prolonging American aid to Western Europe are taken into account, the conclusion seems justified that the political objective of ERP can be attained only if the economic target is reached within the period originally planned. If the tapering off of outside aid gravely obstructs the progress of recovery, there will be much reason to fear dangerous political instability within Western European countries and a breakdown of military and political cooperation among them and with the United States.

Some impression of the overall dimensions of the adjustment

problem may be gained by an examination of Western Europe's balance of payment on current account.

(In billions of dollars)

	1947	*1948*
Imports	−13.9	−15.3
Exports	6.7	9.0
Invisibles	0	0.7
Deficit	−7.2	−5.6

(Source: Economic Commission for Europe, *Economic Survey of Europe in 1948*, p. 117)

It is estimated that in the next few years income from invisibles (tourists, shipping, investment income) may increase to double the 1948 figure. If one assumes (1) that the proceeds of exports are fully available to pay for imports, and (2) that the relationship between prices of exports and prices of imports remains the same as in 1948, an expansion of the volume of exports to the outside world of about 55 per cent would be required to pay for a volume of imports equal to that of 1948.[2] This would mean closing the gap in external payments.

Western Europe's exports, measured by volume, showed an increase of about 30 per cent between 1947 and 1948. In the latter year they had attained 94 per cent of the 1938 volume. Imports meanwhile showed a slight decline.

Western Europe's imports in 1948 still included a considerable volume of shipments relating to temporary reconstruction needs. Moreover, the recovery programs of Western European countries

(1938 = 100)

	Exports	*Imports*
1947	73	97
1948	94	95

(Source: Organization for European Economic Cooperation and ECE data)

2. Cf. Economic Commission for Europe, *Economic Survey of Europe in 1948*, p. 212.

place considerable emphasis on production of domestic substitutes for imports (agriculture, oil refining, synthetic fibers). Consequently, if total imports could be maintained at about the 1948 volume over the next several years, available supplies of primary products would suffice to permit a continuing expansion of real income. This should not be taken to mean that the continuation of imports at the 1948 rate is, in any sense, ideal. The most advantageous level of imports at which to achieve balance-of-payments equilibrium depends, on the one hand, on the receptiveness of foreign markets and availability of foreign supplies, and, on the other hand, on the cost of expanding domestic production of primary products and of other methods of economizing imports.

All Western European countries achieved substantial recovery of exports in 1948, although only Great Britain substantially exceeded the 1938 level. For Western Europe as a whole the volume of exports was still somewhat below the semi-depressed volume of 1938. An expansion in exports of 55 per cent would bring them to a level 45 per cent above 1938. Given adequate supplies of raw materials, expansion of industrial production to a level at least 30 per cent above prewar levels appears entirely possible by 1952. Thus, the expanded volume of exports required to pay for imports would represent only a moderately larger fraction of Western Europe's industrial output than in 1938. Viewed from the side of production, the necessary expansion of exports seems fairly easy. The cost in real income of providing this increased volume of exports in exchange for a volume of imports still somewhat below the 1938 level would be extremely slight in comparison with the contribution to real income resulting from high employment and rising productivity. Under the conditions assumed, the process of restoring balance-of-payments equilibrium would not seriously impede Western European recovery.

The significance of this conclusion depends, of course, on the validity of the assumptions underlying it. The importance of the first assumption—that the proceeds of exports are fully available to pay for imports—is strikingly illustrated by Great Britain's present balance-of-payments difficulties. During the twelve months ending June 1949, the volume of British exports was 45 per cent above prewar, while imports were almost 20 per cent below the prewar level. As a result, the British balance of payments on current account was approximately in equilibrium. Nevertheless, Britain had a dollar deficit of $1.6 billion which was met chiefly by ERP aid and partly by reducing gold reserves. Although a number of factors were responsible for this dollar deficit, the largest single source of the deficit consisted of "unrequited exports" to soft currency countries. The British Government—by adopting a liberal policy with respect to utilization of accumulated sterling balances, by permitting virtually unrestricted movement of private capital from Britain to other parts of the sterling area, and by granting aid and credits to several Continental European countries—has fostered a flow of exports to markets which provide neither goods nor dollars in return.

The second assumption—that the relationship between export prices and import prices (i.e., the terms of trade) remains the same as in 1948—is, of course, arbitrary. Indexes of the average prices of Europe's imports from and exports to the outside world are shown below.

The table shows that in 1948 a unit of European exports exchanged, on the average, for a 9 per cent smaller volume of imports than in 1938. In 1938, however, the terms of trade were exceptionally favorable to Western Europe, owing to depressed prices of primary products. Indeed, although long-term comparisons of price indexes are of dubious significance, the available data suggest that the terms of trade in 1938 were more favorable

(1938 = 100)

	A	B	$\frac{B}{A}$
	Import Prices	*Export Prices*	*Terms of Trade*
1946	177	186	105
1947	217	212	98
1948	244	221	91

(Source: Economic Commission for Europe, *Economic Survey of Europe in 1948*, p. 97.)

to industrialized European countries than at any time in over a century, except for the years 1931, 1932, and 1933. Thus, the moderate worsening of Europe's terms of trade in 1947 and 1948 is not, of itself, particularly serious.

The significant question is whether and how much Western Europe's terms of trade will worsen as she strives to become self-supporting by expanding the volume of her exports. If, for example, an expansion of one-third in export volume were accompanied by a 25 per cent decline in the average price of exports relative to imports, the expansion in volume of exports would merely have diverted goods from domestic buyers while contributing nothing to Europe's capacity to pay for imports. The extent to which it is useful for Western Europe to emphasize expansion of exports depends chiefly on the receptiveness of outside markets to Western European goods. If markets for increased exports are highly unreceptive, the attempt to force exports would result in a substantial worsening of the terms of trade.[3] In this case, Western Europe may be led to rely chiefly on contraction of imports either as the only feasible, or as the less costly, method of adjustment. If unfavorable conditions in outside markets and sources of supply force the adjustment of balance of payments to follow this path, the resulting substantial contraction of imports would halt the progress of Western European recovery. If, on the other hand, markets are receptive to an expansion of European exports, so that balance-of-payments equilibrium can be achieved through expansion of exports without substantially worsening the terms of trade, the adjustment to declining American aid need not seriously obstruct the growth of Western Europe's real income.

The receptiveness of outside markets to increased Western European exports will turn primarily upon whether effective demand for industrial goods outside Western Europe is expanding.[4] This will be considerably affected by such developments as the possible growth of East–West trade in Europe, the extent and rate of recovery of Far Eastern production for export, and the rate

3. Countries such as India, which is running a large deficit on current account financed by drawing down its sterling balances, would be classified as unreceptive in the sense in which the term is used here. India's present capacity to pay for imports through earnings from exports is greatly impaired.

4. Excluding external demand financed by capital outflow from Western Europe.

of expansion of primary products output in overseas areas generally.

It will also depend upon the volume and character of American investment in undeveloped areas. If the present program, which emphasizes technical aid and the encouragement of private direct investment abroad, is broadened to include a substantial volume of "untied" long-term lending to undeveloped countries, the process of European adjustment will be considerably assisted. In part, these loans might replace the present outflow of capital from Britain to such countries as India, thus converting present "unrequited" exports into dollar-earners. In part, such loans would represent a net enlargement of the external buying power of the borrowing countries; expenditure of the proceeds would result in increased imports of industrial goods both from the United States and from Western Europe. Thus, American lending to undeveloped areas, if the loans are not tied, can provide an important indirect source of dollars to Western Europe. Over the longer term, the increasing productivity of the borrowing countries will increase their capacity to export and import.

Most important of all, the receptiveness of external markets to Western European exports will depend upon prosperity in the United States. As our most urgent postwar needs for the replenishment, expansion, and modernization of business and consumer capital are satisfied, and as our export surplus tapers off, shall we be willing to use the instruments of fiscal policy if this should be necessary to sustain an adequate growth of domestic demand? A repetition of the experience of the thirties seems highly unlikely; nevertheless, a situation of prolonged semi-depression is a real possibility and a real danger.

The usefulness of devaluation of European currencies in contributing to adjustment of the balance of payments depends upon whether other conditions are favorable to an expansion of European exports to the United States and to overseas markets now supplied by American manufacturers. If American industry is operating at close-to-capacity levels to meet a strong and expanding domestic demand for its products, this would tend to draw European goods to this country and would increase European opportunities to regain overseas markets now supplied by American exports. Strong domestic demand would restrain American producers from cutting prices to meet European competition, and their demands for higher import duties should not be too difficult to resist. Under these conditions, a moderate cheapening of European exports through currency devaluation would substantially raise export volume, thereby contributing to Europe's capacity to import and to rising levels of real income.

On the other hand, if markets are deficient and American industry is seriously depressed, the effect of currency devaluation in increasing export volume would be insufficient to outweigh its adverse effect on Europe's terms of trade. Within a limited total market, it is difficult to conceive of a marked increase in European exports to this country, at the expense of American producers, or a displacement of American by European goods in other markets. American manufacturers would meet intensified European competition by lowering their prices and by pressing for greater tariff protection.

If Western Europe confronts this kind of situation, restoration of balance-of-payments equilibrium will have to take place to a considerable extent through reduction of dollar imports. Under these conditions the adverse effect on Western Europe's recovery will, in any event, be pronounced; but the burden would be kept down by a policy of maintaining favorable terms of trade through currency overvaluation, import controls, and trade discrimination through non-convertibility of currencies into dollars and bilateral and regional commercial arrangements.

Thus, the progress of Western European recovery and the pattern of economic policy in Western Europe over the next three years depend to a large degree upon external developments affecting her export markets and sources of supply. If these developments are predominantly favorable, one may expect exchange rate adjustments, a large expansion of European exports, continued improvement in real income and standards of living, progress toward more liberal commercial policies, and a further relaxation of domestic rationing and allocations of foods and raw materials. If the development of external markets is unfavorable, one may expect a large reduction in Europe's dollar imports, a halting of the recovery in real income and standards of living, a tightening of direct controls and allocations, and increased discrimination in commercial policy.

4 *Western Europe's Long-Term Balance-of-Payments Problem*[1]

The OEEC report's analysis of Western Europe's long-term balance-of-payments problem contains much that seems to the writer highly questionable. In the OEEC report, the long-term economic problem of Western Europe is defined as one of maintaining a high standard of living for a dense population in a world in which Western Europe is no longer the predominant source of manufactured supplies. At the end of the nineteenth century Western Europe provided 90 per cent of the world's exports of manufactures. World trade in manufactures stopped growing after World War I; it was no larger in 1937 than in 1913. Meanwhile, world output of manufactures had doubled and Western Europe's share in this total had declined to little more than one-half. World War II and its aftermath, besides extinguishing income from overseas investments, permanently deprived Western Europe of a large part of its markets and access to raw materials in the Far East and in Eastern Europe and accelerated industrialization in other parts of the world.

Looking to the future, the report finds that industrialization

1. Written in September 1949 for the Council on Foreign Relations Study Group on Aid to Europe. This analysis is in response to the Organization for European Economic Cooperation's *Interim Report on the European Recovery Program,* Volume I.—Ed.

and growing populations in countries producing primary products will increase the internal requirements of these countries for foods and raw materials and will restrict their demand for imported manufactures. These factors, along with the incomparable rapidity of technological progress in the United States, mean that the semi-monopoly position in world trade in manufactures which Western Europe enjoyed prior to World War I as a result of its head start in the industrial race has been progressively undermined. In the future, the OEEC concludes, the growing relative scarcity of primary products compared with manufactured goods will compel Western Europe to accept increasingly adverse terms of trade, paying relatively high prices for its necessary imports and receiving relatively low prices for its exports. This unfavorable price relationship will deprive Western Europe of much of the benefit which it formerly derived from international trade. The pressure of relative prices will reduce real income and force a readjustment of Western European economies in the direction of greatly reduced dependence on imports. However, unless the necessary adjustments are expedited by affirmative government policies, the OEEC warns that the process of readjustment will involve dislocations and crises.

The foregoing analysis is plausible, but, to the writer, not convincing. It implies that there exists a fundamental conflict between the economic interests of Western Europe and the interests of world economic development, unless economic development outside Western Europe is confined to agriculture and mining. This has not been borne out by the economic history of the past forty or fifty years. The gains which Western Europe has derived from the growing diffusion of modern technology and capital have greatly outweighed the costs resulting from loss of its former semi-monopoly position in manufactures. The long-term trend of real income in Western Europe has continued upward apart from wars and depression; this growth of real income and living standards in Western Europe has been due not only to technological progress and expansion of capital within its borders, but also to economic progress in the rest of the world. When the necessary qualifications and amendments are taken into account, this part of the OEEC's analysis does little more than explain why economic progress in the twentieth century has been less rapid in Western Europe, an area already highly developed by 1900, than in some other parts of the world which were then less highly developed.

Considerable point is made by the OEEC of the failure of world trade in manufactures to expand in the inter-war period. This fact, however, is not analyzed, and without analysis it seems to prove too much. The central question, not discussed in the report, is whether this was due to industrialization of raw-material-producing countries or to other causes. In this connection the following points should be mentioned:

a. The prices of primary products were lower in the twenties and much lower in the depressed thirties in relation to manufactures than in 1913. If the relative prices of primary products are as high in the future as the OEEC predicts, this will greatly strengthen the demand for manufactured goods in raw-material-producing countries.

b. The decline in Western Europe's manufactured exports to the outside world was to a large extent the result of economic policies and trends in the industrial countries, such as European agricultural protection, the development of substitutes (e.g., synthetic nitrogen and fibers, light metals) and, in the thirties, the world depression.

c. It has been observed everywhere that as real income rises, foods and raw materials become a diminishing part of the total demand for goods and services. This long-term trend means for Western Europe declining relative dependence on imports.

The only point of practical significance in this part of the OEEC's analysis is its forecast that food and raw materials will be relatively scarce in the future and manufactures relatively abundant. If this forecast proves correct, the effect on real income in Western Europe will be adverse, and the strain may be expressed in chronic balance-of-payments difficulties. Adjustment will have to come about largely through reduction of imports. The plans of agricultural exporting countries are based upon precisely the opposite expectation, namely, that after abnormal postwar demands have been met the world will revert to the position of oversupply in agricultural products which characterized the inter-war period. The danger is not so much that the plans of agricultural importing and exporting countries will not mesh but rather that they will mesh—with misallocation of resources and lower real income all around.

The writer would reject the OEEC's analysis of past trends affecting Western Europe's economic relations with the outside world and would reserve judgment on its forecast of future terms of trade. One is not entitled, however, to conclude that the *Interim Report* necessarily exaggerates the seriousness of the external factors affecting the Western European balance of payments. Along with its forecast of adverse basic trends affecting the relationship of producers of manufactured goods to producers of primary products, OEEC mixes in an essentially distinct analysis of Western Europe's balance-of-payments difficulties based upon the economic relationships between Western Europe and the United States.

Viewing the pattern of world trade as a whole, Western Europe's present balance-of-payments deficit has its counterpart in the United States surplus. It is a truism of double entry bookkeeping that the elimination of Western Europe's deficit must be accomplished by (1) a large increase in American imports, or (2) a large decrease in American exports, or (3) a large net deficit, financed by the United States, in the external trade and payments of the rest of the non-European world, or (4) an adequate combination of (1), (2), and (3). This point, although not extensively treated in the *Interim Report,* underlies the report's balance-of-payments forecasts and its recommendations for drastic economy in imports. The authors of the report doubt the United States' willingness to accept greatly increased European exports or greatly intensified European competition in other markets. They doubt also that the United States will extend sufficient financial aid to underdeveloped countries to enlarge quickly the total world market for manufactures and the available supply of raw materials.

It is because of these doubts that the OEEC advises the participating countries to scale down their forecasts of exports and to impose further economies in imports. European uneasiness regarding American developments cannot be dismissed as groundless.

It would be highly desirable if the simple interconnection between the Western European balance of payments and that of the United States were more widely understood in the United States. The United States, as well as Western Europe, must be prepared to adjust to a substantial shift in its balance of payments during the next several years. Tapering off of ERP aid must be matched by a combination of increased imports, increased financial aid to other countries, and reduced exports. Particularly if business activity is sagging in the United States, but perhaps even if it is not, the increasing competition of European exports, both in our domestic market and abroad, will put our present policies to a difficult political test. Moreover, business depression in the United States would automatically impair Europe's export possibilities, and the decline in the prices of her imports would be only a partial offset.

On the other hand, it seems to the writer that these dangers are too well understood abroad. In some countries long-term pessimism is providing an excuse for postponing immediately necessary but difficult internal measures. It is not the intention of the OEEC report to provide excuses for inaction, but its pessimism may have this effect in some countries. If one looks at the situation today, the United States has substantially reduced its tariffs, has proposed a long-term program of technical and financial aid to undeveloped countries, and—so far—has maintained internal prosperity. In Western Europe, on the other hand, internal economic, political, and social factors have combined to limit the recovery of exports. The predominant factor now limiting Western European exports is inflated internal demand and overpriced exports, not deficient external markets.

If the OEEC's pessimism proves justified, its general emphasis on drastic economy in imports is undoubtedly justified. However, it would seem better for the Western European countries, before accepting this emphasis as the basis for their plans, to test more fully the capacity of export markets.

One further point is worth noting. If the OEEC's doubts about the United States are based upon an expectation of business depression in the United States, they are difficult to reconcile with its forecast of increasingly adverse terms of trade for Western Europe. Business depression has invariably caused a sharper decline in the prices of foods and raw materials than in manufactures.

5 *The Mechanism for Adjustment in International Payments–the Lessons of Postwar Experience*[1]

I

The grand design for the machinery for adjusting international payments in the postwar period, embodied in the Bretton Woods agreement, was derived from the lessons of the thirties. The task of establishing a new international economic and financial framework was regarded as one of reconciling the requirements of domestic and international equilibrium. Domestic equilibrium meant chiefly full employment. International equilibrium meant chiefly the avoidance of large and persistent national surpluses and deficits in external accounts. The two guiding principles were that no country should be prevented by balance-of-payments difficulties from pursuing domestic policies of full employment, and that no country should be permitted to adopt "beggar-thy-neighbor" measures for exporting unemployment. These principles were adopted to assuage the widespread fear that after the war the United States economy might sink back into depression and that the United States government might not take adequate compensatory measures to correct deficiencies in aggregate demand. One central objective was to develop a postwar framework which would prevent American depression from again becoming world depression. Another was to free trade from the trammels of quan-

1. Written with C. P. Kindleberger. Reprinted from the *American Economic Review: Papers and Proceedings,* May 1952, pp. 332-44.—Ed.

titative and price interferences and to establish a framework conducive to the development of world trade and investment.

The methods for reconciling these parallel objectives were (1) the creation of an international pool of liquid reserves to help meet cyclical balance-of-payments difficulties; (2) exchange control to prevent "hot-money" movements, thus eliminating speculative amplification of balance-of-payments disturbances; (3) discriminatory restriction on dollar imports if cyclical disturbances in the balance of payments were of sufficient size and duration to exhaust available reserves; (4) exchange rate adjustments to correct persistent or "fundamental" disequilibrium; and (5) with the two foregoing exceptions, the rule of fixed exchange rates with current payments free of quantitative restrictions and discrimination.

Some of these rules, acceptable in principle, proved difficult to effect in practice. Thus, for example, speculative capital movements were proscribed in many countries but took place nonetheless as the ingenuity of the speculators exceeded or led in time that of the exchange controllers. Some took on the character of a rule of thumb, clung to even at the sacrifice of its objective. The emphasis on par values of exchange established to promote trade, for example, led to the conclusion in some quarters that it was desirable to protect par values at whatever cost, even if it meant severe restrictions on trade—a point which was put in this way by Guy Orcutt.

For the most part, however, discussion in Britain and the United States revolved around the question whether the new facilities and new rules would be adequate to prevent a repetition of the experience of the thirties. Some considered that the rules conceded too much to the predilections of American exporters for multilateralism and left insufficient room for the use of discriminatory direct controls; others felt that too much had been conceded to the planners and neo-Schachtians. Initially, however, there was general agreement that the problem was to maintain balance-of-payments equilibrium on the one hand and the domestic level of effective demand on the other.

It would be easy to conclude that the Keynesians, in their international as in their domestic planning, were concerned with imaginary rather than real dangers and that the fault was not with their economics but with their judgment. The postwar difficulty on this showing was not lack of effective demand but a plethora. Consumption rose to a new relationship with income, because of backlogs of demand, liquidity maintained by wartime accumulations of money and government debts which could not be repudiated, and, in some countries, a shift of income in favor of spending and against saving groups in the society. Investment responded to the shortage of capital, which had been seriously underestimated, and, at least through 1948, to postwar reconstruction needs. Government expenditure and business investment were then held at high levels by the unforeseeable military expenditures which followed the invasion of South Korea.

But the fault with the Keynesian tradition has not been solely one of forecasting. Two other demerits can be charged against it. In the first place, in the thirties it produced near unanimity that deflation was a wrong method of correcting balance of payments under all circumstances. Cultural lag carried this view into the late forties. Secondly, the economic problem in a world of excess demand is not simply the obverse of the problem in a world of depression. Exports come to be thought of less as added employment than as a cost; and imports lose their character as producers of unemployment and are regarded as real income. More than this, however, the world of full employment is a classical world where the problems of allocation of resources and the distribution of the gains of trade, neglected in depression, come into their own. The roots of present balance-of-payments difficulties do not lie solely in excess demand, as some anti-Keynesians and even pro-Keynesians think, but in this fundamental area. The real questions today are structural.

II

Before we turn to these structural problems which involve the price system, however, a further comment may be in order concerning income adjustments and the effects of depression.

The Keynesian view of the world of depression was limited to industrial countries where the impact of depression is different from its impact on producers of primary materials. Under the system which evolved in the nineteenth century, a large part of the burden of maintaining interregional and international equilibrium was borne, not by the financial centers, but by debtor, primary-producing regions at the periphery. A reduction in the flow of capital to the periphery usually preceded or accompanied a decline in external demand for primary products, thus subjecting their balances of payments to double pressure. The effect, however, was not chiefly upon the level of employment, owing to short-term inelasticity of output, but upon terms of trade, volume of imports, and, consequently, real income.

Primary-producing countries frequently adjusted their external accounts through exchange depreciation rather than deflation, but this did not obviate the loss of real income. The only choice open to them was to accept the loss through lower export prices or higher import prices. Meanwhile in the industrial regions the cheapening of imports subject to inelastic demand bolstered expenditure for domestic goods and helped to counterbalance the loss of employment resulting from the falling off of exports.

Insofar as industrial countries are concerned, however, it is ironical that Britain and Western Europe should be so fearful of another American depression. Capacity to control effective demand—at least to the extent of preventing it from declining—could be used to offset secondary income effects resulting from loss of exports. If economic assistance were not forthcoming or were available in insufficient amounts to finance deficits, the dollar deficit could be reduced or removed by devaluation or discrimination. The overall position of Western Europe, however, would be improved by the movement of the terms of trade in favor of manufactures and against agricultural products and raw materials. It is the primary producers rather than Western European industrial countries which should fear American depression.

Popular confusion on this point has been caused by the behavior of the sterling area, which lumps the United Kingdom industrial balance of payments with those of Commonwealth primary producers and hides the separate movements in each. Rising raw material prices build up the sterling balances of the primary producers; declining prices bring them down. Britain, as banker for the area, gains gold and dollars from rising prices as in 1950; loses from falling as in 1949. But high raw material prices, after primary-producing countries have adjusted real consumption to them, no longer benefit the banker qua banker; if the adjustment is excessive, so that balances are drawn down, as has been the case in 1951, the banker may suffer. And Britain and Western Europe suffer from high prices of primary products and gain from low in their other capacities as producers and consumers. Only a partial offset to these fundamental effects is afforded by the change in income from overseas investment, now much reduced from prewar and from the nineteenth century.

III

The exclusion of deflation from the armory of weapons for adjusting balance-of-payments disequilibrium has not been rigorously maintained. Room was found in the postwar period for what is not an unrelated process—disinflation; and deflation which produced unemployment, while perhaps less effective in limiting imports from the dollar area, has been found useful in reducing balance-of-payments deficits within the European trading area. For the most part, however, economists have searched elsewhere and for a relatively painless device to bring about balance-of-payments adjustment. In advocating restriction of investment, Harrod assumed that much of the investment taking place was of low productivity. Proponents of exchange rate adjustment have expressed faith in the elasticity of demand for industrial goods. Advocates of discrimination have assumed that reciprocal discrimination could easily be negotiated. There is, however, nothing in economic theory to support the faith that balance-of-payments maladjustments of a structural nature can easily or cheaply be corrected, even if the appropriate mechanism be chosen.

An impressive technical literature (e.g., Lerner, Mrs. Robinson, Metzler, Hirschman, and Meade) has developed during and since the war, stipulating the conditions under which devaluation improves the balance of payments of a country. To this has been added an expanding series of articles—especially by Frisch and Alexander—comparing the efficacies of devaluation and discrimination and suggesting the optimum method of discrimination. Broadly speaking, devaluation will improve the balance of payments of a country only when, including real-income effects, the sum of the elasticities of its demand for imports and the world's demand for its exports is greater than one; and import restriction improves the balance of payments of a country more economically than devaluation, i.e., with less loss in real income, so long as the gain in welfare from an additional dollar spent on imports is less than the welfare cost of earning an additional dollar through exports. If, on the other hand, the domestic value of the added imports is greater than that of the goods which must be foregone as exports in order to obtain them, then it pays to devalue rather than to restrict imports further.

These developments in theory were accompanied by a spate of work in the field of measurement (e.g., Tinbergen, Adler, and Chang) culminating in the conclusion, rather widely accepted, especially by Orcutt, Machlup, Haberler, and Viner, that the pioneering efforts in this area left much to be desired. Few economists are willing nonetheless to hazard the judgment that the elasticities are high overall, except perhaps in the long run.

It is important to observe, however, that this is partial-equilibrium analysis and therefore of limited relevance. Modern proponents of devaluation are prepared to concede that the elasticities of demand may be low in the short run, but they count on their being higher over time. This involves a reversal of the older view of the matter. It used to be thought that depreciation would be effective in correcting balance-of-payments disequilibrium only in the short run. Over time, when full equilibrium had been reached, it was thought that this transitional gain would have been lost because of the long-run inflation of costs and prices. The job is not only to "halt the inflation and adjust the exchange rate," if this can be done, but also to keep down domestic prices and costs as resources are transferred into export and import-competing industries and in the face of the rise in import prices. Partial-equilibrium analysis is not sufficient. With its use, depreciation assumes too readily that the price system will be effective in persuading countries to accept the loss in available goods and services entailed in getting rid of balance-of-payments deficits.

The advocates of discrimination fall into two none-too-clearly divided groups. One would ignore the price system altogether as a guide to the allocation of resources and maximization of real income. Bulk buying, discriminatory promotion of high-cost production to save foreign exchange, and quantitative restrictions in general are viewed as the prerequisite to effective internal planning. The difficulty with this view is that price comparisons lose their meaning as a guide to resource allocation. The criterion of "economizing foreign exchange" in directing new investment and allocating resources may waste productive energy, lower real income, and even worsen the balance of payments. Since the balance-of-payments problem is one of achieving the least costly adaptation to changed external conditions, i.e., of minimizing the loss of real income, discard of the price system may leave the planners without effective guides to the allocation of resources and distribution of output.

The other group chooses to use the price system rather than discard it, to take advantage of inelasticities to improve real income. An extreme example of the attitude employed is found in the advocacy of exchange appreciation, not discrimination, by Harrod and by the Economic Commission for Europe to secure more favorable terms of trade for Britain and Western Europe. If there are low elasticities of demand for exports and of supply for imports, then monopoly and monopsony gains are possible from restricting exports and imports respectively. The monopsony gain from restricting imports may be at the cost of increasing unemployment due to loss of complementary resources rather than leading to a gain in employment, as in a depressed world. But the beggar-thy-neighbor tactic of subsidizing exports, which flourishes in a depressed world, is replaced by that of holding them back.

There are a couple of things wrong with this prescription for world trade. In the first place, it leads to retaliation. The neo-Schachtians and the liberal critics of German bilateralism failed alike to recognize that the system persisted because it had real attractions for Germany's trading partners. In a depressed world, additional exports produced additional employment, additional imports, and additional real income, at whatever terms of trade.

Second, the all-around adoption of restrictions on exports and imports leads to an impasse in trade negotiations—witness the difficulties of the Andes Agreement between Britain and Argentina —and involves the loss of real income all around. Some monopoly gains are possible for raw material producers, particularly vis-à-vis the United States and by means of the multiple-exchange rate device. But there are limits to these gains, as Argentina knows in linseed and Canada in newsprint. And the possibility of Western Europe effecting monopoly or monopsony gains at the expense of either the United States or primary-producing areas may be excluded in a world of full employment.

This concludes what little we have to say about the adjustment mechanism in a narrow sense confined to the balance of payments. The rest of our paper focuses attention not so much on the balance of payments as on the underlying phenomena within the country experiencing balance-of-payments disequilibrium.

IV

In a classical economic world of full employment, two questions present themselves. One, from the point of view of the world as a whole, is whether the resources of the world and of each country are allocated to the production of the right goods. A second, which is related to the first, is how total income is distributed among factors within a country and among countries. A world concerned with real income, as ours now is, must have regard to both these questions.

As an aid to the analysis, we may perhaps distinguish between structural disequilibrium at the goods level and structural disequilibrium at the factor level. Disequilibrium at the goods level means that relative goods prices do not reflect the allocation of factors among various industries appropriate to existing factor prices. Disequilibrium at the factor level may arise either because a single factor receives different returns in different uses or because the price relationships among factors are out of line with factor availabilities.

Some of the difficulties at the goods level are due to monopolistic competition, already discussed in connection with discrimination. Included among these by a number of writers is the increasing-returns case. This is a favorite of the underdeveloped countries. In addition to monopolistic competition, however, the price system may suffer because of excessive factor response, typically found in the cobweb theorem, or in factor rigidities which permit no response. Part way between, perhaps, is the difficulty which occurs in products of long gestation, like coffee, where short-run inelasticity is combined with long-run excessive response, occurring years after the cause of the stimulus is forgotten. These defects in the price system have recently been examined by Professor Haberler.[2] While the price system admittedly falls short of its smoothly efficient ideal, he concludes that in the absence of any superior alternative its defects do not constitute an argument for its abandonment. It must be conceded, further, that the demerits of the price system by no means constitute a positive argument for planning. If private enterprise is too little responsive to increasing-returns situations, public authorities find many which ultimately prove illusory. Planners face the same rigidities in factor responses that price will encounter, and in the absence of large windfall profits will provide little stimulus to correct allocation. And planners, perhaps more than entrepreneurs but certainly as much, are as likely to infect each other in particular situations with their own enthusiasm and overrespond to price stimuli and their underlying significance.

The price system never operated without making mistakes. Economic Darwinism regarded the losses under competition as the price paid for progress. With large units directing resources, however, whether under oligopolistic competition or under planning, the penalties of error are increased manyfold and a lower tolerance for mistakes has been developed.

The workability of the price system, however, depended on submission to its verdicts. The invisible hand carried out the judgments of an impersonal fate from which it was impossible to appeal and against which it was useless to struggle. The growth of monopolistic competition and government interference, which ex-

2. See especially "Some Problems in the Pure Theory of International Trade," *Economic Journal,* June 1950, pp. 223-40, and "Real Cost, Money Cost and Comparative Advantage," *International Social Science Bulletin,* Spring 1951, pp. 54-58.

posed the hand and showed the fate to be personal, has changed this. The price system has been undermined in a fundamental respect. Its decisions are known not to be *ex cathedra* and infallible.

Structural disequilibrium at the factor level involves questions both of resource allocation and use on the one hand and of income distribution on the other. We shall discuss first the case of disequilibrium between factor prices and factor endowments, and then the case of unequal remuneration to one factor in different uses despite mobility between uses. Both cases, it need hardly be pointed out, are different from the classical case of non-competing groups, where immobility exists among occupational groups.

The disequilibrium of Italy and Germany arises from lack of complementary resources. Given the technology in use, these countries lack capital and have an overabundance of labor. In one view, the solution to their problem is capital imports and emigration, to establish the factor proportions appropriate to prevailing factor prices. An alternative is a change in relative factor prices. This would result in changing the least-cost combinations of factors in all uses and the relative prices of goods, thus altering the volume and composition of exports and imports. In the absence of change in either factor endowments or factor prices, balance-of-payments adjustment means unemployment of the redundant factor, and full employment leads to balance-of-payments deficit.

Factor disequilibrium in which factor proportions are out of line with factor prices poses a problem which is out of reach of measures of discrimination and for which devaluation is likely to provide an inadequate solution. Except in the case of slight disequilibria, moreover, capital imports and emigration are not likely to occur to the extent necessary to justify existing factor prices and technology. Strenuous deflation with high interest rates, which will raise the return to capital and lower that to labor, is hardly attractive as a social and political policy. In addition, it faces the disability that elasticities of substitution of labor for capital are almost certainly low. Capital, for example, can be shifted among industries only slowly, as depreciation takes place. The alternative aspects of the disequilibrium, however—the deficit and the unemployment—require solution urgently.

Germany and Italy are, in a sense, special cases. But it must be remembered that most Western European countries have been hovering close to the same type of structural unemployment. The combination of a full employment level of domestic demand for manufactures, limited exports, and American aid to finance a part of the needed primary products is providing a sheltered market for Europe's output. But when and if Western Europe must shift from domestic capital formation, military production, and American aid to exports and self-support, it is questionable whether Europe's full employment requirements for food and raw materials can be paid for by exports of manufactures. At best the process will produce a marked worsening of terms of trade. If external grants and loans are not available, other European countries may face structural unemployment or underemployment, of the work-relief type.

A similar disequilibrium, partial in nature, may be detected in underdeveloped countries. In these, the export sector of the economy, which may have access to foreign capital, will frequently employ factor combinations which yield relative marginal productivities different from those in the subsistence sector. In consequence, labor and land will receive a higher return in exports in combination with foreign capital than in the rest of the economy where it works with scarce domestic capital. In Venezuela, for example, labor will earn more in oil than in domestic enterprise. In Cuba, foreign capital participates in the sugar export economy but not in tobacco; so that different factor proportions and factor returns exist side by side in exports.

The existence of different returns in different sectors of the economy need raise no particular problems for the balance of payments. It may, however, raise serious problems of other kinds, both economic and social, as pointed out by F. Ortiz in *Cuban Counterpoint: Tobacco and Sugar* (New York, 1947), pages 1-93. The difficulty, however, is that these countries are tempted to use the technology and factor proportions appropriate to the export sector in development projects for which foreign capital is not available. In these cases, the result is structural disequilibrium which is reflected either in balance-of-payments deficit or in a large degree of unemployment or underemployment in the subsistence sector of the economy.

The dual-economy case is representative of the first type of disequilibrium in which factor prices are out of line with factor proportions if we focus attention on the subsistence sector of the economy. If, however, we look at both sectors and if labor moves between the subsistence and export sectors as production for export fluctuates, we approach the second type of disequilibrium: unequal prices for one factor in alternative uses. Wage rates are higher in the export sector than in the subsistence economy. The general case of failure of factor prices to reach equality in different uses, however, is that presented by Manoilesco (*Theory of Protection,* London, 1931), which has recently received renewed discussion in connection with underdeveloped countries.[3] In this model, the level of wages in the manufacturing or import-competing sector of the economy is assumed to be higher than in the primary area engaged in exports and subsistence, owing simply to wage rigidity in manufacturing. There are no barriers to entry and the supply of labor for manufacturing is highly elastic at the established wage rates. On this assumption, the marginal transformation ratios between primary products and manufactured goods deviate from the corresponding price ratios.

Manoilesco regarded this situation as one calling for protection of manufactures, to induce a shift of underemployed agricultural labor into industry. It should be pointed out, however, that if expansion of industrial output requires additional capital as well as labor, it is necessary to weigh the gain in real income from such investment against the gain which would result from an equal amount of output-increasing investment in agriculture. But it is also important to examine the position in demand. If the elasticity of demand for primary-products exports is low and the marginal terms of trade lower than the average, the higher apparent return to capital in agriculture at the average terms of trade is illusory. In this case a further reason exists, from a national point of view, for shifting resources from an overcrowded, underemployed agriculture.

The following analysis, overdrawn for emphasis, may be sug-

3. See Gottfried Haberler, "Real Cost, Money Cost and Comparative Advantage," *loc. cit.*, and Jacob Viner, "Lectures on the Theory of International Trade" (mimeographed, 1950), pp. 60 *et seq.*

gestive of how the Manoilesco case may apply to the real world and its structural disequilibrium at the factor level. Western Europe has been a densely populated area with limited natural resources. Its relatively high real income per capita in the past has come in large part from its gains from trade. Western Europe has concentrated in the production and export of industrial goods in exchange for primary products; the exchange ratios have overvalued industrial goods and undervalued primary products in comparison with their transformation ratios. Rostas' comparison of prewar productivity in the United States and the United Kingdom, for example, shows that real income in the United Kingdom was much higher relative to the United States than industry-by-industry comparisons of productivity would suggest. A major element in the explanation for this phenomenon was the relatively greater concentration of British resources in "high value-added" items; i.e., a more favorable product mix.[4] Colin Clark indicated the same phenomenon in another light when he showed the far lower average return available in the United States in agriculture as compared with industry (see *Conditions of Economic Progress*, London, 1951, second edition, Chapters IX and X, especially pages 395 and 440 and following). This lower return reflects disguised unemployment, not throughout agriculture as a whole, but in some major sectors of American agriculture.

In the last ten years, there has been a considerable narrowing of the gap between the returns in occupations in which wages and prices are relatively high and rigid and those in which they are low and flexible. This narrowing has been almost world wide, in developed and underdeveloped countries alike. Its importance for income distribution, present and prospective, should not be underestimated. With some notable exceptions, both industrial and primary-producing countries have attempted to increase their real income by directing labor and capital into those lines which are characterized by high and rigid wages. A large part of the problem of international equilibrium turns on the question whether, if these trends continue, manufactures can be exchanged at their customary terms for primary products.

4. L. Rostas, "International Comparisons of Productivity," *International Labor Review*, September 1948, pp. 283-305, especially pp. 295-96.

The question has been postponed for a time by the prolongation of American aid to permit the expansion of military production. The military program provides an outlet for highly fabricated goods at the same time that it intensifies the demand for raw materials. When and if there is a return to a more nearly peacetime economy and if the output of manufactures is sustained through domestic full employment policies, it may well be that the share of world income going to primary producers will be much larger and that of fabricators much smaller than in the past.

The demand for full employment in the industrial countries is irresistible. In practice, full employment means a level of demand sufficient to keep high-wage industries operating at close to capacity, and a concentration of investment to expand these industries. As a result of full employment, along with expansion of manufacturing plants, restricted immigration, mass education, and growing labor mobility within countries, industrial countries are drawing a larger and larger share of their resources into the traditionally high-wage lines of activity. In this the underdeveloped countries insist on joining, through emphasis on industrialization. At the same time, they are unwilling and will not need to accept the former terms of trade. The scarcity premium which manufactured goods have enjoyed over most of the last 150 years is in process of being lost.

V

A smoothly functioning system of international payments requires that all countries follow the same set of rules. This will be done if the interest of each of the separate countries, as each views it, is identical or parallel with the interests of all others; or if each country is prepared to carry out measures against its interest, either because of ignorance or because of faith in the ultimate identity of the national and the cosmopolitan interests.

The present full employment world is one in which neither of these conditions holds. On this account alone, no return to gold, nor to flexible exchange rates, to regional free trade, to bilateral monopoly, or to anything else, by itself, will provide the basis for a successful system of international adjustment.

Even if there were a consensus, a major difficulty would remain. The two major schools of thought—the price economists and the planners—have accepted too simple a view of the nature of the problem. We have examined structural disequilibrium at this length because of our view that neither therapy, universally accepted and skillfully applied, would fully meet the maladjustment nor the balance-of-payments problem. International capital movements and migration of labor are unlikely on an adequate scale, as both schools would agree. While the record in governmental loans and grants has been remarkable, no accepted criteria have been evolved in surplus countries, and they remain a limited and unreliable substitute for the international capital movements of the nineteenth century.

Fundamentally, the mechanism of adjustment includes all the processes by which new patterns of resource use and the distribution of gains from trade emerge in response to continual changes in technology, resource endowments, and demand. Price economists tend to focus exclusively on the problem of resource allocation; planners on that of international income distribution. But these problems are inseparable. A workable system of international payments must both allocate resources and distribute income in some fashion which countries and factors within countries are willing to accept.

More time is needed after the breakdown of the nineteenth-century system to see how a new workable mechanism will evolve. If one kind of consensus should emerge, the world may settle on new terms of trade, preferably after increases in productivity have converted an absolute to a relative decline in the standard of living for Western Europe. Another possibility is a shift of resources in both industrial and primary-producing countries into raw materials and foodstuffs, and an increase in relative efficiency in these lines, to restore the terms of trade to which the industrial sections of the world have become accustomed. Still a third alternative is the evolution of some regular system for redistributing income internationally, as this is now done interregionally within a country, to offset the most inequitable results of malallocation of resources where it exists and to ease any hardships of adjustment to appropriate resource allocation and terms of trade.

6 *The Significance of the European Common Market to the American Economy*[1]

Statement:

I have been asked to discuss the significance of the European Common Market for the American economy.

Most of the articles which I have seen on the European Common Market or Economic Community begin by characterizing it as "one of the most important undertakings of the twentieth century" or "one of the most far-reaching economic undertakings of all time." However, in these articles the discussion that follows of the economic effects of the Common Market is often vague and indefinite. One might, perhaps, wonder whether the Common Market will be really so momentous after all.

Before discussing specific economic matters, I should like to make a general comment about this. Vagueness in discussing the Common Market is unavoidable not only because the Treaty of Rome establishing the Common Market contains its share of escape clauses, loopholes, and ambiguities, but, more important, because the plan is incomplete and unfinished in one decisively important respect. The issues concerning commercial and finan-

1. From *Employment, Growth and Price Levels,* Hearings before the Joint Economic Committee, Congress of the United States, 86th Congress, First Session, Part 5; International Influences on the American Economy, Government Printing Office, Washington, 1959. The "Statement" is from pp. 1030-37, the "Testimony" from pp. 1018-27.—Ed.

cial relationships between the Economic Community, on the one hand, and other Western European countries and the rest of the free world, on the other hand, remain unresolved. If this problem is worked out well, the Common Market will both strengthen free-world political unity and stimulate its economic growth. In this sense, the Common Market is a momentous project. If the problem is badly resolved, however, the Common Market may be a source of chronic political tension and disunity and economic disruption. Its results might then be momentous in a radically different sense.

The British proposal of a free trade area, although far from ideal, represented a first, constructive attempt to meet this issue. Now that this scheme has been firmly rejected, the time is ripe for a new effort toward a constructive solution, and this country's role in this effort should be an active one. I shall return to this point later.

I. EFFECTS WITHIN THE COMMON MARKET

In considering the economic effects of the Common Market, the first point to be noted is that, apart from its temporary, psychological impact, which has been one of the factors stimulating a flow of both European and American capital into the Economic Community countries, the fundamental economic effects will be felt only gradually as the Common Market comes slowly into effect over a twelve- to fifteen-year period.

A second major point is that the economic similarities among the countries composing the Economic Community are much more striking than their differences; all are exporters of manufactures and all import primary products. As a result, the classical argument for trade liberalization, that it enables countries to derive mutual benefit from their differences in resources and skills, has limited applicability to the Common Market. The popular view that the removal of barriers and the creation of a large, free market will permit industries to adopt more efficient mass-production methods which would not have been profitable when producing for limited national markets seems to me also to deserve only moderate weight. The principal constructive economic effect of the Common Market is that, as it goes gradually into effect, the market for manufactured goods within the six countries composing the Economic Community will become more dynamically competitive than it has been in the past.

Improvement in technology and growth of productivity has been exceedingly rapid in Western Europe in recent years, and the technological gap between Western European and American industry has narrowed considerably in a number of manufacturing lines. As an illustration, although inflation in the general level of prices has been greater in Western European countries than here, their prices for metal products, machinery, and vehicles have, on the average, gone up much less than ours.

In many manufacturing industries, however, the technological inferiority of Western Europe still remains pronounced. A major cause is the lack of progressiveness and enterprise of many European business firms operating under sheltered conditions and accustomed to low volume and high profit margins per unit. Under the more competitive conditions which the Common Market will gradually create, a strong premium will be placed on managerial efficiency and progressiveness. Production will tend to concentrate in those firms which adopt improved methods and install more efficient equipment. Chiefly through enlargement of competition, the Common Market may be expected to spur technological progress, increased investment, higher productivity, and growth of real income. In this way, it will serve to sustain the strong upward trend of growth evident over the past decade. In this respect, the Common Market, instead of creating a new trend, will bolster a trend already strongly present in the Common Market countries.

This enlargement of competition will not be without limitations and restraints. In the field of agriculture, for example, the substitution of competition for the several national programs of price and income support and production control is not contemplated. Instead, these programs will be gradually coordinated into a community-wide program of subsidization and control under the protection of uniform import restrictions for the Common Market as a whole. In some industries, also, it is possible that present national cartels, cartel-type arrangements, and governmental subsidies will simply be replaced by wider cartels and price-fixing arrangements and coordinated subsidies to protect and sustain inefficiency and backwardness.

Despite this qualification, the general trend in manufacturing will be toward gradual enlargement of competition, disappearance of inefficient firms, and expansion of investment and output in efficient and progressive firms. This promises to be the most important, constructive economic result of the Common Market, just as, at the political level, the strengthening and institutionalization of French-German cooperation appears to be its most constructive long-run potentiality.

Of the countries composing the Common Market, France and Italy may be the largest gainers. Their productivity is likely to benefit most from enlargement of competition, and the postwar evolution in industrial organization and management which has been taking place in some important branches of French and Italian industry will be broadened and extended.

II. EXTERNAL EFFECTS OF THE COMMON MARKET

The questions of the effects on trade between the Common Market and other countries in general, and on our foreign trade and balance of payments in particular, are matters of particular interest to the members of this committee. In considering trade and payments between the Common Market and the outside world it is necessary to distinguish two opposing types of effect—a growth effect and a displacement effect.

In the first place, there will be the group of effects associated with growth of productivity and real income in the Common Market countries. Growth of productivity and real income in these countries will be accompanied by expansion both in their volume of exports and in their demand for imports. To be sure, rapid technological progress in import-competing lines tends to reduce dependence upon imports. However, unless the gains in productivity are narrowly concentrated in this group of industries —and there is no reason to expect this in the case of the Common Market—this tendency will be overshadowed by the increase in exports resulting from other gains in productivity and by the rising aggregate demand for goods, including imported goods, resulting from growing production and real income. Thus, the net effect of growth is to expand import and export trade with the outside world.

The displacing effect, on the other hand, results from the discrimination which is in some degree inherent in any customs union or preferential trading arrangement. It will occur in the Common Market whenever the lowering of trade barriers within the Community induces a member to purchase from another member goods which would otherwise have been imported from outside. As barriers within the Community are progressively lowered, the inducement to diversion or displacement of outside trade becomes stronger. Generally speaking, such diversion of trade is likely to be uneconomic not only in its effects on outside countries but even in its effects on the members of the Community themselves.

The net resulting effect on the trade of Common Market countries with the outside world will depend upon the comparative strength of the opposing forces of growth and of displacement. Two highly important general conclusions may be drawn.

First, the relative strength of these two opposing forces will be chiefly determined by the level of the import barrier surrounding the Common Market. If the import barrier is high, the displacing effect will be large and the general effect on external trade will tend to be restrictive. If the barrier is low the growth effect will be predominant, and the effect on external trade will be expansive. It is for this reason that the unresolved issues concerning the future commercial relationships between the Economic Community and other countries are of crucial importance.

It should be noted, in this connection, that a low import barrier against outside trade would not only serve to reduce the displacement effect; generally speaking, it would also enlarge the growth effect by further enlarging competition and giving further momentum to growth of productivity within the Common Market. Thus, the effectiveness of the Common Market in stimulating the economic growth of its own members, far from being strengthened by high external tariffs and quotas, would be considerably weakened.

Second, the specific geographical impacts on outside countries of the growth and displacement effects, respectively, will be highly diverse. Although a comprehensive analysis of country-by-country effects would be out of place here, it is necessary to make some general observations on this matter. Even if high import barriers should surround the Common Market, the growth effect is likely to remain important in the case of trade with exporters of complementary products. Outside countries exporting primary products which the Common Market needs and cannot readily produce for itself are likely to benefit from the Common Market's increasing demands for their products as well as from its growing role as an exporter of machinery and other manufactured goods. Although for trade with outside countries exporting primary products growth effects will predominate in most cases, displacement effects will not be wholly absent. The Common Market plan contemplates eventual free entry into all Common Market countries of French and Belgian colonial products as well as increased investment to expand production in their African territories. This has possible displacement implications for outside producers of such products as oil, coffee, cocoa, tobacco, and bananas. Moreover, it should be emphasized that in the case of imported agricultural products of which production within the Common Market countries can be expanded, even if at higher cost—for example, butter from Denmark, or grain from America—the outcome will depend on the evolution of the Common Market's agricultural policy and the degree of protection accorded to agriculture.

In contrast to the situation of outside countries exporting complementary products, the skills of Western European non-members are similar to, rather than complementary to, those of the Common Market countries. Consequently, even a moderate degree of tariff preference can have rather large trade displacement effects. This shifting due to discrimination is not only contrary to the interests of Western European non-members but is also against the long-term interests of the Common Market countries themselves.

The exports of eleven OEEC countries not belonging to the Common Market to the six Common Market countries amounted in 1956 to $3.8 billion, or 23 per cent of their total exports to all countries. The percentages ranged from 14 per cent for Britain to 31 per cent for Denmark, 39 per cent for Switzerland, and 49 per cent for Austria. The postwar expansion in inter-European trade was fostered by the steady extension of measures for liberalization of inter-European trade initiated under the Marshall Plan. The movement for inter-European trade liberalization embraced the whole group of OEEC countries. Trade liberalization, besides its important economic benefits, contributed importantly to Western European political solidarity. Whether this solidarity will be greatly weakened or greatly strengthened by the Common Market depends significantly upon whether the Common Market adopts a level of import barriers against outside countries which produces substantial trade displacement. The dangerous possibilities inherent in this issue have been foreshadowed in the prolonged and finally bitter discussion in OEEC of Great Britain's free trade area proposal, and in the strain imposed on British-French relations following France's rejection of this proposal. Trade discrimination within Western Europe, if substantial, may be difficult to reconcile with political solidarity.

This is the essential reason why the European Common Market is so difficult to evaluate. Its favorable effects on growth of productivity in member countries, the strengthening and institutionalizing of French-German cooperation, and the possible development of effective supranational instrumentalities and loyalties are its positive potential benefits. However, if, at the economic level, the Common Market inflicts serious injury on Western European non-members by introducing a substantial degree of trade discrimination, and if, at the political level, the Common Market should become merely an instrument for increasing French prestige and influence in Europe at Great Britain's expense, the costs of the Common Market, both economic and political, might outweigh its important benefits.

There is, of course, no reason why this must happen. It will not happen if a healthy structure of commercial and financial arrangements between the Common Market and outside countries is negotiated. Two points, however, deserve emphasis. First, the negotiations should not be delayed. As trade discriminations are permitted to develop, vested interests in their continuation are built up, and they become increasingly difficult to liquidate. The common tariff provisions set forth in the Treaty of Rome, if actually applied, would result in a high degree of trade discrimination, but the treaty also leaves open the possibility of downward revision through negotiation with outside countries. Second, the failure of Britain's free trade area proposal strongly suggests that the prospect for success of the next round of negotiations will be much enhanced if the United States takes an active role in formulating new proposals and in conducting trade and financial negotiation with the Common Market countries. This would also be of direct economic interest to us. Before presenting certain specific suggestions concerning the kinds of proposals which we should make, it is important to consider the effects of the Common Market on the American economy.

III. U.S. TRADE AND PAYMENTS

Dollar-short Europe has found it necessary to discriminate against American exports since the early 1930's, and marked discrimination has been practiced during most of the period since World War II. Despite the progress toward currency convertibility and some relaxation of discriminatory import quotas in the past few years, considerable discrimination remains. Partly because our trade with Western Europe already reflects this discrimination, any further trade displacing effect of the European Common Market in curtailing our exports to its members should be comparatively slight. Our exports to the six Common Market countries amount to about $3 billion annually ($2.8 billion in 1956) or roughly one-sixth of our total exports. About one-third of our exports to the Common Market consists of manufactures, with the remainder primary products. Most of these exports are complementary to rather than competitive with the goods produced within the Common Market. In this respect our situation differs sharply from that of the Western European countries outside the Common Market.

With respect to the foreign trade and balance of payments of the United States, growth of productivity and real income in the

Common Market countries is likely to be the factor of greatest importance. Here the long-term effects of the Common Market should serve merely to reinforce a trend already under way. A continuing, strong trend of growth in the Common Market impinges on the American economy in a number of ways. Speaking broadly, intensified competition will be felt in those branches of American industry in which productivity in Common Market countries is increasing most rapidly relatively to ours. For this group of manufactures, one may expect (1) some reduction of American exports to the Common Market, (2) increased exports of this class of Common Market products to the United States, and (3) intensified competition from Common Market products in the markets of third countries. Automobiles are a familiar example of this general class. At the same time, one may anticipate a general tendency toward increased capital outflow to the Common Market countries, owing to repatriation of private foreign funds hoarded in the form of dollar balances in order to take advantage of expanding investment opportunities in the Common Market, direct investment by American corporations in Common Market countries, and some purchases of European securities by individual American investors.

It is important to remember, however, that growth of productivity and growth of real income are opposite sides of the same coin. (This assumes—correctly, I believe—that the effects of growing productivity will not be substantially dissipated through mounting unemployment and idleness.) In assessing the overall effect on our foreign trade and balance of payments, both sides of the coin must be taken into account. While increasing productivity means that American manufacturers will face increasing competition from Common Market products, increasing real income within the Common Market carries with it an increasing demand for American goods.

Both sides of the coin must be taken into account, but there is no necessary implication that they will be equal and that our net balance of payments will remain unaffected. The increase in Common Market demand for American goods will be felt most strongly with respect to our exports of primary products, both agricultural and mineral, which now account for two-thirds of our exports to

Common Market countries. The favorable effect of expanding energy requirements in the Common Market on American coal exports needs no emphasis, although in the long run much depends upon the rate at which alternative sources of energy (oil, including African oil, and nuclear energy) are substituted for coal.

In the case of our agricultural exports, it is clear that the underlying long-run economic possibilities for expansion are extremely large. Just as the growth of productivity in Western Europe has been most marked in such fields as metal products, machinery, and vehicles, the broad sector of our economy which in the past two decades has shown the most spectacular gain in productivity, both absolutely and in relation to productivity trends abroad, has been agriculture. If actual patterns of trade were permitted to adjust to these divergent trends in productivity, and to the resulting shift in the structure of comparative advantage, there can be little doubt that the increasing competition of Western European manufactured exports in world markets would go hand in hand with rapidly growing demands in Western Europe for imported agricultural products, and that the United States would be the largest beneficiary of this growth of demand. Comparison of Western European with American food consumption patterns shows their much higher caloric intake from potatoes and grains, with correspondingly lower consumption of meat and dairy products. Since growth in real income carries with it an increasing demand for costlier foods, it is clear that the combination of expanding manufacturing activity and real incomes abroad and strikingly rapid gains in agricultural productivity here create vast underlying, long-run economic possibilities for expansion of American agricultural exports to the Common Market countries (and to other Western European countries).

Unfortunately, however, realization of this underlying possibility is inhibited by serious obstacles. A sizable expansion of agricultural exports to the Common Market may reasonably be expected, but one major obstacle to the realization of the very large basic potentialities for expansion of agricultural exports—and the obstacle most pertinent to the committee's present discussion—is European agricultural protectionism. On this score, the agricultural provisions of the Treaty of Rome are not encouraging. A permanent policy of high protection, subsidization, and official control is clearly contemplated. In future commercial negotiations with Common Market countries, a strong effort should be made to induce them to adopt a long-term program of gradual reduction of import barriers and domestic agricultural subsidies. It must be admitted that our own past position, and the special exceptions for agricultural products which we have included in our past trade liberalization proposals, will be a source of some difficulty in any such negotiations. Nevertheless, this opportunity should not be neglected since the underlying possibilities for expansion of our exports to Common Market countries are much greater for agricultural products than for manufactured goods.

In addition to the prospective increases in some of our exports to the Common Market resulting from its growth in real income and in import requirements, increased Common Market purchases from other exporters of primary products, e.g., Latin America, will serve indirectly to increase our exports to third countries.

On the whole, however, the guess may be ventured that, so far as the Common Market countries are concerned, and indeed for all Western Europe considered as a single unit, the persistent problem of dollar shortage is at an end. Considering the combined balance of payments for the Common Market countries, or for all Western Europe, on the one hand, and the United States balance of payments, on the other hand, it seems exceedingly difficult to maintain any longer, as so many economists and others have maintained during the postwar period, that for deep-seated structural reasons there is a chronic tendency toward deficit in Western Europe's balance of payments and a chronic surplus tendency in our balance of payments, resulting in chronic dollar scarcity. On the contrary, the underlying tendency for a number of years ahead may even be somewhat the other way. Today's basic international disequilibrium, however, is not dollar shortage but the limited ability of most underdeveloped countries to pay for the imports necessary for their development. This problem involves the whole structure of relations between the whole group of industrially advanced countries and the underdeveloped countries.

My reasons for judging the problem of Europe's dollar shortage to be at an end are (1) the progressive narrowing of the technological gap in many important manufacturing lines, with the expectation that this will continue for some years; (2) the serious obstacles which, for many years at least, will limit the potential expansion of our agricultural exports; and (3) the growing movement of investment capital from the United States to Western Europe.

In order that this assessment of the present position and tendency may be properly interpreted, two explanatory comments are necessary. First, it does not mean that individual Western European countries will be freed from balance-of-payments difficulties. Indeed, reasons were given earlier for anticipating that unless the import barrier surrounding the Common Market is definitely low, serious strains will be imposed on Western European non-members. Second, the judgment that Western Europe's dollar shortage disequilibrium is at an end refers only to the underlying position and tendency. Wide short-term fluctuations in international payments and receipts resulting in large surpluses or deficits can result from many causes such as temporary, speculative international movements of funds from one financial center to another, cyclical business fluctuations, divergences between countries in their rates of internally induced inflation or deflation, or revaluations of individual currencies. But there is no longer any reason to consider the demand for dollars as persistently striving to outrun the supply, with Western Europe under chronic pressure to restrain its dollar expenditures.

This progress toward international equilibrium is a development of far-reaching importance, with salutary effects for us and for the free world as a whole. Since this committee has a special interest in the problem of American economic stability and growth, it is worth pointing out that increased competition of European manufactures has been both an important anti-inflationary factor in our markets and a spur to increased efficiency and innovation on the part of American industry. Enlargement of competition is not only a good prescription for the Common Market countries; it is also good for us. European competition is now being keenly felt chiefly in those fields of manufacturing where until recently increases in administered prices and upward wage pressures have been most strongly evident.

IV. SUGGESTED POLICY IMPLICATIONS

The disappearance of dollar shortage and the launching of the European Common Market mark a major turning point in the structure of free-world economic relationships. They create both a highly promising opportunity and an urgent need for (1) commercial arrangements to achieve genuine liberalization of trade, and (2) some modifications in financial and monetary arrangements. Adequate adaptation of commercial policies and financial arrangements to the changed tendencies of the free-world economy can come about only as the result of sustained consultation and negotiation. To facilitate continuing discussion and negotiation, consideration should be given to new institutional arrangements such as, for example, transformation of the present OEEC into a new organization including the United States and Canada as full members.

In the field of commercial policy, our objective of non-discriminatory, multilateral trade has been persistently frustrated during the past twenty-five years by the inescapable fact of dollar shortage. Foreign countries have resorted to discrimination against American exports, chiefly through import quotas and currency inconvertibility, as a means of keeping their dollar disbursements within their available dollar resources. Although, as the dollar problem has eased, progress toward currency convertibility has been substantial, and some relaxation of import quotas against dollar goods has occurred, the disappearance of dollar shortage will not automatically assure the removal of long-established discriminations.

The reciprocal feature of the reciprocal trade agreements program, although of political value at home, also had limited actual significance in a dollar-short world. In the condition of dollar shortage which has generally prevailed since the passage of the original Trade Agreement Act in 1934, any reduction in American import barriers, and any resulting increase in foreign earnings of dollars, automatically increased our exports, since foreign purchases of urgently needed American goods responded at once to any easing of the supply of dollars available to them. Thus, the expansion of our exports flowed automatically and promptly from the reductions in our import barriers, whether reciprocal concessions were granted or not. The reciprocal concessions which were obtained in trade negotiations were, in this sense, somewhat superfluous.

With the disappearance of dollar shortage, the connection between increased American imports and increased exports to foreign countries is much less direct and automatic. By the same token, the reciprocal feature of our trade agreements program now takes on a wholly new importance. Under present conditions it becomes of great importance, in future commercial negotiations, to use our tariff-reducing powers as a real bargaining instrument to achieve the substantial trade liberalization which disappearance of dollar shortage has made possible.

One objective in these negotiations should be to facilitate the evolution of the European Common Market as an integrated, single market with a low external tariff. We should join actively with Western European non-members in pressing the demand for a low tariff, especially as the breakdown of discussions on the free trade area proposal suggests a need for an active American role in the negotiations. Since France and Italy have very high tariffs, Germany high tariffs, and only Benelux has a low tariff, the broad formula for the common tariff proposed in the Treaty of Rome—an average of the present tariffs of member countries—would yield a highly disruptive degree of trade discrimination between members and non-members. An external tariff at any such level must be prevented. In these negotiations, the Western European non-members must also be prepared to reduce tariffs substantially.

A second urgent objective is to secure the further liberalization and, within a reasonable period, the complete elimination by Western European countries of their remaining quantitative import restrictions on manufactured goods. So long as these quantitative import restrictions remain in effect, currency convertibility alone remains of somewhat limited significance. With the "dollar shortage" justification for these restrictions no longer present, full compliance with the GATT's general rules against quantitative restrictions in non-agricultural products is called for.

In the matter of Western European agricultural protection, our objective should be to negotiate long-term agreement with the

Common Market for a substantial relaxation of barriers in successive, moderate steps. The importance of this for our agricultural exports has already been emphasized. It should also be pointed out that gradual relaxation of agricultural protection would further strengthen the growth of real income within the Common Market.

In the financial and monetary field, there are three major areas where modification of existing arrangements requires consideration.

First, the present allocation of the financial burden of NATO defenses should be reconsidered in the light of the changing economic condition, balance-of-payments position, and fiscal situation of its members. From the point of view of an economist, the present share borne by the United States appears somewhat high in relation to today's conditions. It is recognized, of course, that on this issue political and strategic factors may be decisive. Moreover, Britain's lack of success in her negotiations with West Germany on this matter is not particularly encouraging. Nevertheless, changes in economic and financial capacity of NATO members should be taken into account. It is even possible that the unity of the NATO alliance might be strengthened by a greater assumption of financial responsibility by some Continental European members.

Second, some Continental Western European countries have begun to participate in the financing of underdeveloped countries both through subscriptions to International Bank flotations and through extension of export credits. Much further expansion along these lines is now possible. Indeed, this provides a promising means of absorbing a part of West Germany's large and persistent balance-of-payments surplus. Apart from investment in French and Belgian territories in Africa, the financing of underdeveloped countries has been hitherto almost exclusively an American and British responsibility. Broader West German participation would be highly desirable.

Finally, with the elimination of inconvertible currencies and relaxation of import quotas, large swings in national balances of payments in response to speculative movements of funds, cyclical business fluctuations, or other temporary causes must be expected.

Although monetary and fiscal policy must today be influenced by balance-of-payments considerations, it may be taken for granted that neither the United States nor other advanced industrial countries will accept severe and sustained inflation or deflation to correct disturbances in the balance of payments.

The greatest danger inherent in the present situation is that essentially minor departures from equilibrium can become major crises through speculative movements of "hot money." The British crisis of 1957, in which the Bank of England's discount rate was raised to 7 per cent, was essentially of this nature. Neither other Western European countries nor the United States can be confident of future immunity from crises of this sort. This is the most serious element of vulnerability in the more liberal trading and financing system which is now evolving.

I suggest that the Tripartite Monetary Agreement which finally evolved in the 1930's as a means of meeting this type of problem should be revived in new form, its membership to consist of the United States, Great Britain, and the Common Market countries.[2] Through informal consultation on balance-of-payments developments and through concerted support of currencies subject to exaggerated speculative pressure, the resources of this group of countries available for meeting speculative runs would be sufficient to forestall unnecessary crises. The International Monetary Fund alone does not meet this problem, partly because its resources might well be insufficient to meet the massive flights which can develop from one financial center to another, and partly because resort to the Fund is itself a crisis measure and a symptom of crisis. In situations of the type which Britain faced in 1957, the task is not to overcome a crisis, since the crisis should not have been allowed to develop. The problem, essentially, is to prevent such crises by supplementing present arrangements for international monetary cooperation. Without some supplementary arrangement among the financially important countries for concerted support and, if necessary, massive support of any major currency subject to speculative runs, the danger of further crises will remain present; with adequate supplementary arrangements of this sort, the speculative runs are unlikely to gain momentum and, in any event,

2. See Paper 1, note 3, p. 9 above.—Ed.

can be easily overcome by concerted support of the currency under speculative pressure.

Testimony:

The CHAIRMAN. The next witness is Mr. Emile Despres, professor of economics at Williams College.

We are glad to have you, sir.

Mr. DESPRES. Thank you, Mr. Chairman.

The most general point I have about the Common Market is this: that it contains highly constructive unifying potentialities both at the economic and at the political level, and also contains divisive potentialities, and that it is in the interests of the United States to emphasize the positive: that is, to minimize the divisive dangers that cannot be wholly ignored today.

A good deal of my paper talks about the divisive potentialities. The reason for that is this: I think Americans who have been interested in these matters have been so very greatly impressed by the high-mindedness and the dedication of the individuals in Europe who have been in back of this movement that they have tended to overlook the divisive dangers. With respect to these dangers, I do not think that they are unavoidable. I do think that the chances of avoiding them depend a lot on U.S. policy.

This is a general observation, and I think it explains the emphasis of the detailed points which I am about to make.

First of all, so far as the economics of the Common Market are concerned, I think that the main economic effect to which we may reasonably look forward in the Common Market countries themselves is a reinforcement of the growth trend, the increases in productivity that have been evident over recent years, and that this will be achieved essentially through enlargement and broadening of competition within the Common Market.

The reason I stress this point is this: that ordinarily in the theory of international trade, the usual argument for liberalization of trade is that it enables the trading countries to take advantage of the differences in their endowment of resources and of skills. In the case of Common Market countries, the economic similarities are more important than the differences, so that the classical comparative-advantage argument does not deserve much emphasis here.

In the popular discussion of the Common Market, a great deal has been made of the point that a larger market will enable European industry to adopt mass production methods which were not possible or profitable for them before. I think also that this point is overworked a good deal, though there is something to it.

The main point is that by the freeing of markets, the broadening of competition, you will get a very powerful, dynamic spur to technological innovation and improvement, and that it is through the dynamism of increased competition that I think we may look forward to a reinforcement and perhaps a strengthening or broadening of the existing strong upward trend of growth in productivity and income in this group of countries.

That is the main point I have as regards the economic effects in the countries comprising the Common Market themselves. So far as effects on their trade with the outside world are concerned, I have tried to analyze this in somewhat elaborate fashion by distinguishing between two types of effects.

What I called the growth effect is the effect on external trade of the Common Market countries of their own internal growth and productivity. Here, in some cases, the growth in productivity will mean that some goods formerly imported from outside will now be produced domestically. On the whole, however, the growth of productivity and of real income within the Common Market means a net increase both in their exports and in their demand for imports. Often when these matters are discussed, it is the increased export competition which is talked about, while the effect of the rise in real income, in increasing demand for imports, is overlooked.

This is the growth effect. The other effect I have called the displacement effect. This occurs in any customs union, whenever as the result of the removal of internal barriers some goods that one of the member countries formerly bought from outside, it now buys from another member of the customs union.

The effect of this kind of trade displacement is, of course, on balance restrictive, so far as trade with the outside world is concerned. It ought also to be said that this kind of trade displacement is in general, not invariably but in general, uneconomic, both in its effects on the outside country and in its effect on the Common Market countries themselves.

I have so far talked about trade with the outside world as a whole. It is important to try to break down a little bit the geographical impact of the two types of effect: the growth effect and the displacement effect.

The trade displacement effect, the restrictive effect, will be most sharply felt in trade between the Common Market countries and the Western European countries outside the Common Market, unless the common external tariff and other barriers of the Common Market are very low.

The reason I say this is that owing to the similarities of the resources and skills of the Common Market countries and the Western European countries outside the Common Market, a degree of tariff discrimination which is only moderate may have a rather large trade-displacing effect. To the extent that this happens, the effect is essentially to draw a line of division within the Western European group itself.

Of the countries likely to be affected by this, most of the Continental European countries outside the Common Market have 30 per cent or more—up to about 50 per cent for Austria—of their exports going to Common Market countries today. For the United Kingdom, the percentage is much smaller. I think it is about 14 per cent. The impact, therefore, if this problem is not well resolved, is likely to be most serious for the Continental Western European non-member countries, but also serious for the United Kingdom.

So far as the effects on our own trade, U.S. trade, with the Common Market countries are concerned, I think it is fair to say the displacement effects of the discrimination element in the Common Market will be slight, largely because the major portion of our exports to these countries is of complementary products, not competitive products. About one-third of our exports to the Common Market countries are of manufactures. The rest are primary products—agricultural goods, coal, and so on.

The main effect, so far as U.S. trade is concerned, will be the growth effect. This means merely a continuation and perhaps a strengthening of the tendencies that have been apparent, that have been operating in the past few years.

American manufacturers, therefore, may expect intensified competition, as they have been experiencing in the past few years, from European manufacturers. But as I pointed out in my general discussion of the growth effects, the effect is not merely intensified competition on the part of the European countries. The effect is also a growth in their real income, and, therefore, intensified demand for imports.

So in analyzing the effects on American foreign trade you have to weigh these two factors, the intensified competition and the growing demand for imports.

The real question is: Which will outweigh the other?

I am inclined to answer this by saying that on a realistic assessment of today's probabilities, the competition effect for some years is likely to outweigh the effect of rising demand in these countries for American products.

The rising demand for American products would impinge chiefly, I think, on those complementary goods which we are now exporting to Europe. This means to a large extent agricultural products.

At the same time that in industry you have had a very rapid growth of Western European productivity, especially in certain branches of industry, you have had in agriculture an extremely rapid growth of productivity in the United States, so that if trade in the real world followed the lines of comparative advantage, we might expect a very, very large increase in American agricultural exports to Europe.

The only joker here is in the phrase, "if trade followed the lines of comparative advantage." The point, of course, is that agricultural protectionism in Europe is very high. Moreover, as you read the agricultural provisions of the Treaty of Rome, there does not appear to be any intention of lowering external barriers here appreciably. In other words, a controlled and subsidized domestic agriculture within these countries is to be maintained.

So that although I would expect, despite European agricultural protectionism, some appreciable increase in our agricultural exports to these countries, nevertheless, in relation to the true underlying economic potentialities, the increase that we are likely to get, unless agricultural protectionism is very considerably reduced over the years, is likely to be small.

The conclusion I reach, therefore, is that for the short or even the intermediate run, the effect of intensified European competition is likely to be more strongly felt by the American economy than the effect of an enlargement of their demand for our products. The reason I say this is the high import barriers so far as agriculture is concerned.

Senator BUSH. May I ask one question, Mr. Chairman?

The CHAIRMAN. Yes.

Senator BUSH. Is it fair to paraphrase that, then, by saying that these conditions should tend to increase our imports more than our exports?

Mr. DESPRES. Yes.

Senator BUSH. That is the net of it?

Mr. DESPRES. Yes.

Senator BUSH. There is no way of measuring the relative increase of one against the other, I suppose?

Mr. DESPRES. There are ways of doing a lot more work on this subject than I have done, sir, but I have not attempted to quantify it. It would be an elaborate kind of an undertaking to do so. But it is true, I think, that the effect on our exports is going to be limited by the fact that there are very severe barriers abroad to expansion of our agricultural exports. It is also true that the agricultural policies of all of the industrially advanced countries, including our own, are to support agricultural income, support agricultural prices, and to develop a kind of a controlled agriculture.

Senator BUSH. May I ask the question another way, Mr. Chairman?

Would you conclude that both our exports and imports would increase as a result of the Common Market existence, or would you suppose that its existence would cause a decline in our exports, an increase in our imports? Or would both increase? Do you see what I mean?

Mr. DESPRES. Yes; I see what you mean.

Some of our exports will increase; that is, despite everything I have said, we can expect a trend of increase in our agricultural exports. It is just a lot lower trend than we could have if barriers were lower. Also, I would say with respect to coal, even though there is excess capacity in Europe today, on the whole, expanding energy requirements in Europe seem to me to suggest that there is a real possibility, for some years at least, of a trend of growth in our coal exports to these countries, although for the longer run one would have to talk about some substitution of atomic energy and also other forms of energy—oil and so on.

Representative BOGGS. Mr. Chairman?

The CHAIRMAN. Yes, Mr. Boggs.

Representative BOGGS. You are, of course, assuming, Mr. Despres, that the six will proceed in a more protectionist fashion than a liberal fashion, are you not?

Mr. DESPRES. No, sir. I am assuming that—well, as a matter of fact, I have some policy recommendations at the end. Let me put it this way:

I fear that the relaxation of agricultural protection by these countries, and by Western European countries in general, will at the very best be slow, and this I think is very clear in the Treaty of Rome provisions. I think that on a realistic assessment of how fast it is possible for democratic governments to move, say, in the taking away of subsidies from an important group like their own agricultural people, one has to assume that these barriers in the agricultural sector are not going to disappear overnight.

I think it is highly important that we urge their reduction, and I would be hopeful that through active U.S. negotiations on the matter we might be able to induce them to develop a long-term program for gradual easing of these barriers. I think this would be a notable accomplishment, and that would be fine.

Representative BOGGS. Are they not trying to do this? Dr. Hallstein, the president of the Common Market, was here recently, and we met with him. This was one of the main things we discussed with him, whether or not the six would move ahead in a protectionist fashion insofar as the rest of the world is concerned or whether the direction would be more liberal.

It is his contention that their whole direction is liberal, and that much more is involved than just their relationship with the other eleven in Europe. He also says that they plan to operate through GATT and all the existing arrangements.

Mr. DESPRES. I do not mean to sound cynical, because I do not feel cynical about this, but I would say only this: that this is certainly an aspiration, I feel, of men like Professor Hallstein. And even though the general direction is a liberal one, just as the general direction of our commercial policy has over the past twenty-five years been a liberal one, it has to be noted that we have made important exceptions for agricultural products, and the Treaty of Rome makes important exceptions for agricultural products, and this is a really tough problem. I think something can be done about it, but I think it would be very helpful to the Europeans who would like to see this kind of development if the U.S. Government took an active role in attempting to bring about a long-term program of tariff reduction.

On the assessment of the long-term prospects, all I can say is that I think it would be naive to expect these barriers to come down very fast of themselves.

That is about all I had in mind.

Representative BOGGS. I do not think anyone expects that. I think it is a question of direction.

Mr. DESPRES. That is quite right.

Representative BOGGS. Another thing. In connection with Senator Bush's question on this point, the increment of American investment in the Common Market is increasing tremendously. This is a direct investment in these countries: West Germany, France, and elsewhere. This, of course, has some effect on exports and imports, because American capital is going to the market frequently. Is that not a fact?

Mr. DESPRES. Yes, it is. The Common Market has been certainly a factor contributing to this flow of American capital. But, as Mr. Ball pointed out, the movement was already under way, and it is essentially a reflection of the strong trend of growth and of the active and lively potentialities for further growth in these countries.

In addition to the trade effects that I mentioned, there is the important effect of the increased movement of American capital to Western Europe and to the Common Market countries.

Representative WIDNALL. Mr. Chairman?

The CHAIRMAN. Mr. Widnall.

Representative WIDNALL. Professor, I take it from scanning your statement that you think time is of the essence in completing financial arrangements and trade negotiations; that there will be built into the operation of the Common Market such discriminations that if we do not complete our negotiations soon, it can be in a very bad way. Is that not one of the main points you make?

Mr. DESPRES. It is, yes; or, I would say, if we do not begin to launch them soon. I regard the negotiation process as a prolonged and indeed a continuing process, just as the Common Market is an evolving institution. But I think we ought to begin the negotiations soon, because otherwise vested interests begin to get built up in the wrong direction, and it gets harder to undo things after they have been established.

. . .

Mr. DESPRES. The next point I wanted to make was made yesterday; namely, Western Europe's dollar-shortage problem is in my judgment at an end, and it is indeed possible that the trend for many years may continue to be somewhat in the other direction. This is, on the whole, a highly welcome and salutory development. It is exactly the thing we were trying to achieve through the Marshall Plan, and we ought to be delighted that it has been so very well achieved.

The reasons why I make this assessment of the existing position to a large extent duplicate those that were made yesterday. There is one other reason I would like to add; namely, the agricultural point. If this were a world of freer trade, the effect on our foreign trade of the increased European competition in industrial goods would be much more largely offset by increased American exports of agricultural goods, because here is where our productivity is growing most rapidly. But unfortunately, the barriers will tend to limit this expansion of our agricultural exports, so this is a further reason for thinking that the balance-of-payments picture has undergone a major shift.

I would like to make a comment about the "pricing ourselves out of the market" line, which is very fashionable today. I do not know exactly what the phrase means, but if it means that inflation in the United States is causing us to lose export markets, and if by inflation you mean a rise in the average general level of prices, it is dead wrong, because the general level of prices in the countries of Western Europe has on the whole gone up a good deal more during this period of rising European competition than the American price level has gone up.

The cause of the increased competition is that in some important industrial lines, their productivity has been rising a great deal more than ours has. You have a table in the President's Economic Report showing that for the prices of certain classifications of machinery our prices have gone up more than Western European prices, even though the general average of prices has gone up more there than here.

So if our trade balance were moving in response to the relative degrees of inflation here and abroad, we would be having increasing exports and reduced imports today. This inflation line, therefore, does not stand up as an explanation of the changes in our trade balance.

I have a few policy recommendations I would like to mention.

First, I agree with the people who spoke yesterday on the desirability of attempting to bring about a reallocation of the costs of NATO defense to some extent.

Second, I agree with the people who spoke yesterday on the desirability of the Germans taking on a larger share of the financing of underdeveloped countries.

In addition to that, I have four points of my own I would like to make:

First, because of our changed balance-of-payments position, we are in a much stronger position today to use the Reciprocal Trade Agreements Act as an effective bargaining instrument than we have ever been since the passage of the first act in 1934. At a time when the world was suffering from dollar shortage, to tell them to reduce their barriers against American goods was all right, but they were entirely ready to import more American goods if they had the dollars to pay for them. So we were not able to expect them to do more than that in any event.

The CHAIRMAN. How would you define "dollar shortage"? May

I define it for you? It is a desire to import American goods for which the foreign country has neither the means nor the desire to pay.

Mr. DESPRES. I was slow on the uptake. I would be glad to take your definition.

Senator BUSH. I would object to part of that, but I think it is a good start.

The CHAIRMAN. Excuse me, sir. This is an aside. But I have often been puzzled by these rather glib phrases, that the European countries have had "a dollar shortage."

Mr. DESPRES. This is a wide-open subject, but I would say, just historically, there has been, since the early thirties at least, and some would carry it back to World War I, what might be called a chronic tendency for our external receipts to exceed our external payments; other countries were more or less continually under pressure to find new measures to cut down on their use of dollars or to expand their dollar receipts. This has been the kind of problem that people have been discussing in using the phrase "dollar shortage." The rest of the world did not have a genuine payments equilibrium with the United States. Things were kept in line, after a fashion, by such devices as foreign exchange rationing and import quotas, currency devaluations and, at times, severe domestic deflation and unemployment.

The CHAIRMAN. What you are saying is that whatever the dollar shortage was, it has largely disappeared?

Mr. DESPRES. That is right. And this is an important change, even if we might disagree about its definition.

The other point would be: And, therefore, we have a new opportunity in our trade negotiations; the change in our balance-of-payments position and in that of Western Europe means we have a stronger bargaining position than we had before, since Western European countries have much greater leeway for reducing their trade barriers.

I think we ought to use this bargaining position for two main purposes: (1) to try to get the Common Market to adopt a very low external tariff; (2) to abolish as soon as possible—and it will take a while, certainly—the quantitative import restrictions on manufactured goods which are against GATT but were justified under the GATT provision that these could be used to meet balance-of-payments problems. The quantitative restrictions are still on, even though the balance-of-payments problem of the countries using them is gone.

But we ought to press hard for their removal.

II *INTERNATIONAL DEVELOPMENT*

7 *Dimensions and Dilemmas of Economic Development*[1]

The title of this paper, provided by the organizers of the seminar, gives the author great leeway, indeed too much leeway. The section which follows, entitled "General Perspective," presents one or two general observations regarding the pace of economic progress of the underdeveloped countries during the past decade. The subject of the subsequent section, "Strains in Economic Development," was selected for analysis chiefly because it has been less extensively written about than other aspects of the development process.

General Perspective

During the decade of the 1950's the annual growth rate of gross national product of the free world's underdeveloped countries was probably in the neighborhood of 3½ per cent; with population growing at 2 per cent, this meant an increase in per capita real income of about 1½ per cent annually. Of course, these averages hide wide variations in the experience of individual countries. For example, growth rates for Brazil, Mexico, Turkey, Ma-

1. Presented to a seminar at the Aspen Institute for Humanistic Studies, September 1963. Participants represented government, the business community, the World Bank, and the Agency for International Development.—Ed.

laya, Taiwan, and Israel were well above the average; the rates for Egypt, Pakistan, Indonesia, Bolivia, and Argentina were distinctly below. Nevertheless, the average figures, taken in conjunction with marked improvements in public health and expansion of educational facilities in most countries, reveal a rate of economic progress which, viewing the underdeveloped countries as a group, is probably unprecedented.

It is easy to understand why the low-income countries regard their rates of progress as unsatisfactory. First of all, they are highly unsatisfactory in relation to urgently felt aspirations. An annual growth rate of 1½ per cent means a doubling of per capita real income in two generations. At this rate it would take India a century to reach the level of per capita income which Mexico and Colombia enjoy today. (And, if their income per head grew at only this rate of 1½ per cent, it would take Mexico or Colombia half a century to reach Italy's present level.) Second, growth rates have been unsatisfactory in relation to those of the rich countries. The rate of growth of GNP in the underdeveloped countries during the 1950's was lower than in the industrially advanced countries of the free world, while their rate of population increase was higher, so that disparity in income per head between rich and poor countries widened further. Finally, much higher rates of growth were achieved in Communist China and in the Soviet Union.

If, as I believe to be the case, informed opinion in the United States is becoming increasingly disparaging of the economic performance of underdeveloped countries and increasingly skeptical of their development prospects, this attitude is less easy to understand than the feeling of dissatisfaction which prevails in underdeveloped countries. It is difficult to see how, taking into account the historical growth experience of the industrially advanced countries and the impediments which exist in today's underdeveloped countries, a larger accomplishment could reasonably have been expected. The average growth rate actually attained in the 1950's by the free world's underdeveloped countries, besides being unprecedented for them, does not compare unfavorably with the long-term growth trends of most of the industrially advanced countries of the free world. It is unlikely that many specialists a decade ago would have predicted—not only for the above-average performers such as Brazil or Taiwan but also for average performers like India—the rates of economic progress which have, in fact, been realized.

The contribution of foreign aid to the recent economic progress of low-income countries deserves recognition. The flow of aid from the industrially advanced to the underdeveloped countries of the free world, including governmental grants and net long-term lending as well as net private long-term investment, rose to $7.9 billion in 1961 as compared with an annual average of $3.5 billion in 1950-55. The contribution of foreign aid to the development process may be viewed from three aspects.

First, it supplements the domestic saving of the underdeveloped countries, thus supplying additional resources for capital formation. Viewed in this aspect, the approximately $8 billion of foreign aid furnished in 1961 was equivalent to about 30 per cent of the gross capital formation of the underdeveloped countries.

Second, foreign aid supplements export earnings, thus adding to the aid-receiving country's ability to import. Aid in 1961 was equivalent to 28 per cent of the export earnings of the underdeveloped countries.

Finally, certain types of foreign aid—technical assistance, "project" aid, and private direct investment—serve as vehicles for transferring technology, skills, "know-how," and organization to the underdeveloped countries.

For many of the underdeveloped countries, external aid made the decisive difference between economic growth and stagnation or decay. Nevertheless, the figures given above somewhat exaggerate the quantitative contribution of aid to the resources available for development. The 1961 figure was a new high. Aid other than grants generates some reverse flow of future interest and dividends. Finally, allowance should be made for the fact that a substantial amount of aid went to military or political "trouble spots," often with minimal effects on economic growth. The flow of governmental aid into the whole group of underdeveloped countries averaged $4 per capita in 1961, but official aid to the "trouble spots" ranged from $10 to $40 per capita.

Only a few of the underdeveloped countries are nearing a point where they can maintain self-sustaining growth in per capita income on the basis of their own resources plus the private foreign capital which they can attract on commercial terms. However, provided the flow of aid from the advanced countries is moderately increased and the special barriers which they have maintained against imports of manufactured goods from poor countries are somewhat reduced, there are strong reasons for believing that the rate of growth of income per head of the 1950's can be somewhat accelerated in the 1960's, despite rising rates of population growth.

It may well be felt that the preceding observations, dealing with the underdeveloped countries as a group and relying upon rather uncertain estimates of growth rates in per capita income, are too general to be of much significance. Nothing has been said about specific countries or regions. Nor has any reference been made to the serious impediments to economic development created by the policies, attitudes, and institutions of the underdeveloped countries themselves.

Nevertheless, economists in particular should stress, as a starting point, that recent progress in productivity and real income of most of the underdeveloped countries has been surprisingly good in relation to what might reasonably have been expected. In studying and writing about underdeveloped countries, they have given attention chiefly to the analysis of difficulties, problems, impediments, and shortcomings. Quite properly, they have been chiefly concerned with what is wrong rather than what is right. Although this is the way that economists can be most useful, its unfortunate side effect is often to give a distorted general picture. In this way economists have probably contributed to the increasingly skeptical attitude which now prevails in many influential quarters regarding the overall effectiveness of the development effort of recent years. Today's attitudes with respect to the economic progress of underdeveloped countries closely resemble attitudes during the period of the Marshall Plan regarding Western European prospects. In the middle phase of the Marshall Plan, after the initial enthusiasm had worn away, there developed a growing body of opinion in the United States, supported by a number of eminent economists, that the program could not possibly fulfill its central objective of making Western Europe self-supporting at rising levels of productivity and real income. Ironically, these views gained adherents at a time when the actual record showed an unexpectedly rapid rate of progress toward the objective. The distortion caused by the economist's necessary preoccupation with specific problems and difficulties—inflation, currency overvaluation, inadequate self-help measures—was probably a major reason for this earlier loss of perspective.

Political Strains in Economic Development

One basic postulate underlying the United States foreign aid program is that if underdeveloped countries achieve a healthy rate of economic growth, their pattern of political and social evolution is more likely to be compatible with United States interests and objectives than if they suffer economic stagnation or decay. I believe this postulate to be correct. Under conditions of economic stagnation, the prospects of a political evolution compatible with our primary interests appear slight indeed. Economic growth not only provides material benefits; it also may yield feelings of accomplishment, generate hope, and relieve feelings of inferiority and subordination. On the other hand, economic progress alone probably will not be sufficient to assure favorable political evolution. Economic progress itself often helps to generate rapid and sometimes turbulent political change. Since, however, a static and placid "normalcy" probably is not in the cards for the underdeveloped countries in any event, we shall have to accept the fact of rapid political change and proceed on the hypothesis that under conditions of economic progress the direction of political change, although perhaps disturbing, will not conflict in essential respects with our most basic interests.

Although this hypothesis seems reasonable, our understanding of the relationship between economic progress and political change is uncertain and limited. Economic progress generates economic strains and tensions which in low-income countries are in important respects different from those in industrially advanced countries. In the following paragraphs some (not all) of these differences will be examined. Although no attempt is made to provide the answer to the basic question mentioned above, some partial insights may be provided. The subject will be approached from the point of view of an economist, without attempting to trace the political consequences.

Income distribution is probably much more unequal in poor countries than in rich countries. The most basic reason is the relative abundance of common labor and the relative scarcity of manual and professional skills and of capital and entrepreneurship. The conventional subsistence wage leaves a large margin of unemployed urban labor and usually an even larger margin of underemployed agricultural labor ready to enter the urban labor market if even intermittent employment is available. Some of the scarce factors of production, on the other hand, are frequently priced below their scarcity value, for a variety of institutional reasons, thus leaving a margin of unsatisfied demand for these factors. Although relative rates of remuneration do not reflect fully the scarcity of skills and capital and the abundance of common labor, even the incomplete reflection of the underlying supply situation results in extremely wide income difference.

This is most clearly evident with respect to the structure of wages and salaries. Skill differentials are extremely wide, much wider than in the rich countries. In some of the top professional and administrative categories, salaries and fringe benefits are not far below Western European levels, and in a few cases they are actually higher. As one descends to the semi-professional and skilled manual occupations, the gap widens greatly, and for common labor it becomes extreme.

It is much more difficult to generalize about the rate of return realized by owners of industrial and commercial capital. This is partly because rates of return vary widely from firm to firm. It may be permissible, however, to venture the generalization that realized rates of return depend more largely upon dynamic than upon static factors. Even under conditions of moderate economic growth and capital accumulation, the underlying scarcity situation for capital is actively felt, and even moderate growth frequently generates very high rates of return. If, however, the economy becomes stagnant, rates of return are often strikingly low.

In the agricultural sector, only a few generalizations will be ventured. Where land ownership is highly concentrated in a few large holdings, this is obviously a major source of inequality. In the overpopulated low-income countries, the range of income in the agricultural sector is exceedingly wide, even in regions where the largest individual holdings are only a few acres. Finally, the average incomes of farmers and village artisans appear to be well below the lowest urban incomes of employed workers, except in the case of plantation workers producing export crops.

The greater inequality of incomes in poor than in rich countries is probably less significant than the fact that the economic process of development in low-income countries sets up tendencies toward increasing inequality. To be sure, these tendencies do not predominate throughout the whole range of the development process. If they did, economic inequality would be more marked in rich than in poor countries.

Perhaps the turning point with respect to income distribution comes when the excess supply of underemployed labor "backed up" in subsistence agriculture is fully absorbed through the cumulative expansion of the urban, commercial, and industrial sector and commercial agriculture. So long as common labor remains in excess supply, this tends to hold down wages of common labor. This turning point may already have been reached or may soon be reached in some of the countries which are not overpopulated. It remains a very distant point for the overpopulated regions of the Middle East and South Asia. In India and Pakistan, for example, the outflow of labor from agriculture into non-agricultural employment remains well below the additions to the agricultural labor force through population growth, so that despite the growth of the non-agricultural sector, the backlog of surplus labor continues to grow. With this labor supply situation, the critical turning point referred to above seems very distant.

So long as wages of common labor are held down by excess supply, the major portion of the increase in average output per worker resulting from capital accumulation, improved technology and organization, and expanding markets will flow to profits rather than wages or agricultural incomes, and the share of national income going to profits will increase.

To be sure, the whole increase in productivity will not be added to profits. If, for example, the growth in demand for skilled labor exceeds the growth in its supply, skill differentials may widen and a portion of the increase in profits will be diverted to skilled wages. Again, if the expansion in marketed supplies of foodstuffs from the agricultural sector of the economy does not keep pace with the expanding demand of the growing non-agricultural labor force, food prices may rise relative to the price of manufactured goods. This may in turn lead to higher wages at the expense of profits.

The increasing share of income going to profits should play a critically important role in the growth process. Provided a major fraction of profits is saved and productively invested, the rising share of profit makes possible a rising investment ratio and presumably an acceleration of economic growth.

The communist countries utilize far more powerful instruments to mobilize resources for investment purposes than non-authoritarian countries could apply. In non-authoritarian private enterprise economies, voluntary reinvestment of profits must provide a major portion of development resources, without which self-sustaining growth seems unattainable.

Even when a high proportion of profits is ploughed back, the growth in the share of income going to profits, the lag in wages, the steady inflow of unskilled rural labor into growing urban communities even in the face of widespread unemployment, and the appalling contrast between rich and poor in major cities of developing countries are a source of acute political and social tension. In many countries these strains tend to increase rather than decline until development reaches a somewhat advanced stage.

In a variety of ways, governmental measures in the low-income countries serve to reinforce these automatic tendencies towards growing inequality which characterize the prolonged initial phase of the growth process. Even the welfare measures undertaken to alleviate hardships most commonly benefit a small group of relatively well-paid workers working in large-scale organizations and enjoying fairly steady employment, thus widening the gap between the unskilled common laborers and others.

Although the problem is graver in some countries than in others, the phenomenon of markedly divergent regional rates of growth in developing countries is sufficiently widespread to be described as a general characteristic of the development process. The political strains resulting from regional inequalities in development are in some countries more severe than the strains enumerated above. This is the problem which Albert Hirschman has characterized as the North-South problem, referring to North-South contrast in the United States and in Italy.

At the beginning of the growth process in a previously stagnant economy, growth gets under way in a particular region rather than uniformly throughout the country. Whatever the initiating causes—natural resources, ports, historical and cultural factors, or sheer accident—the growth process itself makes the growing region an easier, more attractive, and more profitable place for most industries to undertake new investment. This is due to a variety of causes—transportation, communication and power facilities, a broad labor market, the availability of business and financial services, and proximity to a large and growing market. Consequently, the more developed and higher income regions enjoy relatively rapid growth while the poorer regions remain nearly stagnant. To be sure, offsetting tendencies may set in when the high-income region reaches full maturity and experiences retardation of growth. At this stage low wages in the poorer region may attract industry from the highly developed area. Even at this stage, however, the result may be uncertain unless positive action by public authorities to provide infrastructure, subsidize new industries, train workers, or pump in purchasing power are undertaken. The phenomenon of cumulatively widening disparities in income between regions within a country reproduces the international phenomenon of divergent growth rates between rich and poor countries.

A few outstanding examples of backward regions within underdeveloped countries are Northeast Brazil, the Northern region of Nigeria, East Pakistan, and Sumatra and the Celebes. The political consequences of the North-South problem are likely to be particularly severe and the difficulties of achieving a viable federalism particularly great when labor mobility between regions is restricted by cultural or other factors and when the backward region happens to be the country's principal foreign exchange earner. The importance of labor immobility scarcely requires elaboration, but the importance of the second factor should be explained. Through such devices as export taxes, government marketing, or currency overvaluation, the producers of exported primary products receive in local currency for their products an amount which fails to reflect the intrinsic value of the foreign exchange which their exports yield. The foreign exchange proceeds are then utilized chiefly to provide raw materials and capital equipment for the industrially expanding regions, while consumers in the backward regions, instead of purchasing in the world market, are limited to purchasing the higher priced products of sheltered domestic producers. This is understandably regarded as exploitation, and proposals of a separatist flavor are covertly advocated.

Of the four regions cited above, all except Northern Nigeria are net earners of foreign exchange. It is ironical that at the federal level the Northern region of Nigeria is strongly influential. In the Brazilian case the representatives of the Northeast are not without influence, particularly in times of crisis in the Northeast, and the Brazilian government has made sporadic efforts over a long period to meet the problem. The present effort is by far the most ambitious, but the state of tension in the Northeast is also most critical. In Pakistan and Indonesia the governments are entirely dominated by men of the relatively advanced region and the underlying strains are severe.

8 *Determining the Size of a Development Plan: Pakistan*

I Informal Lecture Delivered at Lahore University, July 21, 1956[1]

This paper discusses particular analytical problems related to the determination of the size of Pakistan's development plan. Our starting point must be the recognition that the situation in Pakistan with respect to real resources is remarkably uneven. Some resources are in excess supply or underutilized. This is especially true of the unskilled labor that is to be found in rural areas. On the other hand, there are other resources that are acutely scarce. Foreign exchange should be classified under this heading; so too should capital in general; also technological knowledge together with administrative and organizational capabilities. These are all scarce resources. The coexistence of surplus resources on the one hand and acute scarcities on the other influences both the composition and size of the development program. As far as the composition of the development program is concerned, the Plan emphasizes the surmounting of the bottlenecks in an attempt to ease the supply of scarce resources. Secondly, the Plan attempts to make maximum use of the abundant resources. This is the reason why the plan places such heavy emphasis on the saving of for-

1. At the time Despres was serving as advisor to the Pakistan Planning Board. The author owes much to his colleague Moen Qureshi. He also hopes this lecture reflected the moral purpose and insight of Zaheed Hussein, the first Chairman of the Pakistan Planning Board.—Ed.

eign exchange through the production of domestic substitutes for imports and for the various kinds of measures introduced to strengthen organizational administration, the expansion of technical training facilities, and measures that might spread improved technology in agriculture and elsewhere.

Particular attention must be given to the composition of the plan. This is because the problem of composition is in a sense inseparable from the problem of determining the feasible size of the development effort. The rate at which the development effort can grow—and hence the feasible size of the plan—depends upon the plan's success in increasing the supply of scarce resources and in bringing surplus resources into more effective use. In this sense, the size of the plan and its composition are inseparably interrelated.

The actual computation that must underlie the determination of the size of the plan depends chiefly on the assessment of three factors: first, the foreign exchange available for development purposes; second, the administrative and organizational capabilities; and third, the country's general financial resources. As a practical measure it may well be the case—indeed, it is probably the case—that the lower ceiling is set by the first two of these factors—that is, the foreign exchange constraint and administrative and organizational limitations.

I want, however, to discuss in particular the financial limitation. Here I find the greatest confusion with respect to analysis and methods. What do we mean by the availability of general financial resources? This is not simply a question of financial mechanics. The government is able to raise money by borrowing as well as by taxes. If the amount that the public will lend, and the amount of government securities that the public will buy, is limited—as indeed it is—the government must borrow from the banking system. If the amount that the commercial banks are able to lend to the government is limited, the government can borrow from the State bank. It might be said that even the State bank has certain legal reserve requirements and therefore its capacity to create money by lending to the government is also limited. This is true. It is, however, a purely technical limitation. The reserve requirements could be changed if it were desirable to do so. In the last analysis, it is not the limitation of the money-creating mechanism or the financial mechanism that limits the general amount of financial resources. It must be something else. The limitation obviously is inflation or the need for avoiding a persistent inflation. If total spending is excessive, so that a persistently inflationary situation exists, the result will be a flight from money, hoarding of commodities, flight of capital, a disruption of the entire process of production resulting in a reduction in the propensity to save, and not economic development. The need to avoid this flight from money is the basis of our desire to avoid inflation. It is this requirement which in turn imposes the overall financial constraint upon the development plan. In other words, the maintenance of financial balance means maintaining a proper relationship between the real resources required by the plan and the real resources that are potentially available for this purpose. This is the reason why analysis of the availability of financial resources must proceed in terms of the real resources that can support the development performance.

Consider now a basic table, such as appears in the financial chapter of the plan (see Table 5, p. 121), showing on the one side the sources of resources for development purposes, and on the other side the uses of resources. Public saving can be estimated as the excess of public revenue over non-development expenditure. Added to this is an estimate of private savings. The combination of these two can be thought of as the total internal savings of the economy. In other words, they represent an estimate of the unconsumed part of the gross national product of Pakistan. These are domestic resources, the internal contribution to the resources available for development purposes. Added to that is some figure showing the external finances believed to be available over the plan period. This external finance is in the form of private foreign investment and more largely in the form of government loans and grants. These sources of external finance enable the economy to maintain the net import balance of goods and services and thus to add to the aggregate real supply available to the economy.

The unconsumed portion of the country's gross national product plus external finance represent the resources available for development purposes. The absorption of these resources is indicated on the other side of the table under two broad heads of private investment and public development expenditure. This type of analysis is essentially Keynesian in character. In determining the size of the development plan, we have had to assess the potential for aggregate supply on the one hand and aggregate demand on the other and then relate the general concept of equilibrium or financial equilibrium in such a way as to determine whether the level of aggregate demand is high enough to make the fullest possible use of available resources. The nature of the overall financial constraint can perhaps be best considered by assuming that there is no shortage of foreign exchange and also that the development program is not hampered by administrative and organizational limitations. In other words, apart from these two bottlenecks, we assume that the demand for foreign exchange is equated to the supply of foreign exchange without the necessity of exchange controls to ration demand, and we also assume that the administrative and organizational capabilities are adequate to undertake a development program of any size that we want to undertake. If aggregate demand should exceed aggregate supply, total spending will increase, prices will rise, and we know that a danger point will be reached.

As a practical measure, however, the quality of statistical information now available in Pakistan is still inadequate for assessing currently the level of aggregate demand and aggregate supply. We do not know very much yet about the actual levels of consumption, saving, and private investment. How do we then judge excess demand? The judgment has to be a "symptomatic" one and has to depend largely on our observations of price behavior. What prices should be observed for symptoms of undesirable inflationary conditions? It might be submitted first that we ought not to pay primary attention to the prices of securities and real estate. It is a characteristic of a developing economy or a rapidly growing economy under conditions of private enterprise that from time to time rather large windfall gains accrue to holders of these types of assets, and that these types of assets become periodically subjected to intense speculative activity. It should be the function of a good tax system to capture a major share of these excessive windfall gains. The fact now, however, must be faced that there are still going to be for some time fairly large gains of this sort as development proceeds. In other words, speculative development and a rise in prices on security and real estate markets are not by themselves a serious danger signal. We have to regard this kind of speculation under present conditions as, to a considerable extent, an inescapable feature of economic development. I would also submit that in assessing inflationary development we ought not to pay primary attention to the prices of imported luxury goods, however close these goods may be to the hearts of the assessors of inflationary development. They are really not terribly important from the point of view of the economy as a whole. The same kind of analysis that I offered with respect to security prices applies here also. With a rise in national income there will probably be a rise in the share of income going to commercial and industrial profits. It is therefore to be expected that not only will the demand for luxury goods grow but that it will grow more than in proportion to the rise in income. The income elasticity of demand for these goods is very large. A country attempting to undertake an ambitious development program cannot allow the demand for luxury goods and services to become excessive. If the demand grows more rapidly than the supply, then exchange controls ought to be utilized to keep down luxury imports, and other internal controls on this sector will be necessary in order to channel investment into more socially productive channels. Here again if the tax system were more progressive and had a larger impact, the rise in prices would be less serious because some of the growing demand would be mopped up through increased tax revenue. These prices in the normal conditions of economic development in a country like Pakistan can be expected to show an upward trend. My conclusion, therefore, is that the prices of consumer essentials are the most important indicators to observe. If a persistent rise in the prices of consumer essentials can be avoided, then the situation is not dangerously inflationary, and I would submit that the desirable size of a development program should be established at that level which will be consistent with the avoidance of a steep rise in the prices of consumer essentials.

If Pakistan should have a smaller development plan than this, then it would fail to make adequate use of its resources for development. It may of course be that there are other limiting factors, such as the foreign exchange constraint or limited administrative and organizational capabilities, that necessitate a lower ceiling on the attainable rate of development. However, it should be the task of the planners to adjust the composition of the plan so far as possible so that the ceiling set by overall financial resources can be reached.

If the previously stated criterion is accepted—namely, the avoidance of sustained and substantial rise in the price of consumer essentials—what then are the major problems confronting Pakistan? Foodstuffs and cotton cloth are the most important consumer essentials in terms of the proportion of total consumer expenditure devoted to them. In the case of the cotton textiles industry, the supply position—the situation with respect to capacity—appears to be rather favorable: it appears that the industry can fairly rapidly keep pace with any reasonable short-term growth of demand. The real problem, therefore, is the possibility of a rise with respect to food. It should be recognized that agriculture from the supply side makes a twofold contribution to the non-agricultural sector of the economy. In the first place, the marketable surplus from agriculture is the chief earner of foreign exchange, the chief means of paying for imports. In the second place, the marketable surplus from agriculture provides the raw materials for feeding and clothing the non-agricultural population. Unless this marketable surplus rises, the growth of the urban industrial sector of the economy is bound to be seriously restricted. Since agriculture provides, in a sense, the major inputs for the industrial sector, the removal of the agricultural bottleneck is crucial for the industrialization process.

I do not want to express now any opinion regarding the notion that the terms of trade ought to be shifted in favor of the agricultural sector of the economy—that is, that agricultural prices ought to be raised in relation to the non-agricultural prices in order to provide incentives for agricultural producers. This may or may not be a sound idea. I think that even if one accepts this notion there is no question but that a cumulative rising spiral in agricultural prices must still be avoided. Therefore a factor of keen importance in determining the size of the development program will be Pakistan's success in expanding its supplies of agricultural commodities.

In sum, I would say that there are really three strategic constraints on the size of the development plan. First, the foreign exchange constraint; second, the administrative and organizational capabilities; and third, the degree of success in increasing agricultural production. These three factors overlap, of course, to a considerable extent. The relaxation of the foreign exchange constraint depends in part on agricultural output. The expansion of agricultural output depends in turn in considerable part on whether the organizational mechanism can be improved for introducing more advanced technology to cultivators. Such operations as agricultural extension services, village AID programs, and so on depend largely upon whether the necessary administrative and organizational capabilities are forthcoming and can be effectively established quickly. Thus the conclusion I reach is that the problem which I initially referred to as the availability of general financial resources really comes down under the present conditions to the development of agricultural production. In an economy such as Pakistan's, the determination of the size of the development plan depends on the intermingling of aggregate and structural considerations.

The general point I should like to make about this part of the analysis that has been followed in the plan document is that the interpretation of the aggregate demand and supply of natural resources is strictly Keynesian in character. In terms of our most recent economic survey, however, we have arrived at a highly Ricardian conclusion. In his *Principles of Political Economy and Taxation,* Ricardo viewed the problem of diminishing returns in agriculture as the key problem in the economy. It was a limitation on the growth of agricultural output that really set the upper limit to the growth of the non-agricultural sector and to capital formation for economic expansion. The Five-Year Plan of Pakistan incorporates a similar notion, and this is a crucial reason for the heavy emphasis that it places on agricultural production.

II Internal Financial Resources in Pakistan's Plan[2]

The role of finance is not merely one of providing money; rather, its fundamental task is to make available the real resources, human and material, necessary for the fulfillment of development objectives. The resources required for development in the plan period, in the monetary sector of the economy, amount to 10,800 million rupees, at present prices, consisting of real resources valued at 7500 million rupees to meet the requirements of the public sector program and 3300 million rupees of resources for gross private investment.

The size of this program was determined after the potential availability of aggregate real resources for development purposes had been assessed. A basic objective of financial policies must be to assure, on the one hand, that the scale of the plan is sufficient in magnitude to utilize, as fully and effectively as is practicable, the margin of real resources which the economy can provide for development, and on the other hand, that the plan's total requirements do not exceed the real resources potentially available for development. This is the essential goal of financial balance; it means, fundamentally, avoiding any serious excess or deficiency of claims in relation to the real resources which can be made available. Perfect precision in this matter is impossible. Fortunately, such precision is also unnecessary. It is essential, however, to prevent any sustained and substantial imbalance between resources and claims. A large and persistent imbalance, whether it resulted from an excess or a deficiency of claims, would jeopardize the achievement of the development goals.

It is difficult enough to make reliable forecasts of the availability of aggregate real resources even for a very short period ahead. It certainly cannot be done for periods as long as five years. This is one reason why it is impossible to treat any plan as fixed and rigid in all its details. Provisions must be made for continuous analysis of performance under the plan and of the evolving eco-

2. Written for Government of Pakistan, National Planning Board, *The First Five-Year Plan, 1955-60,* December 1957, Chapter 9, pp. 129-42. This chapter was written with Moen Qureshi, and Abdul Shahoor assisted in preparing the tables.—Ed.

nomic situation in the country. A "safe" plan, which underutilizes resources because it is based upon overcautious assumptions, is just as unsatisfactory as one which is based on overoptimistic assumptions about resources and exceeds capabilities. Planning should be done on the basis of reasonable projections of available resources, subject to appropriate adjustments if sizeable shortages or surpluses develop.

It should be recognized also that although overall financial balance is a necessary feature of a sound plan, such balance alone is not sufficient to assure the feasibility of the program. Financial balance relates to the availability of real resources of different kinds being aggregated for this purpose on the basis of their market values at present prices. In addition to the requirements of overall balance, it is also necessary to adjust the scale and composition of the development program to the limitations of our supply of certain specific resources, such as foreign exchange, and entrepreneurial, organizational, and technical capabilities. Problems of specific resources are considered elsewhere in this report; financial balance alone, the balance of real resources in the aggregate, is the subject of this chapter.

The potentially available supply of goods and services in any year consists of the gross national product which can be produced plus the net import balance in current transactions with the rest of the world which can be financed. The bulk of this total supply will be currently consumed. To arrive at the resources available for development, one must deduct the consumption goods and services used by the private sector as well as by the public sector for purposes other than development, such as civil administration and defense. The remainder represents the margin of resources available for development.

This margin contains two elements—internal saving (gross) and external finance. Saving is performed both by individual action in the private sector and by collective action through the public sector. The term public saving, as used in this chapter, denotes the excess of the public sector's gross income (revenues from taxation and from such non-tax sources as the gross profits, before depreciation charges, of government-owned enterprises) over public expenditure for non-development or "consumption" purposes.

This excess of revenues represents a levy imposed on the community for the purpose of restricting private claims against available resources, thus freeing these resources for development.

Private saving, on the other hand, is the result of individual decisions to refrain from consuming some portion of income. It consists of the margin of personal income (after tax) over personal consumption, plus the undistributed profits and depreciation accruals of private firms. It is, in other words, the unconsumed portion of the private sector's gross income. Internal saving (gross), which is the sum of public saving plus private saving, represents the excess of gross national product over private consumption plus public non-development expenditures; it is the margin of gross national product available for development.

External finance adds to the aggregate physical supply of goods and services by permitting a surplus of imports in the balance of international payments on current account. The sources of external finance are (a) foreign grants and loans to the public sector, (b) the utilisation of reserves of gold and foreign exchange, and (c) foreign investment in and credits to the private sector. Although temporary fluctuations, upward and downward, in reserves are bound to occur, it has been assumed, in framing the development program, that external reserves, which have been very substantially reduced in recent years, should not undergo further net depletion during the plan period. Consequently, apart from transitory deviations, the deficit on current account should be limited to the external finance made available by foreign governments, international agencies, and private investors and lenders abroad. The import balance on current account made possible by external finance provides additional resources for the development program above what is available from internal saving.

In determining the size of the development program, we have estimated the magnitude of each of the main sources of resources available for development purposes—internal saving, public and private, and external finance. The original estimates presented in the draft plan have been revised and are presented below. The revised estimates take account of the changes in the economic situation and in the price level up to 1956. In projecting the potential availability of internal resources we have not provided for any further rise in the average level of prices after 1956. Another assumption is that the real national product will increase by 15 per cent during the plan period. The national product, as it grows, should provide a larger and larger volume of saving, thus permitting further expansion of the scale of development, and laying the basis for continued growth in the national product. If this automatic tendency for saving to rise as national income grows is reinforced by vigorous public measures the successive increments of resources for development can be substantial.

Public Saving

Our projections of public saving, and of the consolidated revenues and non-development expenditures of the central and provincial governments for the plan period are given in Table 1. For the plan period as a whole, revenues are estimated at 11,410 million rupees and non-development expenditures at 10,410 million rupees, leaving a net balance of public saving available for development purposes of 1000 million rupees.

TABLE 1 ***Public Saving***
Consolidated revenues and non-development expenditures of central and provincial governments. 1955–60

(Million rupees)

	TOTAL	ANNUAL AVERAGE
Revenues	11,410	2282
Less Non-Development Expenditure	10,410	2082
Public Saving	1000	200

Revenues exceed non-development expenditures by only a small margin in the early years of the plan. The major portion of public saving will be concentrated in the latter years of the plan. The increase in public saving reflects a projected rise in revenues of 29 per cent with only a small increase in non-development expenditures. This growth in public saving will come about partly as the automatic result of expansion of production, incomes, and external and internal trade. But to achieve it fully a series of positive measures will be needed to augment revenues and to prevent unnecessary expansion in non-development expenditures.

It was mentioned earlier that the concept of public saving which we have used has been framed for the specific purpose of measuring the contribution of public revenues to the resources available for the plan. The public development expenditures projected by the plan include expenditures for the replacement as well as for the expansion of publicly owned physical capital. Correspondingly, public saving has been computed on a gross basis, by including as an element of revenue the depreciation accruals of public enterprises from which replacement can be financed. Moreover, the development outlays embraced by the plan are not confined to investment in fixed capital, but include outlays on certain new or expanded schemes in the fields of education, health, Village Aid, and other social services which, although not resulting in the creation of new physical facilities, serve to increase the community's intangible productive capital, by raising the fitness and skill of the people. Accordingly, in computing public saving available for development purposes, we have deducted from gross revenues only public expenditures which we have classified as non-developmental. The figure for public saving derived on this basis is considerably higher than the figure which would be obtained if we were measuring merely the resources available for net investment; our estimates should not be interpreted as measuring public saving in this latter sense.

Moreover, public saving, as the term is used here, should not be confused with a surplus in the revenue budget. The distinction between development expenditures and non-development expenditures, upon which our concept of public saving rests, differs from that between revenue disbursements and capital disbursements in the official budget tables of central and provincial governments. Our definition of revenues also differs to some extent from that used for budget purposes.

Private Saving

PROJECTION AND DEFINITION

Our projection of potential private saving for the plan period is 5600 million rupees. The annual rate of saving is expected to rise as national income grows. Our projection for 1959-60 is estimated to be 32 per cent above the level of 1954-55.

Several points with respect to the meaning and scope of private saving, as the term is used in this report, should be noted. First, our concept of private saving includes depreciation accruals on privately owned physical plant and equipment.

Second, our projection of private saving excludes such saving as will be absorbed by the normal expansion of privately owned stocks of raw materials, goods-in-process, and semi-finished and finished products. Owing solely to lack of data, our estimate of private investment in recent years and projections for the plan period cover only investment in fixed capital. The investment needed to increase stocks of raw materials, goods-in-process, and semi-finished and finished articles is not included in our figures as part of the development program. The need for working stocks will rise as a result of the growth in national product and the broadening of the monetary sector of the economy, and saving is just as necessary to expand working stocks as to enlarge fixed capital. Since we have not been able to include any estimate for this type of investment in the development program, it was also necessary to omit the saving which will be absorbed by normal expansion of working stocks from our estimates and projections of private saving.

Third, the estimates of private saving used in this chapter relate to the monetized sector only. Similarly, the figures for the development program given in this chapter refer only to money expenditures for development purposes. We have not here included any estimates of the saving which takes place in the non-monetized sector, nor have we included in our development program the corresponding private investment in the non-monetized sector. This omission does not imply that this form of saving and investment is unimportant; on the contrary, one of the main objectives of the Village Aid program is to stimulate such saving and investment through voluntary, cooperative effort in improving village facilities. The unpaid work undertaken by families and villages to improve local facilities should become a most significant element in our whole development effort, and in this sense it is an important part of the plan. However, such saving and investment involve no specifically financial problems and it is for this reason that the non-monetized sector has been excluded from the estimates of private saving and private investment presented in this chapter.

Fourth, it should be stressed that our projection of private saving, like that of public saving, refers to potential rather than actual saving. In other words, these projections represent the amount of saving which would be forthcoming if development expenditures were maintained at the highest level which the economy can support without inflating the price level of essential consumer goods. Development expenditures provide money incomes to those who are engaged on the development schemes as workers or as suppliers of materials. A level of development expenditures which makes inadequate use of all potential resources tends directly to restrict private incomes resulting from construction work and other development activities. As a consequence, the flow of private money payments by those whose incomes have been restricted is cut, and money income declines throughout the economy. An inadequate level of development expenditure restricts both consumer spending and private and public saving. This may cause a decline in consumer goods prices, but lower prices resulting from restricted consumer purchasing power rather than from increased production and supplies are not a net social benefit. If development expenditures are not sufficient to absorb present productive capabilities, current income and present rate of actual saving are below what is possible, and the future growth of the development effort is also restricted. For forecasts of resources available for development, it is potential saving, rather than actual saving, which is relevant. Whether actual saving will come up to, or fall short of, potential saving depends upon the adequacy of the plan in relation to available real resources.

Finally, our projection of potential private saving, as well as the projection of public saving, should be interpreted as an estimate of underlying trend values. The savings potential in any one year may temporarily be substantially above or below its trend value. The national product is subject to sizeable year-to-year fluctuations, arising chiefly from variations in harvest or from fluctuating market conditions for export products. Although these short-term upward and downward movements are accompanied by movements in the same direction in total consumption of goods and services, the variations in consumption are usually smaller in absolute magnitude than the variations in real income. Since saving consists of the small excess of real product, or real income, over total consumption, a somewhat smaller movement of consumption than of income necessarily means a relatively wide percentage change in saving. In years of abundant harvests or favorable export markets, a slower increase in consumption than in real income would generate abnormally large saving, which should be used to build up foreign exchange reserves and internal stocks of goods. In bad years, the severity of the decline in consumption is usually moderated by such means as using external reserves, drawing upon domestic stocks, obtaining emergency aid, or, as a last resort, curtailing capital goods imports, to provide exchange for the purchase of essential consumer goods. All these devices serve to bolster consumption in the face of declining income, thus reducing saving below its trend value.

It is, of course, impossible to take account, in our projections, of these large short-term changes in the rate of saving. It is for this reason that our projections must be presented as five-year totals rather than annual estimates. Sizeable temporary deviations from the underlying trends must be expected in abnormally good or abnormally bad years. These wide short-term variations in the rate of saving, resulting from fluctuations in harvests or in terms of trade, are a major obstacle to the execution of an orderly development program. It is highly important, therefore, to build up substantial stocks of foodstuffs, and, if possible, increase reserves of foreign exchange, in order to protect the development program from the disruption which these fluctuations in saving might otherwise produce.

METHOD OF ESTIMATION

The computation of our estimate of potential private saving involved two main steps. The initial step was to obtain a base figure by estimating the trend value of potential private saving in 1954-55. The second step was to project this figure for the plan period, taking into account the effect both of growth in national income and of certain measures which we recommend as essential for encouraging thrift.

To arrive at a base figure, we began by estimating the average annual rate of actual private saving during the four-year period from 1951-52 to 1954-55. This computation is shown in Table 2. The actual rate of private saving in any past period may be inferred by use of the following relationship:

Private saving equals
- (1) Private investment domestically financed *plus*
- (2) Public expenditures financed by increase in domestic liabilities or liquidation of assets, *minus*
- (3) Decrease in gold and foreign exchange reserves and other balances abroad.

This formula was used in our computation. The estimate of private investment in fixed capital required for this calculation is that of the Planning Board.

TABLE 2 Private Saving, Annual Average, 1951-52 to 1954-55

(Million rupees)

1. Domestically financed private investment:	
Private investment (gross)	593
Less—Foreign investment in and credits to private sector	43
Domestically financed	550
2. Public expenditures financed from domestic non-revenue sources:	
Through increase in domestic liabilities (permanent, floating, and unfunded debt and increase in deposits, etc.)	370
Through decrease in assets (sale of land and PIDC assets and decrease in cash)	186
Total (1) and (2)	1106
3. *Deduct*—decrease in foreign exchange (and gold) holdings	177
Private saving	929

Table 2 shows that private investment annually absorbed, on the average, an estimated 550 million rupees of domestic funds. Public expenditures financed through domestic borrowings, liquidation of assets, and allied methods averaged 556 million rupees. Thus, total domestic financing, both to expand fixed capital in the private sector and to provide funds for public expenditures, averaged 1106 million rupees. The absorption of real resources through such internal financing exceeded the resources made available through private saving, as is revealed by the reduction of external reserves at an average rate of 177 million rupees. Subtracting this figure, private saving may be estimated to have provided annually an average of 929 million rupees of resources.

To arrive at a figure for the trend value of potential private saving in 1954-55, expressed in rupees of 1955 post-devaluation buying power, this figure should be adjusted to allow for a number of factors. These factors include the upward trend of real income during the four-year period, the distinction mentioned earlier between actual and potential saving, and adjustment to rupees of 1955 post-devaluation purchasing power. After roughly evaluating these factors, we have estimated the trend value of potential private saving for 1954-55, expressed in rupees of 1955 post-devaluation purchasing power, at 900 to 1000 million rupees. Consequently, we have adopted 950 million rupees as our base figure for 1954-55.

The projection of private saving for the plan period involves two further assumptions. First, we have assumed that real national product will increase by 15 per cent from 1954-55 to 1959-60. Second, we have assumed that one-tenth of the rise in gross national product will be devoted to increased private saving.

It should be clearly understood that a 15 per cent growth in national product can be achieved only through a vigorous implementation of the plan. Without a substantially enlarged and balanced development program which concentrates limited resources upon schemes of highest productivity, an annual rate of growth in real income approaching 3 per cent would not be possible. Allowing for growth of population, it would permit a rise in per capita income of nearly 1.4 per cent per year. Of this it is expected that roughly one half will be absorbed by increased private consumption and the balance will go into increased public non-development expenditures and increased savings.

Moreover, our assumption that as much as one-tenth of the increment of national product will be devoted to increased private saving requires for its fulfillment the strengthening of existing governmental measures and the adoption of certain new measures to encourage thrift and discourage non-essential expenditure. Private saving, at 950 million rupees in 1954-55, represented about 5 per cent of gross national product. Thus, an incremental ratio of 10 per cent implies that as real income increases, a rising fraction of the total income will be saved. A considerable portion of saving in recent years was performed by recipients of temporary windfall profits. The expansion of cotton spinning and weaving capacity has already reached a point where mill margins have been somewhat reduced from earlier inflated levels. Devaluation of the rupee, while raising the incomes of producers of export crops, has reduced the disparity between the external prices and the domestic prices of imported goods, thus lowering the extremely wide profit margins of importers. The diminution of the previously inflated profits of mill owners and of importers may well reduce the saving of these groups.

Along with these developments, the gain in tax revenues during the plan period resulting from improved tax collection, from devaluation, and from customs receipts on foreign aid imports, and the further increase in revenues to be expected from adoption of the recommendations made in the following chapter will be partly at the expense of private saving. Taking all these factors into account, our assumption of a 10 per cent incremental saving ratio represents a goal to be achieved; it should not be taken for granted as an automatic and assured by-product of economic growth.

MEASURES TO ENCOURAGE THRIFT

To assure the required growth of private saving, it is necessary, in the first place, to impose deterrents to non-essential consumption. This requires tight import controls and a rigorous denial of exchange permits for the imports of non-essential consumer goods. As the availability of foreign exchange is increased, it is of the utmost importance that external buying power should be concentrated upon increased imports of raw materials, repair parts, and new capital equipment, and that none of it be diverted to the importation of luxuries, on avoidable travel spending abroad, and similar uses. Strict exchange controls, by limiting the opportunities for luxury consumption, are a potent factor for conserving foreign exchange and promoting private saving.

It is also of importance that expenditure on domestically produced luxuries should be appropriately curbed. Although the tax proposals which we have recommended will have a mild restraining effect by absorbing some of the growth in income of the well-to-do groups, these proposals must be supplemented by more direct measures. Restrictions on the scale of ceremonial and other sumptuous entertaining should be reimposed and strictly enforced. It is also important that a general surveillance should be exercised over new private investment, both to encourage the establishment and expansion of enterprises which will contribute to economic growth and to the raising of general living standards, and to discourage costly investment in forms which, instead of strengthening the economic foundations for a broad rise in living standards, cater only to the taste of a small well-to-do group. This would include restriction of luxury construction of all sorts, whether for houses, high-class shops, expensive amusement places, or elaborate public buildings. In Western Europe the growth of commercial and industrial wealth was aided and promoted by the frugality of the middle class. As this class gained in wealth and power, the lavish practices of the older land-owning aristocracy came increasingly into disrepute. In this country also a growth of frugality is essential in order that a major portion of the growing incomes from industry and trade and the incomes of landowners may contribute to further economic growth.

The restrictive measures taken to curb non-essential consumption should be accompanied by other steps to encourage saving. Measures for the development and expansion of the operations of the life insurance companies are proposed in the chapter on credit, banking, and insurance. We also recommend that, while interest rates on government securities held by the banking system should be kept low, substantially higher rates should be put into effect on securities designed to attract the funds of other investors and on saving deposits.

Internal Saving

Our projections of public and private saving are combined in Table 3, which shows the resources available for the development program from domestic sources.

Table 3 Internal Saving (Gross)

(Million rupees)

	TOTAL	ANNUAL AVERAGE
Public saving	1000	200
Private saving	5600	1120
Total	6600	1320

Total internal saving during the plan period, according to our projection, represents about 6 per cent of estimated gross national product in these years, as compared with about 5 per cent in 1954-55. As was noted earlier, saving as the term is here used refers to the total internal resources available for development uses, including replacement as well as expansion of fixed capital and certain expenditures on development schemes which do not result directly in physical capital formation. It excludes, however, non-monetized saving and the savings absorbed by normal investment in working stocks. Using the conventional definition of saving—internal resources available for net investment—the ratio to national income during the plan period may be roughly estimated to be in the neighborhood of 5 per cent.

During the plan period the projected rate of growth of internal saving averages about 12 per cent annually, in comparison with an annual rate of growth of national income of slightly below 3 per cent. Almost one-fourth of the increase in gross national product will be absorbed by increased gross saving, public and private. Gross internal saving in the final year of the plan will be equivalent to about 7 per cent of the country's gross product, against about 5 per cent in 1954-55. It should be kept in mind that we have treated as saved that portion of public revenue which finances increased social service and research outlays, and that we have assumed a total defense expenditure of 4775 million rupees during the plan period.

External Finance

We estimate that new foreign investment in the private sector will amount to about 500 million rupees during the plan period. On the other hand, repayment of deferred credits previously granted to finance the import of machinery will absorb nearly 100 million rupees, leaving a net import of capital into the private sector of 400 million rupees.

Any projection of foreign loans and grants to the public sector is necessarily conjectural, because the amount depends largely on future decisions of foreign governments and lending institutions. The estimates of foreign aid and loans, 3800 million rupees, shown below exclude receipts from import of food grain under aid. This amount of non-food aid is believed to be well within the range of possibilities. Our expectations of foreign loans are based on the rate at which it has been possible to borrow from abroad in the past few years as well as on the existence of suitable projects which can be made the basis of negotiations for foreign loans in the future. Our estimates of foreign aid assume a considerable increase in the rate at which aid has been received so far.

We consider that foreign exchange reserves, although showing temporary fluctuations, should not be permitted to undergo further net depletion during the plan period.

Our projection of external finance is shown in Table 4.

External finance performs a dual role in the economy. By permitting a surplus of imports in the balance of international pay-

TABLE 4 External Finance, 1955-60

(Million rupees)

	TOTAL	ANNUAL AVERAGE
Loans and grants to public sector	3800	760
Investment in and credits to private sector	400	80
Total	4200	840

ments on current account, it adds to the aggregate physical supply of disposable goods and services, thereby permitting development expenditure to exceed internal saving. This would be the main significance of external finance if the economy were not faced with a special limitation with respect to imports. As is well known, however, the country faces also a specific shortage of foreign exchange. It is for this reason that the plan places heavy emphasis on the expansion of domestic production to replace imports and, so far as possible, on the development of exports. In view of the special shortage of foreign exchange, external finance has a double significance; it serves both to increase the aggregate resources and also relieves a specific shortage of key importance to the economy. In this chapter external finance is treated only in the first of these aspects, as an addition to the aggregate physical resources available for development purposes. The specific balance of availability and requirements for foreign exchange is the subject of a separate chapter. It should be mentioned here, however, that the role of external finance is of far greater strategic importance to the execution of the plan than a comparison of its monetary magnitude with that of internal saving would suggest. A large curtailment of foreign aid or a sizeable shortfall of export earnings would necessitate halting work on many schemes. Most of the development schemes involve considerable expenditure on imported capital equipment and technical aid. It is obvious that external aid and credit in these forms contribute directly to the development program. Moreover, external aid in industrial materials and foodstuffs permits an increase in the tempo of the development effort both by freeing some foreign exchange earnings, which would otherwise have to be used for these purposes, for financing capital goods imports, and by adding to the total supply of these goods. With additional supplies of goods, it is possible to increase internal expenditures for development without producing inflationary consequences.

The Sources and Uses of Resources for Development

It is now possible to summarize our projection of the real resources available for development purposes during the plan period and to compare the aggregate availability of resources with the requirements of the plan. This comparison is made in Table 5. The potential availability of real resources is estimated at 10,800 millions, consisting of 1000 millions of public saving, 5600 millions of private saving, and 4200 millions of external finance.

TABLE 5 Sources and Uses of Resources for Development, 1955-60

(Million rupees)

SOURCES:		USES:	
Public saving	1000	Private investment	3300
Private saving	5600	Public development expenditure	7500
External finance	4200		
Total	10,800	Total	10,800

We consider that the foregoing projections of the trend of availability of resources for development purposes provide a reasonable guide in setting the magnitude of the development program. It has already been noted that our trend projections will undoubtedly require future periodic revisions in the light of experience under the plan, and that even with such revisions internal saving may be expected to deviate markedly in exceptionally good or exceptionally bad years from its estimated trend.

These considerations lead to two important conclusions. In the first place, the plan must not become fixed or rigid. A considerable measure of flexibility must be preserved with respect to its tempo, magnitude, and composition. Adjustments should be made whenever indicated by the periodic revisions of the projections of resources available. Secondly, even though the required balance is maintained between the size of the program and the trend of available resources, year-to-year fluctuations in harvests or in export markets may produce sizeable temporary discrepancies or gaps between resources actually available and the requirements of our program. Such temporary gaps are to some extent inevitable. Although flexibility in programming is essential, adjustments, upward or downward, must be carried out in an orderly and efficient manner. Large revisions cannot be executed suddenly without great administrative difficulty, and the disruption and waste resulting from abrupt changes in tempo would be exorbitantly costly.

It is the function of reserves, both foreign exchange and internal stocks, to bridge the temporary gaps which will arise from time to time. If these reserves are insufficient to meet periods of strain, any development program which adequately utilizes resources may be seriously disrupted by transitory shocks to the economy, such as a poor harvest or a temporary slump in world markets for exports. We wish to stress the need for building up foreign exchange reserves and internal stocks, particularly of foodstuffs, whenever this is feasible, in order to provide a more nearly adequate cushion against temporary shocks. This is essential for a development program of adequate size, to be sustained without disruptions and setbacks.

Although the country should rely chiefly on reserves instead of attempting fully to adjust the tempo of the development program to merely temporary fluctuations in internal saving, it is of the greatest importance to prevent any large and persistent disparity between the potential real resources for development purposes and the requirements of the plan. Failure to utilize fully the potentially available resources is grossly wasteful; the obvious remedy for such waste is energetically to expand the development effort. A very strenuous effort to accelerate the development program is needed in order to activate the resources which can be brought into use for this purpose.

Although the present urgent task is to step up the tempo of the development effort, it is also true that a development program whose requirements outrun the real resources which can be made available for this purpose is, equally, to be avoided. If money expenditures for development purposes were allowed to rise at a more rapid rate than the real resources provided through internal saving and external finance could expand, the result would be an inflation of the price level. The need for avoiding price inflation sets an upper limit to the size of the development outlays which can prudently be undertaken.

It has sometimes been urged that a gradual and continuing inflation of prices is desirable, on the ground that, by squeezing certain classes of consumers and increasing the share of national income going to profits, inflation actually increases real saving and thereby enlarges the margin of resources for development. Such a policy, although it may work for a time, is full of danger. It rests on the hazardous assumption that price inflation, even though persistent, will be so gradual that it will pass unnoticed. In the economic realm matters can seldom be arranged with such delicate precision. Moderate short-term movements in the price level are not seriously harmful and can hardly be avoided, but an upward trend of prices, if it persists for a considerable period, is unlikely to remain gradual and unnoticed. Once the trend becomes recognized, and further price increases come to be generally expected, the result may be a flight from money into goods, thus accelerating the rise in prices. It causes a withholding of marketable supplies and a disappearance of goods into speculative holdings and hoards, resulting in a disruption of production and normal trade. This deprives both the development program and the vast majority of consumers of essential supplies and resources. Internal inflation also curtails exports, and, despite exchange controls, causes leakages of foreign exchange. Inflation, if carried to an extreme, far from stimulating development, disrupts the whole process. It is for this reason that an attempt to carry out a development program whose requirements substantially exceed the resources which can be made available from internal saving, public and private, and from external finance may actually set back economic growth.

Although short-term fluctuations in the price level can hardly be prevented and should not cause alarm, a sustained upward trend must be avoided. The correction need not invariably be made through a reduction in government expenditures for development. Alternative measures to increase revenues, to reduce non-development outlays, to encourage private thrift by restricting the supply of non-essential goods, imported or domestic, to curb luxury private expenditure, and to secure additional external aid should first be considered. Government expenditures for development should be curtailed only if action in these other fields cannot be taken on a sufficient scale to correct a major imbalance.

The best indicator for detecting the presence of inflationary tendencies is a general index of the prices of goods and services bought by low-income consumers. This means chiefly basic foods, cotton cloth, kerosene, and a few other articles of mass consumption. If the average level of prices of goods of this class remains approximately stable, one can be confident that available resources are not being subjected to inflationary strains; if, however, an upward tendency not ascribable to purely temporary causes becomes evident, this is a danger signal and indicates the need for corrective action.

The Financing of Government Development Expenditures

AVAILABILITY OF RESOURCES

As a guide in budgeting government development expenditures under our plan, it is useful to project the real resources for development uses available to the public sector alone. Such a projection may be readily obtained by deducting the resources allocated to private investment from our previously presented estimates of total resources available for the whole development program, shown in Table 5 above. The deductions consist of the external finance and private saving absorbed by private investment. The remaining resources, available for the development program of the public sector, are shown in Table 6.

TABLE 6 Resources Available for Government Development Program, 1955-60

(Million rupees)

	ESTIMATES	
ITEMS	TOTAL 1955-60	ANNUAL AVERAGE
Public saving	1000	200
Foreign grants and loans to public sector	3800	760
Excess of private saving over internally financed private investment	2700	540
Total resources available	7500	1500
Government development expenditure	7500	1500

According to these estimates, the total resources available for government development expenditure during the plan period amount to 7500 million rupees, averaging 1500 million rupees per year. These estimates emphasize the urgency of substantially expanding government development expenditures if potential resources are to be effectively used. The task of executing a large and rapid increase in the development program will call upon all the resources of organization and enterprise which the central and provincial governments can bring to bear.

THE USE OF PRIVATE SAVING FOR GOVERNMENT DEVELOPMENT EXPENDITURES

Of the total resources available for government development expenditures during the plan period, we estimate that public saving will furnish 1000 million rupees, or 13 per cent, and foreign grants and loans 3800 million rupees, or 51 per cent. The plan envisages that the remaining contribution of resources, amounting to 2700 million rupees or 36 per cent, will come from private saving.

This utilization of private saving by the public sector is an essential feature of the plan, and is indispensable to any adequate and effective development program. The circumstances which make it appropriate for the Government to perform the role of channeling a large share of the voluntary saving of the private sector into productive uses are deeply rooted in the present economic situation. If these circumstances, and the resulting need for an active government policy for putting private saving to work, were not clearly recognized in the plan, the development effort would be needlessly restricted and the pace of economic progress would be feeble indeed.

This arises from the fact that the process of economic development, at its present early stage, requires heavy emphasis on public expenditures for development purposes. Of the total development expenditures under the plan, the public sector accounts for 69 per cent and gross private investment for 31 per cent. This does not reflect any predilection for public enterprise; on the contrary, public outlays will broaden the opportunities for private activity. We envisage that the percentage of private investment will tend to grow as a more advanced stage of economic development is reached.

A large portion of projected government development expenditures are for needed expansion of "social overhead" capital, in such fields as irrigation, power, transport, and communications. Public investment in facilities of this type is essential to the growth of private industry, agriculture, and commerce. Increased expenditure on education will help to provide the trained men and women whom an expanding economy requires. The Village Aid program is designed to promote private co-operative activities on a broad front, contributing to rural development. The program of the Pakistan Industrial Development Corporation in launching new industries will extend industrial growth into new and productive fields which private enterprise, for various reasons, is not yet equipped to initiate. After these PIDC undertakings have become successfully established as going concerns, they will normally be transferred from public to private ownership. Finally, the development program of the public sector includes provision of the capital funds for credit institutions to finance agriculture and private industry. Viewed as a whole, therefore, government development expenditures required under the plan are designed to supplement and promote, rather than displace, private economic activities. Meanwhile, with the falling rate of large-scale private investment in the cotton textile industry, new avenues and opportunities for private investment in other sectors must be developed. Consequently, the role of government development schemes is now of crucial importance, and this accounts for the relatively heavy emphasis on public outlays under the plan.

The most fruitful allocation of development resources between the public and private sectors, as envisaged by the plan, actually results in a level of private investment which is well below potential private saving. This excess of private saving over internally financed private investment provides a sizeable margin which is available for the development expenditure of the public sector. Government must channel this saving into productive channels if the resources potentially available are to be adequately and effectively used. Owing to the surplus of private saving available, this does not create inflationary dangers. Inflationary pressures would be created only if development expenditures exceeded the margin of real resources available to the public sector for this purpose.

METHODS OF FINANCING

The voluntary saving of private firms and individuals is used by them to increase their assets or to reduce their debts; it is embodied, therefore, in an increase in the net assets or net worth of firms and individuals. Consequently, the operation of mobilizing private saving for use by the public sector is carried out by increasing the public sector's domestic liabilities and by liquidating some of its assets. These operations add to the net assets of the private sector, thus providing outlets for potential private saving.

In considerable degree, the Government's financing methods must be dictated by the preferences of firms and individuals with respect to the types of assets which they wish to hold. Rough estimates are given in Table 7 of the channels through which private saving may be mobilized for the development program of the public sector. The projection of private saving available to the public sector, shown in the first line of Table 7, is taken from

TABLE 7 Financing Methods in Absorption of Private Saving by Public Sector, 1955-60

(Million rupees)

ITEMS	ESTIMATE TOTAL 1955-60	ESTIMATE ANNUAL AVERAGE
Private saving available to public sector	2700	540
Methods of financing:		
1. Increase in provident funds, postal saving, Postal Life Insurance; sale of land and PIDC assets; repayment of advances to private borrowers; increase in deposits of local bodies, etc.	1200	240
2. Increase in permanent and floating debt	1500	300
Total	2700	540

Table 6. In the second line of Table 7, we have attempted to estimate roughly the amount of funds which may flow into the public sector through increase in unfunded debt, the sale of publicly owned assets, repayment of outstanding advances due from private borrowers, and increase in the funds of local bodies and others held on deposit with central and provincial finance offices. The third line, designated "Increase in permanent and floating debt," shows the remaining amount of private saving to be mobilized though borrowing operations.

In this computation it is assumed that no net change takes place in the consolidated cash balances of central and provincial governments, and that there will be no net accumulation of unspent counterpart funds. Thus the amounts taken under borrowing represent what the Government would borrow to finance its development expenditures rather than to build up cash balances. If cash balances or counterpart funds are accumulated, the amount of borrowing consistent with the avoidance of inflation would be correspondingly increased. The public sector does not absorb private saving through the act of borrowing itself, but rather through the expenditure of borrowed funds. Hence, our figures for borrowing are to be taken net, after deducting any increases in working balances and counterpart funds.

If the portion of available private saving reaching the public sector through growth in unfunded debt, sales of assets, and allied channels should prove to be smaller or larger than we have estimated, the amount which can appropriately be raised through expansion of permanent and floating debt would be correspondingly increased or reduced.

EFFECTS ON MONEY SUPPLY

Most of the expansion of internal public debt will take place through government borrowing from the banking system, including both the commercial banks and the State bank. Any increase in the loans and investments of the banking system results in an approximately equal increase in currency and bank deposits. Thus the banking system creates deposits and currency whenever bank credit expands, whether such credit expansion occurs through advances to private borrowers or through purchases of government securities. Through the process of government borrowing from the banking system, a substantial portion of the saving performed by the private sector will take the form of increased holdings of bank deposits and currency by firms and individuals.

This expansion of currency and bank deposits is a normal and necessary accompaniment to economic growth. A growing economy needs a growing stock of money for transactions, and this need is heightened by the broadening of the monetized sector. The private sector, therefore, retains a part of its current saving in monetary form in order that working balances may keep pace with the growing real volume of transactions. Moreover, money is accumulated beyond transactions needs as one of the major methods of storing or holding wealth. In this respect, of course, the situation differs radically from that of highly advanced industrial economies; in those economies there exists an extensive system of specialized intermediary financial institutions such as life insurance companies, savings banks, building societies, and investment trusts. Savers are accustomed to putting their unspent income largely into life insurance, retirement annuities, savings deposits, the shares of buildings and loan associations, corporate shares and debentures, and government or municipal obligations. Such financial institutions and habits for employing savings have had only a rudimentary development in this country, where money inevitably plays a very large role as a medium for the accumulation of savings.

It must be recognized that the holding of a significant proportion of private wealth in the form of inactive money balances is not wholly without possible unstabilizing effects. The accumulation of wealth in the form of currency and bank deposits is, of course, greatly preferable to its accumulation in the form of bullion and jewelry. Moreover, it is not the inactivity of these money balances which creates difficulties. It is rather the possibility that, under some circumstances, they might suddenly become active. This need not occur; as the economy grows and the rate of saving increases, there is no reason why the stock of both transactions money and inactive money should not continue to grow, even though as other media for accumulating savings become more widely available and better understood, the fraction of current saving going into accumulation of money may be expected gradually to decline. If, owing to other causes, a price inflation were allowed to develop, however, the inactive balances might suddenly become active, thus creating a danger of runaway inflation. This merely emphasizes the need for preserving financial balance and preventing inflationary tendencies from gaining a strong foothold. Exaggerated fears of inflation should not, however, be allowed to interfere with full use of real resources available for development.

Government borrowing operations and the credit policies of the State bank must be geared to providing an expansion of money supply sufficient to create adequate outlets for the community's present disposition to accumulate its savings in monetary form. That portion of current saving which is not directly "ploughed back" by the savers into real investment of their own seeks its principal outlet in the accumulation of money balances. The accumulation of money balances will occur and potential saving will be fully realized in actual saving only if money creation takes place through the expansion of bank credit.

Of course, this does not mean that government borrowing from the banking system should be undertaken without restraint and in unlimited amounts. The appropriate amount of expansion is determined by the principle previously stated, namely, that the public sector's total absorption of private saving, both through borrowing from banks and other means, should be adjusted to the potential margin of private saving over domestically financed investment. If this principle is observed, the money supply will expand at the appropriate rate, the necessary financial balance of the economy will be preserved, and inflation will be avoided.

Once the decision has been reached about the amount of private saving which can prudently be mobilized by the public sector, the debt management and borrowing operations of the central and provincial governments must be framed to a large extent in the light of "market conditions"—in conformity with the revealed asset preferences of the private sector. Institutional and private investors other than banks should be encouraged to buy government securities, and yields and maturities of new security offerings should be as far as possible adjusted to attract such purchases. Moreover, life insurance, retirement annuity systems, and other savings schemes should be developed and expanded both as means of encouraging thrift and in order to divert savings into forms less liquid than money. As the institutions develop and as habits change, the market for government securities outside the banking system will broaden.

It is also appropriate to weigh the advisability of increasing interest rates on long-term government securities as a possible means of (a) encouraging thrift, (b) stimulating the flow of savings into government securities, life insurance, and other similar assets, and (c) exerting some restraint on real estate speculation. The main disadvantage of higher interest rates would be in raising government debt service charges; but if short-term interest rates were kept low, this increase would be small.

Since changes in habits with respect to the forms in which the private sector accumulates its savings will be gradual, the central and provincial governments, although taking active measures to broaden the non-bank market for their securities, must continue for some years to rely chiefly on the banking system as a source of finance. Expansion of credit, both by the commercial banks and the State bank, is essential if the saving potential is to be fully and effectively channeled into productive uses. No useful purpose is served by pressing the commercial banks to purchase long-term securities. To the extent that the Government depends upon bank borrowing, it is far better to issue short-term obligations suited to their liquidity requirements.

In this situation, the policies of the State bank should necessarily be oriented towards facilitating credit expansion to the full extent that this is compatible with the avoidance of serious price inflation. So long as the Government's borrowing program does not outrun the real availability of private saving, there will be no conflict between the State bank's responsibility for assisting government financing operations by expanding credit, and its responsibility for protecting the purchasing power of the currency.

The financing of government expenditures through borrowing from the banking system is sometimes referred to as "deficit finance." Under a different usage, this term is limited to government borrowing from the central bank. The preceding analysis of the availability of resources has demonstrated that, under either definition, deficit finance, within limits indicated above, is a sound and necessary instrument of government finance in the present phase of economic and financial development. Private saving potential exceeds the private investment which can at present be fruitfully undertaken. This surplus must be absorbed by the public sector to achieve full and effective utilization of the real resources available for development purposes. Because the private sector desires to accumulate a considerable portion of its savings in the form of currency and bank deposits, the banking system must serve as intermediary by creating the desired amounts of additional currency and deposits. The chief means of doing so is government borrowing from the banking system. Since currency bulks large in relation to bank deposits, the State bank, as well as the commercial banks, must play a substantial direct role in absorbing government securities. These operations do not become inflationary unless the volume of bank-financed government expenditure results in a rate of expansion of currency and bank deposits which outruns the public's desire to save in these forms.

9 *Price Distortions and Development Planning: Pakistan*[1]

There appears to be an assumption that government must plan and regulate all aspects of economic life in detail, even though the regulations are applied without coordination or clear objectives and without adequate data or efficient administrative apparatus. Many factors are responsible for this, including a rather paternalistic view of the role of government.

There are many portions of the private sector, such as agriculture and cottage industry, in which positive governmental stimulation is essential. There are others, such as luxury construction, in which more restrictive governmental controls would be highly desirable. But there is a broad area which could best be left to semi-automatic decentralized regulation through the mechanism of the market. In this area the apparatus of direct controls, including import licenses, licensing of new firms, capital issues authorizations, and many others, is a major impediment to economic efficiency and growth.

I have used the term "semi-automatic" in the previous paragraph because the government's role in spheres which are left to the working of the market mechanism should be by no means

1. Memorandum to Chairman, Planning Board, Government of Pakistan, December 1956. This was written in the capacity of advisor to the Pakistan Planning Board.—Ed.

completely passive. In the first place, government should continually investigate the prices of major commodities to detect promptly cases in which they are being held substantially above competitive levels, through collusive practices or otherwise. Cotton cloth and vegetable ghee seem, for example, to be good candidates for investigation. If existing laws do not enable the government to take corrective action, these laws should be strengthened.

In the second place, there are many cases which do not require direct controls but in which the impact of market forces can usefully be modified through the use of taxes and subsidies. Taxes and subsidies are frequently preferable to direct controls as instruments to influence the uses to which existing resources are put, the structure of production, and the direction of new investment. To some extent these devices are already used for this purpose, as in the case of protective tariffs. Many of the present tax devices, however, are not well calculated to improve the use of resources. The tax concessions on new investment, even if originally justified, have become unnecessary and wasteful since new capital is already grossly underpriced and existing demands for capital equipment for repair and replacement, as well as for modernization and expansion, cannot be fully satisfied. The present sweeping concessions, instead of providing a needed stimulation to investment, merely augment this excess demand and provide an unnecessary windfall to the taxpayer.

On the other side, the whole policy of taxation of exports should be carefully re-examined, both in general and for specific export products, in order to determine whether these taxes are not seriously interfering with the most productive use of the country's resources. The need for revenue is not a sufficient justification of continuation of these taxes if their larger economic effects are found to be adverse, since the revenue lost could be more than recovered by a new levy on imports, as is proposed later in this memorandum. In considering the economic effects of export taxes, the main questions are the following:

1. To what extent would the physical volume of exports be increased by removal of the tax?

2. Would increased export volume be fully translated into increased foreign exchange earnings, or would much of the benefit be wiped out by the depressing effect on world prices? (This question, which relates to the elasticity of world demand, arises chiefly in the case of jute.)

3. Taking into account both the increased export volume and the possible adverse effect on world jute prices, would the net gain in foreign exchange earnings be sufficient to compensate for the internal costs involved in additional production of goods for export? In the case of cotton and jute, the chief element of internal costs would be the loss of other agricultural production through diversion of acreage. Would the additional export earnings be more than sufficient to make good this loss of other agricultural output?

4. Should the cotton textile and jute textile industries continue to be subsidized, or should they now be required to stand on their own feet without subsidy? If a continued subsidy is deemed necessary, are export taxes which depress the internal prices of raw cotton and raw jute the best means of subsidizing their manufacture?

It is easier to raise these questions than to answer them, and even when further research has been carried out, difficult questions of judgment will still remain. The main point, however, is that a decision regarding these taxes should be based on full assessment of their economic effects rather than upon direct revenue considerations. If the economic effect of a removal of some or all of these taxes would be to increase the overall productivity, it should be possible to make good elsewhere the loss of revenue directly involved.

Once this point is clearly recognized, there are many opportunities to use taxes instead of direct controls as a positive regulatory device. For example, market demands for cigarettes appears to be high and growing. If the government feels that scarce capital, instead of being used to expand the capacity of this industry, should flow into other fields of greater social value, the tax on cigarettes could be increased to a point where demand for cigarettes is held within the limits of existing capacity. If, instead, new investment is merely curbed through denying import licenses for the machinery while demand for cigarettes continues to grow, the price of cigarettes will rise and manufacturers and distributors will gain an unjustified windfall. This price increment might better be captured as taxes than be permitted to accrue as private profits. A price ceiling at the manufacturer's level cannot meet the problem, since it would merely transfer the profit to the distributors. If placed at the retail level, the ceiling would be widely evaded. Nor is rationing a workable solution for articles like cigarettes. Rationing, when administratively feasible, is probably the best course where essential consumer staples are in short supply, but it should be limited to such goods. In other cases, the tax device proposed above is greatly preferable.

With respect to direct controls, import controls are the worst offender of all. They are said to be justified on the ground that foreign exchange is short. But if foreign exchange ever reaches a condition of abundant supply, it will be a sign, among other things, that the development effort is grossly inadequate and that the country is not making full use of a key resource. Foreign exchange should be short. The fact of shortage, by itself, does not justify continuation of the present system, which misuses resources and provides easy monopoly profits to established, favored firms and established industries. It favors proximity to Karachi. It greatly hampers small and medium-sized firms and cottage industry. On the whole, it favors capital-intensive projects. It creates needless bottlenecks and waste of resources, owing to shortages of repair parts or key materials. It impedes the entry of new firms, thereby stifling entrepreneurship, restricting competition, and retarding industrial diversification. It provides easy profits to a favored group. It deprives the government of much revenue which it could easily and properly obtain. Although gradual strengthening of administration and the slow development of more detailed statistical data might somewhat mitigate these shortcomings, they are largely inherent in the system itself.

The present dependence on direct controls of all sorts prevents prices from fulfilling the regulatory role which they can perform. There is a widespread attitude in official quarters that things should be kept cheap even when they are scarce. This attitude, which is justified in the case of basic necessities which can be rationed, causes needless difficulties in other areas. Since there is not enough to go around at the controlled, cheap price, the favored firms or individuals, who are able to buy at the controlled price, are able to enjoy a quite unjustified windfall gain. In the case of scarce productive resources, the advantage of allowing their prices to rise to a level which reflects their scarcity is that users generally will be induced to economize in their use, and, generally speaking, only those who can make the most profitable use of the scarce resources will buy them. Although the most profitable uses are not invariably the most productive uses, the criterion of profitability should be accepted in most fields. Under the present system of low prices, those who are fortunate enough to receive the necessary permits often use the resources extravagantly, while others whose needs are, in many cases, of higher economic and social urgency are denied access to the supplies. The result can scarcely be called a system of private enterprise; it tends, rather, towards a restrictive type of state capitalism.

There are many examples of this unwillingness to let prices perform their appropriate function. I am told, for example, that coal prices are equalized among the main consuming centers, so that prices in Lahore and Karachi, for example, are the same although Lahore is closer to the source of supply. There is simply no reason for this. Rail haulage of coal is costly; it is capital-intensive; railroad capacity is strained. A higher price for coal at Karachi, which would encourage the use of other fuels here and encourage industries using much coal to locate closer to the supplies, seems appropriate. It is also said that the price of Sui gas, instead of being placed well below coal, has been fixed "competitively" with coal, which has retarded substitution of the cheaper for the dearer fuel.

The Planning Board has given much attention to the problem of overcentralization in public administration. The problem discussed above is a closely allied one. Under the system of direct controls, the function of decision-making in the private sector of the economy has been to a considerable extent transferred to government. Although decentralization of initiative, with coordination through market processes, is perhaps the major advantage of a system of private enterprise, this advantage is now largely lost through the pervasiveness of official controls. The result is that the decision-making process for both the public and private sectors is characterized by government overcentralization. Moreover, the application of the separate controls is largely uncoordinated, with resulting large impairment of productivity through disturbances of economic balance.

The draft plan stressed the general principle that national income could be raised not only by expanding total resources through new investment but, even more important, by using existing resources at higher levels of productivity. The plan mentions several ways in which the use of existing resources can be improved. In addition to the methods cited there, one should add an increased degree of reliance on the market mechanism, with reduced dependence on an uncoordinated use of centralized controls.

In this connection the most important single step would be a substantial modification of the present system of import controls (while retaining present exchange regulations to prevent flight of capital, restrain vacation travel abroad, and provide an additional check on luxury imports). The change would consist of the imposition of an import license surcharge roughly sufficient to eliminate the present excess demand for imports. This level need not be accurately estimated in advance, since it can be found by successive trials. A single rate of surcharge would apply to most imported goods. A few goods, such as food grains and pharmaceuticals and necessary remittances to Pakistanis studying abroad, might be exempt from surcharge, partly for social reasons; a few, such as private passenger cars and other imported luxuries, might be subject to a special penalty rate. With these exceptions, a uniform rate would apply. Generally speaking, differentials in the levies on particular imports should continue to be confined to their rates of custom duties.

An effort would be made to fix the surcharges at a level high enough to allow all remaining demand for import permits to be met except, perhaps, for luxury imports. There would be no need, however, for a precise balancing from day to day. The surcharges might be fixed at annual or semi-annual intervals, and the foreign exchange reserves of the State bank might serve, as at present, as a buffer stock to absorb surpluses or meet deficits. The surcharges should be paid not only by private importers but by government departments. It is understood that the IMF, while opposing the auction system, does not look with disfavor on a system of the type proposed above and considers it in many respects preferable to the present type of licensing system, which relies on official rationing rather than surcharges as a means of allocating scarce foreign exchange.

This system possesses two basic advantages. In the first place, scarce foreign exchange would be put to more productive use than at present. Access to import permits would be greatly broadened. Apart from importers of luxury goods, who might be denied licenses even if willing to pay the penalty surcharge, all those who were willing to pay the customs duties, sales tax, and general surcharges would be granted licenses to import. The decisions of buyers based upon their willingness or unwillingness to pay the surcharges would be substituted for the decisions of government officials in determining the allocation of scarce foreign exchange among competing claimants. Although it cannot be held that those who are willing to pay the highest price will invariably be those who would put imported goods to their most productive uses, it is strongly probable that a much better result would be obtained than if the matter is left to government allotment. As an example, the benefits to cottage industry are readily apparent. Many such industries must have imported equipment in small amounts. Since the price of the equipment, even if high, is not a major element of cost, the price is usually of quite secondary importance to the prospective buyer. Many cottage industries today are fettered by their inability to get needed imports at any price. The same line of reasoning applies wholly or in part to many small-scale and medium-scale enterprises, to new firms, and to business lacking representation in Karachi. The proposed liberalization of the import licensing system would go far to remove this obstacle. It would by no means obviate the need for Cottage Industries Centres and other positive measures of stimulation, but it would make the task of stimulation much easier. Cottage industries, as well as small-scale or medium-scale industries which are now unable to obtain licenses, would benefit greatly. Since these industries are generally labor-intensive, the small amounts of capital equipment which they need would be very highly productive.

At the other end of the scale, large established firms, under the system now operating, are sometimes allotted much more foreign exchange than they would choose to acquire under the surcharge system. The result has been that exchange has sometimes been used to purchase unnecessarily elaborate equipment and to set up industrial plants using "advanced" technologies which are needlessly capital-intensive and, therefore, unsuitable here. Along the same lines, imported steel and other metals have been extravagantly used in much construction work. Firms with large uninvested profits, when granted licenses, have purchased imports well beyond their requirements since they would rather hold imports than idle rupee balances. Although it might not be effective in all cases, the imposition of a high import license surcharge would tend to curb many of these low-priority uses of foreign exchange, thus freeing exchange for more productive purposes. It would also help to eliminate many crippling bottlenecks which now arise due to shortages of spare parts or key materials.

The second major advantage of the system here proposed is that it would provide large government revenues which could be used for economic development. The producer of export crops receives a price in rupees which depends upon the official rates of exchange at which the foreign exchange proceeds of the exports are surrendered to the State bank. If the producer of exports were allowed to sell the foreign exchange proceeds in a free market, instead of at the official rate, his income would be greatly increased. In effect, therefore, the requirement that the exporter surrender exchange at the official rate imposes a large hidden levy on the producer of export goods. Although a part of this levy is captured by the government through customs duties and sales taxes on imports, and through income and profits taxes, the major portion accrues as profits to private firms and individuals who sell industrial goods, imported or domestic, at the prevailing scarcity prices. Just as a levy is imposed upon the exporter who is required to sell foreign exchange at the official rates, a gift is bestowed upon the importer who receives a license and is allowed to acquire foreign exchange at these rates. For example, the manufacturer possessing an import license is permitted to buy his capital equipment and raw materials with foreign currencies purchased at low official rates and to sell the resulting product at prices which fully reflect internal scarcities. Much of his profit emerges from this spread between world prices and internal prices. His gain is not essentially different from that of the importing merchant who merely resells at high internal prices the same goods he has been licensed to purchase abroad at much lower world market prices.

Favored access to cheap foreign exchange is one of the major sources of the large industrial and commercial profits of recent years. Even though continuation of the hidden levy on exports represented by present exchange rates is necessary unless a situation is reached where devaluation would substantially increase foreign exchange earnings, the proceeds should be collected and used by government for economic development. The levy becomes difficult to justify if it is chiefly transferred to private profits in the industrial and commercial sector.

The internal price structure for industrial goods contrasts markedly with that for agricultural products. The effects of the official exchange rates and of export taxes on agricultural exports have been mentioned. In addition, governmental procurement of food grains and other official measures have been used to hold down the prices paid to producers of domestically consumed agricultural products. Consequently, the domestic terms of trade between the rural agricultural sector and the commercial and industrial urban sector are markedly unfavorable to agriculture and highly favorable to industry and commerce, in comparison with corresponding price ratios in the world market. Although this is to some extent characteristic of underdeveloped agricultural economies which export agricultural products and import manufactures, it is markedly accentuated in this country by government policies.

These policies, although they bear most heavily on the poorer, backward sector for the benefit of the wealthier, developing sector, should not be drastically reversed. In a predominantly agricultural country striving for economic development, a substantial share of the internal resources needed for development uses must come, directly or indirectly, from agriculture. The question, therefore, is one of degree. It is not whether agriculture should bear such levies, both direct and disguised, but how large these levies should be.

My answer would be that the direct levies, chiefly land revenue and water rates, are now too low, that the hidden levies probably are somewhat too high, and that too large a share of the hidden levies is emerging as private industrial and commercial profits rather than as public revenue. Such private profits, if predominantly reinvested in high-priority fields, can contribute decisively to economic development. This contribution was of first-rate importance in stimulating and financing urgently needed industrial expansion in the initial phase of Pakistan's development. At present, however, these profits are not being so usefully employed. Top priority should today be given to agriculture rather than industry, and most of the high-priority investment needed at the present stage is public investment. A somewhat higher level of agricultural prices as a whole in relation to industrial prices would probably reinforce the effectiveness of the schemes for raising agricultural productivity, although this cannot be stated with certainty. In any event, the growth of urban buying power may make it gradually more difficult to maintain present price relationships, even if crop yields recover to normal levels. Whatever view may be taken on this question, it is clearly necessary that commercial profits be more heavily taxed in order that these funds may be funneled through the public sector into agricultural schemes and public investment projects which today deserve top priority. An import surcharge appears to be the most effective single measure for this purpose.

Another serious case of underpricing of an acutely scarce resource is that of capital. Underpricing in this case results from a combination of direct and indirect causes. The direct causes are: (1) the import licensing system, under which the price in rupees of imported equipment paid by firms granted licenses is held down; (2) low interest rates to these restricted classes of borrowers who can obtain funds through security flotations, bank credit, loans from insurance companies, and similar sources; and (3) substantial tax concessions on new investment. Thus, the businessman who obtains an authorization to build or expand his plant, an import permit, and bank credit or permission to issue securities gains command over a scarce and highly profitable resource at extremely favorable terms. At these favorable terms, there exists today a sizeable unsatisfied demand for import permits, for credit facilities, and for other official authorizations.

The general disadvantages of this system of underpricing and official rationing have already been pointed out. Official restraints on certain types of profitable but undesirable investment, wherever possible through taxation or, if this is not possible, by more direct means, should be continued and, in some fields, strengthened; government should encourage and promote private investment in other fields which, although potentially of high productivity, are held back by lack of entrepreneurship or special obstacles. But the present attempt at pervasive regulation of the whole field of new investment results in wasteful and distorted use of resources. Although the market mechanism does not yield ideal results, the results, apart from special cases, are likely to be much better than under the present system of pervasive regulation.

Revision of the present import licensing system has been proposed above. The draft plan contains proposals for curtailing present tax concessions on new investment. There remains the problem of broadening credit facilities and the closely related problem of interest rates. The rates paid on government loans and loans to first-class private borrowers are at a level with or below those now prevailing in most advanced countries. The volume of funds which can be made available for lending without producing dangerous inflation is narrowly limited, however. Under present conditions, financial facilities are inadequate and loanable funds are available to only a few restricted classes of borrowers, so that most of the productive demand for funds from credit-worthy borrowers remains unsatisfied. Thus, low interest rates go hand in hand with a restrictive rationing of financing facilities, partly through government action and partly through the narrowly restrictive lending practices of the banks.

The draft plan contains recommendations for a comprehensive broadening of credit facilities to both industry and agriculture. As this is achieved, the total demand for loans would greatly exceed the amounts which could be made available without leading to serious inflation. An obvious solution would be to permit interest rates to rise in order to discourage marginal borrowers and limit demand to those productive borrowers whose uses for funds promised sufficiently high returns to enable them to meet the higher interest costs. High interest rates, besides channeling funds into uses promising the highest returns, might also be conducive to increased thrift.

Since high interest rates are generally deemed objectionable on religious and moral grounds, this method of meeting the problem probably must be rejected. An alternative approach, which, although providing no inducement to increased thrift, would be as effective as higher interest rates in making it possible to broaden the availability of credit to borrowers who at present cannot obtain funds at any price, would be to impose an annual tax on a borrower's average outstanding indebtedness above a stated minimum figure. The annual carrying charge on a loan would then consist of the interest paid to the lender plus the tax paid to the government. The exemption limit should be placed high enough (1) to exempt the borrowing of small- and medium-sized cultivators and individuals borrowing small amounts to meet temporary personal needs; and (2) to keep down the costs of collection by excluding a large number of small assessments. Enforcement of the tax would be aided by utilizing the loan records of banks, insurance companies, and other major lending agencies. In explaining the tax to the public, it would be justified both as a measure for capturing the windfall profits which some businesses get through low interest rates and as a measure which must go hand in hand with the broadening of credit facilities in order to avoid the dangers which a marked broadening of credit facilities would otherwise involve. The tax might perhaps be waived on a highly selective basis, for a few new industries deserving of high priority and needing special inducements to expand.

An increased measure of reliance on the price mechanism is

the unifying thread linking the proposals in this memorandum. They run counter to much accepted practice in the subcontinent and will doubtless be resisted for this reason, among others. I suspect, however, that in actual practice India has moved a considerable distance in recent years towards freeing private industry from a network of official controls, while controls in Pakistan have increased. Although the ideology of Pakistan is rather friendly, and that of India rather unfriendly, to private business, the actual scope for private initiative may well be broader in India than in Pakistan.

The proposals in this memorandum may be objected to on the ground that by reducing profits, they will restrict private business. While it is true that private enterprise responds to the incentive of profit, it by no means follows that greater profit always invokes greater enterprise. When easy profits for a few are the result of government policies which exclude other potential bidders for resources, they are a deterrent to enterprise.

The present situation in Pakistan appears somewhat analogous to that which prevailed in Western Europe in the late mercantile period. In the preceding stage of European development the grant of subsidies and monopoly privileges to selected commercial interests appears to have provided a powerful stimulus to commercial expansion. By the eighteenth century, however, these traditional devices obstructed development by favoring a few long-established and strongly entrenched interests and handicapping new enterprises and new activities. Although in Pakistan there are many specific fields which still require government assistance, the economy has reached a stage where the present pervasive system of controls exerts a similar restraining effect.

10 *The Welfare State and Development Expenditure: Pakistan*[1]

The subject of this paper is the welfare state in the West. It may be well, first of all, to indicate what the term "welfare state" does not mean, in contemporary Western usage. The preamble of the Constitution of the United States, for instance, adopted one hundred and seventy years ago, includes the objective to "promote the general welfare." Indeed, it is not a distortion to say that the welfare of the people was the central objective and that all other objectives mentioned in the preamble derived importance through their contribution to welfare.

This idea—that the basic objective of government is the welfare of the people—had its origin in the Western world in the seventeenth and eighteenth centuries, and was expressed in the writings of many of the political philosophers of that period. Thus the broad notion that the state should serve the welfare of the people, instead of pursuing some different aim—such as the mere extension of its own power, as an end in itself, or the glorification of the monarch, or the fulfillment of a religious mission—is several centuries old. This long-established idea provides one possible

1. Text of address delivered at the Seminar on Welfare Administration organized by the Ministry of Health and Social Welfare, Government of Pakistan, September 28–October 1, 1959, at Karachi. This address has also been published in a volume of seminar proceedings, and in Institute of Development Economics (Karachi), *Economic Digest,* Vol. 3, No. 1, Summer 1960, pp. 3-7.—Ed.

meaning of the term "welfare state," although this is not its meaning in the contemporary Western usage of the term. If I understand the matter correctly, however, this older meaning comes fairly close to the meaning which is sometimes given to the term in Pakistan. When the term "welfare state" is used in this country, it sometimes seems to mean simply a state whose government seeks to promote the welfare of the people instead of exploiting them and whose public officials keep this objective continually in mind in their day-to-day dealings with the public.

This is not all that "welfare state" means as this term is today used in Western countries. The concept of welfare which prevails today in the economically advanced, industrial countries of the West is quite different from what the British and French and American political theorists had in mind in the seventeenth and eighteenth centuries, because the specific content and meaning of "welfare" has vastly changed as the Western societies have become wealthy, urban, and industrial.

The term "welfare state," in its Western usage and, frequently, in its usage in Pakistan, refers to the sweeping economic and social transformation which has occurred in many Western countries, largely during the past thirty years, as the result of the extensive series of governmental welfare measures put into effect in this period. These measures have been designed to reduce economic insecurity; to mitigate economic inequalities; to provide the less-privileged members of the community with free or subsidized services such as better housing, greater educational opportunities, and more adequate medical care. These measures have included social insurance plans, the use of fiscal and credit controls to maintain general economic stability and high employment, agricultural price supports and subsidies, minimum wage laws, and much else.

The aggregate effect of all these measures has been to create economic systems in many of the Western countries which can neither be described as private enterprise capitalism, nor as socialism. The phrase "welfare state" has been coined to characterize this type of mixed economy, which diffuses widely among its people the benefits of high productivity and material abundance, and which provides a decent and secure minimum for all. The welfare state has developed farthest in the Scandinavian countries, Great Britain, Australia, and New Zealand. It has proceeded somewhat less far in North America but the general trend has been the same.

Of course, welfare measures did not begin thirty years ago. Their history goes back into the nineteenth century. In Britain the first Factory Act was adopted in the 1830's, limiting the length of the working day for children under fourteen; general elementary education and literacy were largely achieved in the nineteenth century in a number of countries. Social insurance schemes were introduced in some countries in the late nineteenth century. But the scope of the welfare measures designed to improve and make secure the living standards of the less-privileged members of the society has broadened so greatly in the past few decades that, taken all together, they have brought about a profound transformation in the economic and social system of most economically advanced Western countries. The countries which have experienced this transformation are today's "welfare states."

There are two points which I wish to make about this transformation in the Western countries, because I think it is important that these points be understood here in Pakistan. The first point is that the major changes which are embodied in the phrase "the welfare state" did not arise out of a growing humanitarianism; they arose as the result of a process of political conflict. The basic source of the conflict, at the political level, was the institution of political democracy itself. It was universal suffrage, public education, the growing political articulateness of the masses, the strength of labor unions and of farm organizations, and the competition between political parties to secure the support of the rank and file of voters that made possible the series of measures that led to the welfare state. If you examine the history of each one of these measures, you will usually find that it was adopted only after conflict between those groups, on the one hand, who considered that they would be benefited by the proposed measures, and those groups who felt that they would be injured by it. The political process, in other words, involved tension at each step.

To take one example, in the United States a law was passed in

1916 setting an eight-hour working day for railway workers. The eight-hour day was adopted first for railway workers because they were then the best organized large group of workers and they made their demands felt most strongly. The necessary legislation was passed with the representatives of the railway unions sitting as spectators in the galleries of the Congress with telegraph instruments on their laps, ready to signal a railway strike by midnight if the law was not passed. This is, perhaps, an exceptionally dramatic example but it illustrates the general point.

After these measures were adopted, many of them gradually gained general acceptance; they came to be supported by a broad social consensus, apart from small intractable groups. I think one may say that as a result of the development of the welfare state, there is in many Western countries a greater degree of social cohesiveness and integration than existed twenty-five or fifty years ago. If there is today a greater feeling of community in Western societies, which expresses itself in a general acceptance of the main features of the welfare state, this greater feeling of community was a result, and not a cause. Each of the main welfare measures had its birth in active political conflict; the social consensus came later. That is my first main point.

The next major point is that large-scale government programs for reducing the insecurity of livelihood and providing a better and more secure standard of living for all the people are of fairly recent date and followed a prolonged period of substantial, cumulative growth of productivity in the economy. The earlier substantial improvement in living standards, which had occurred before the welfare state emerged, had been the largely automatic result of the growing productivity of Western economies. In the earliest stage of industrial development, however, there was little or no improvement for the workers, and their condition was miserable. In the early stages of the industrial revolution the orthodox doctrine was that every shilling spent for relieving the misery of the poor was a shilling subtracted from the funds available for capital accumulation and economic development. This harsh doctrine remained the accepted orthodoxy until the latter part of the nineteenth century, and it contained an important element of truth in the early stages of Western industrial development.

Although this doctrine, modified and weakened, still exercises influence in some Western countries, it no longer holds the center of the stage. It has lost ground generally, and in some countries it has been wholly submerged by the markedly different ideas and doctrines of the modern welfare state. But it is important to stress that the modern theory of the welfare state gained dominance only after a prolonged period of cumulative economic development had created the foundation for it. The Western welfare state rests upon the material abundance made possible by high productivity. I think that there is some basis for the view that when the welfare state finally emerged, the timing was such that it helped, rather than hindered, future economic growth; this would not have been true if it had been introduced at an early stage of Western economic development.

The timing of the emergence of the welfare state in Western countries is an exceedingly important point to keep in mind. I need hardly say that the situation of the Western countries is not the situation of Pakistan today. An indiscriminate attempt to imitate Western welfare programs before the economic foundation has been created would make things worse rather than better in this country.

The general lesson, I would suggest, is that, for the most part, welfare programs in underdeveloped countries should be treated as one aspect of the general effort to increase productivity. I would suggest also that the same kind of change in organization and administration which is required in this country to promote a broadly based increase in productivity and a self-sustaining process of economic growth is also required to carry out a workable welfare program. The two things go hand in hand and can reinforce each other. The development of a more effective organization for carrying out feasible welfare programs would provide a better organizational framework for executing important, neglected economic programs, and vice versa.

So far, in Pakistan, the economic development effort has been somewhat one-sided. It has been to a great extent concentrated on great government projects and the development of a few large-scale private industries. In other words, it has been narrowly based. The result is that some serious imbalances have developed—an imbalance between the expanding urban, industrial, and commercial sector and the lagging rural agricultural sector. Too large a share of the country's scarcest resources has gone into big government projects and large-scale industry; not enough has been applied to small-scale industry and agriculture.

I have just read with interest and admiration the excellently written and well-reasoned Report of the Panel of Economists on the Second Five-Year Plan. I thought that the things that the report had to say about priorities, about the need for improvements in organization and administration to promote more advanced agricultural methods, foster small-scale industries, and "contain" the demands of the best organized and most energetic claimants for scarce resources, and about prices and government controls were wise and sound.

I hope that the program of development expenditure formulated and carried out in the second plan will be truly in keeping with these principles. Even in the framing of a program of development expenditure, it is extremely difficult to adhere to the stated principles of the plan. There is a tendency to assign too large a share of the resources to those well-organized and established sectors whose demands should be "contained," and too small a share to the unorganized or poorly organized sectors, on whose development future economic progress so largely depends. The figures given in the Report of the Economists on the composition of the expenditure program in the Second Five Year Plan make me wonder whether this distortion has not already crept in. At the stage of implementation and execution, the difficulties of avoiding distortion are even greater.

It seems fair to infer from the Report of the Panel of Economists, first, that the First Five Year Plan has been substantially implemented with respect to the total financial size of investment and development expenditure; second, that it has not been well implemented in the actual distribution of these expenditures among various sectors of the economy, and, finally, that the recommendations have had very little influence in bringing about needed changes in administration and organization and in general economic policies—apart from focusing attention on the need for land reform. The net result was that although financial expenditures closely approached the target figures, the increase in productivity and real income was extremely disappointing.

Perhaps the main difficulty is that when a development plan is published it is interpreted by most government officials and readers generally as, first and foremost, a program of development expenditure. This is thought of as the core of the plan; the other recommendations are regarded as secondary or, at best, supportive.

If these mistakes are repeated either in the framing or in the implementation of the second plan, the results will again be disappointing. The lion's share of the resources would continue to flow into those areas which have received the largest share in the past. Instead of raising national income, this would tend merely to accentuate the existing imbalances.

Perhaps it would be helpful if the second plan were presented so that its central feature was a detailed program of recommended changes in organization and administration and in policies of economic control, and if the expenditure program were given merely a supportive role. This expenditure program should be wholly consistent with the plan's basic principles. It is only through such a radical shift in emphasis that resources can flow adequately into those relatively neglected fields where their contribution to the growth of production will be high.

Unless the basis for economic development is broadened in this way (and this requires more energetic measures than have been taken so far), it will not be possible to bring into more effective use the country's largest resources—its vast surplus of unemployed and underemployed labor. The most important welfare measures that can be taken, as well as the most important economic measures, are to be found precisely in this area. There are some large-scale and costly projects which, when completed, will raise the productivity of a very large number of workers, so that the ratio of the number of workers favorably affected to the investment cost of the project will be big enough to justify the large cost. There are others, however, which lack such justifications. Generally speaking, better use of labor over a broad front requires much more than a few large and costly investment schemes. The program must be far broader than this.

With respect to urban welfare conditions, so long as there is vast rural unemployment and underemployment, it will remain relatively attractive for a young man to come to the city, even if he can get only intermittent and casual employment, picking up a few rupees a week through odd jobs of one sort or another. People will flow to the cities, continually outrunning the jobs and housing facilities. The attempt to solve the problem of urban congestion and distress by expanding urban housing and utilities, building a few large modern facilities that provide jobs to only a relatively small fraction of the working population, and extending urban welfare measures is bound to fail unless the problem is attacked at its roots in the rural areas. It requires, and I think this must be faced, the most radical transformation in organization and administration, and an elastic revision of priorities, to bring these changes about. This must be the chief aim of an effective welfare and economic development program.

11 *Financing of Development: Malaysia*

I The Role of External Borrowing[1]

The main conviction to which I have been led as the result of my conversations with economists, bankers, and officials and a perusal of the documents, memoranda, and statistics which have been made available to me during my brief visit to Malaysia is that unless the present shortfall in external borrowing below needed levels is swiftly eliminated through wholehearted action by the Malaysian authorities to obtain additional external financing facilities and put available facilities to full use, the result may well be not only a marked retardation in economic growth, involving a continuing decline in per capita real income, but also a possibly intractable worsening of the balance of payments with a resulting cumulative drain of external reserves. The first danger appears to be recognized, although judgments concerning its seriousness differ considerably; the second possible danger seems to have escaped much attention.

It will be useful, as a starting point in spelling out the basis for my conclusion regarding the critical importance of adequate external borrowing, to indicate certain basic points of disagreement with the analysis presented in the recent IBRD (International Bank for Reconstruction and Development) Asia Department

1. From a Memorandum to Malaysia's Economic Planning Unit, August 24, 1967.—Ed.

Report reviewing Malaysia's economic situation. In calling attention to several major flaws in its economic analysis, I do not wish to imply that the report is without merit. Besides pulling together, in careful and organized fashion, much valuable information, it contains a number of wise judgments. Nevertheless, its overall effect is to give a picture of the way Malaysia's economy works which is misleading in important respects, and to convey much too sanguine an assessment of the consequences which would necessarily result from a failure to correct the present shortfall in external borrowing.

A recurrent theme, on which the report's conclusions and recommendations largely rest, is that: (1) declining export prices *directly* reduce the domestic saving ratio; (2) domestic saving measures and determines the amount of investment which Malaysia can soundly finance from its own resources; and (3) the role of external finance is merely to provide finance for the excess of domestic investment not covered by domestic saving, private and public. The fallacies contained in each of these points will be considered in turn.

The *direct* effect of declining export prices on Malaysia's saving ratio has certainly been slight. A fall in export prices, other things being equal, does directly reduce Malaysia's real income by worsening its terms of trade. This is the direct channel through which it impinges on saving. A reduction in real income ordinarily reduces the amount of saving and, perhaps, the ratio of saving to income as well. This effect, however, is trivial. A 20 per cent decline in the price of rubber, with no change in the volume of export shipments, causes a decline in the income of foreign factors derived from rubber of more than 20 per cent, since profits are most sensitive to price fluctuations; by the same token, it directly reduces Malaysian incomes from rubber exports by considerably less than 20 per cent. (If the decline in prices is in part brought about, and offset, by increased export volume, the net effect on real income is, of course, smaller.) Since rubber exports represent one-seventh of national income and since the shrinkage of foreign profits provides a buffer, the direct effect of a 20 per cent drop in rubber prices in reducing Malaysia's national income could hardly exceed 2 per cent. This is a considerable reduction, but as a simple matter of arithmetic, its direct effect on Malaysia's potential saving ratio would be nil unless it induced directly a more-than-proportionate reduction in saving. Even if the direct effect on saving, through lower tax receipts and reduced private saving, were a reduction of 3 per cent, i.e., a proportionate reduction of 50 per cent greater than the percentage decrease in real income, the resulting decline in the saving ratio would be only 0.2 of a percentage point. For example, if the old saving ratio was 20 per cent, the new ratio would be 19.8 per cent. This decline is too trivial to deserve the heavy emphasis which the report places upon it.

The report is utterly mistaken in attributing the decline in the actual saving ratio to an impairment in Malaysia's capacity to save brought about by falling rubber prices, and in asserting that the decline in the actual ratio represents a reduction in domestic capacity to finance investment. The primary cause of the decline in the domestic saving ratio is precisely the opposite of that indicated by the report. A decline in the inducement and willingness to invest has brought about a decline in the investment ratio, and, through the elementary laws of double entry bookkeeping, in the saving ratio as well.

Declining rubber prices have contributed to this weakening of the inducement to invest. It is said that foreign-owned rubber plantations, with lowered profit expectations, have curtailed their expenditure on replanting. The Government, with reduced receipts from some taxes, has both raised other taxes and held public investment outlays below planned targets. The people, whose incomes have suffered from reduced income from rubber, from the restraint in public investment outlays, and from higher taxes, have experienced a stagnation of real purchasing power. This stagnation of domestic purchasing power, in turn, has impaired the profit expectations which provide the incentive to undertake private industrial and commercial investment of domestic entrepreneurs and foreign firms. This weakening in incentives to private investment, unless corrected, will have further cumulative adverse effects on domestic incomes and spending.

Although declining rubber prices have been a major influence —perhaps the major influence—in impairing the incentive to invest, it would be more accurate to attribute the decline in the investment ratio primarily to the combined effects of declining rubber prices and an insufficiently expansionary budgetary policy. Other factors, such as the separation of Singapore, the near-completion of replanting on rubber estates, and some evidence of a downturn in private construction, may also have contributed to the decline. Had the weakening of private investment incentives brought about by falling rubber prices been countered by an acceleration of public investment to levels moderately above the previously planned level, supplemented, perhaps, by some additional tax incentives to stimulate private investment, it can be stated with considerable confidence that the combined public and private investment ratio could have been soundly sustained and with it the saving ratio. Although the retardation of growth of real income perhaps could not have been wholly prevented, it could have been greatly reduced, and this remains the case today.

One major error is the report's failure to stress the contribution of public expenditure and tax policy to the retardation of economic growth. Analytically, the error consists in misinterpreting a weakening in the desire to invest (both public and private) as an impairment of the ability to save, and in attributing the restriction of investment to a resource, or supply, constraint (impaired saving potential) instead of an incentive, or demand, constraint (impaired inducement to invest). This basic error is the first of the major errors of analysis in the IBRD Asia Department Report.

The second major error which runs through the analysis is the assumption that domestic saving sets the amount of investment which Malaysia can soundly finance from its own resources and that the role of external finance is merely to provide residual financing for the excess of investment not covered by domestic saving. As the report points out in its factual review of the balance of payments, a portion of private saving is absorbed by remittances of persons of Chinese or Indian extraction to their relatives abroad. Such remittances are most appropriately treated as a charge to the current account of the balance of payments along with imports of goods and services. After subtracting such external, private remittances from domestic saving, an unknown but undoubtedly considerable portion of the remaining domestic saving is absorbed by outflow of Malaysian capital. The dollar amount of some of the components of this outflow is known, but the major portion of this movement is unrecorded and is probably the chief component of the large "errors and omissions" item shown by available statistics.

This outflow of Malaysian capital takes a number of forms, some of which are worth enumerating. Some previously foreign-owned plantations and mines are being wholly transferred to local ownership through "take-overs"; in other cases, foreign-owned rubber estates are selling portions of their properties to Malaysian buyers in small parcels, i.e., "fragmentation." Recent British tax changes on income from overseas investments are helping to induce gradual selling, and there are some indications that the movement has received further encouragement through application of discreet suasion by British financial authorities. In addition to the outflow of Malaysian capital through repatriation of some of the foreign-owned firms and properties, a further portion of this outflow consists of the direct acquisition of foreign assets—bank balances, securities, and other assets—and the retirement of debt by firms and individuals in Malaysia.

Even when saving takes such forms as increased holdings of domestic currency, bank deposits, or life insurance, this normally results indirectly, under the prevailing practices of financial institutions in Malaysia, in an outflow of Malaysian capital. In the case of increasing currency circulation, the outflow is particularly large, since the statutory foreign exchange reserve requirement is 80 per cent and, for the present at least, the Central Bank desires, for confidence reasons, to hold reserves well above this minimum. In the case of bank deposits, the commercial banks continue to hold a fraction of their assets in foreign exchange, particularly in London and Singapore. Although this fraction has been reduced by the terms of the liquidity requirements which the Central Bank has applied to commercial banks, it still remains true that unless this fraction is reduced further, growth in bank deposits carries with it an increase in the balances and funds employed abroad by commercial banks. Although the proportion of their policy reserves which insurance companies are legally required to hold in Malaysian assets has been increased, the fraction which they are permitted to hold and do hold in investments abroad remains considerable. Thus, when domestic savings are used, for example to purchase life insurance, or when expansion of physical capital, external trade, and motor vehicle use requires increasing casualty insurance coverage, the resulting premiums are devoted in part to acquisition of foreign assets. There is perhaps a tendency among Malaysia's financial institutions to regard the ratio of external assets to domestic liabilities as inflexible downward. To the extent that this attitude is controlling, Malaysia's large external reserves are in considerable degree "locked in" and unavailable for balance-of-payments uses except through general financial deflation, which reduces the domestic liabilities against which external reserves are held.

To provide a rough indication of order of magnitude, it may be estimated, using the balance-of-payments and saving estimates for 1966 given in the IBRD report, that an amount equal to about one-third of Malaysia's private gross saving was devoted to personal remittances abroad and to capital outflow by individuals, business firms, and financial institutions domiciled in Malaysia. If, as would be more appropriate, these flows were expressed as a percentage of private net saving, the fraction would be closer to one-half. The foregoing estimates are based on the plausible assumption that in addition to the recorded outflows of Malaysian capital shown in the balance of payments, about 80 per cent of "errors and omissions" consists of private remittances and capital outflows.

Although the main facts regarding financial outflows given above are presented in the IBRD report, their analytical implications seem to have been largely disregarded. There is a failure to recognize that the portion of domestic saving which is absorbed by Malaysian personal remittances and capital outflow provides no financial or real resources for domestic investment. In the absence of foreign capital inflow, an outflow of Malaysian funds would have to be matched by an export surplus of goods and services, depriving domestic investment of the resources which employment at home of the domestic saving would provide. Consequently, a major function of foreign capital inflow is to offset the outflow of Malaysian funds, thus permitting the Malaysian economy to devote to domestic investment uses resources which would otherwise have to be absorbed in generating a large export surplus of goods and services. This two-way flow of capital may be thought of as an international exchange of financial claims. Malaysian financial institutions, firms, and households acquire assets which they desire to accumulate or which foreign owners wish to sell, while the inflow of foreign capital gives foreigners assets representing claims on the Malaysian economy. This two-way flow is, in some degree, a characteristic of every financially open economy; in this financial respect, as in trade, Malaysia's degree of openness is particularly high. Much of Malaysia's saving does not go to finance domestic investment, and even if domestic investment merely equals or even falls somewhat short of domestic saving, dependence on external finance remains heavy. In attributing to external finance merely the role of financing the excess of domestic investment over domestic saving, the IBRD analysis ignores its function, which has so far been predominant, of offsetting Malaysian financial outflows. It is surely a mistake, in analyzing the role of external finance, to treat such finance on a net basis as if it were synonymous with the current-account deficit of the balance of payments.

By treating external finance in this fashion, the IBRD report considerably understates its true economic importance to Malaysia. By the same token, the report underestimates Malaysia's vulnerability to a serious restriction in the use of external finance. Such a restriction could either cause or result from a contraction in the domestic investment ratio to levels greatly below domestic saving, carrying with it a severe contraction of income, output, and employment.

Parenthetically, it should be emphasized that the large leakage abroad of private domestic saving does not provide a valid reason for attempting to plug the leak and conserve domestic saving through imposition of comprehensive exchange controls. First, such controls cannot be effectively enforced; they increase the incentive to export capital without providing an adequately enforceable means of curbing the movement. Second, such controls would greatly impair Malaysia's credit standing and reduce her eligibility for ordinary external finance at a time when "concessional" aid has become extremely scarce. Third, exchange controls to curb Malaysian capital outflow would undoubtedly be supplemented by a tight import licensing system to control the current account. In every country which has used this system, the resulting misallocation of domestic investment into inefficient and costly lines has ultimately intensified instead of relieving the balance-of-payments constraint upon economic growth. If the worst came to the worst and some emergency action became imperative—a contingency which can only be considered highly remote—it would be much less damaging to allow the exchange rate to find its own level in an unrestricted market than to attempt a defense of the official rate through comprehensive direct controls.

Although I disagree sharply with the report of the IBRD Asia Division on the two basic points of economic analysis elaborated above, I fully support its conclusions that external finance is the principal bottleneck to plan fulfillment. Although I strongly share the IBRD view that increased use should be made of external finance, my reasoning, as is implicit from the analysis presented above, is of course substantially different. I believe that the IBRD experts have failed to recognize the critical payments situation which could result if the Malaysian Government continues along its present financial course.

I consider it wrong, for example, to suggest, as the IBRD report at times comes close to doing, that the effects on planned growth of a shortfall in external finance can be made good by increased public saving, i.e., tax increases and restraint in current expenditure. Although external borrowing, tax increases plus restriction of current expenditure, and domestic borrowing are, of course, alternative methods of financing public investment, their respective economic effects are markedly different. It would be dangerously misleading to suggest that external finance and public saving are close substitutes in their economic effects. If external borrowing could not be arranged in the increased amounts now needed to fulfill the plan and if foreign exchange reserves could not safely be further drawn down to make up this shortfall, some combination of a reduction in public investment, reduction in outlays chargeable to the revenue budget, and higher taxes would surely be inescapable.

But when these budgetary adjustments were made, this would by no means be the end of the matter. The moderate impairment of domestic investment incentives which has already occurred has begun to curb foreign direct investment, both in the form of new money and in reinvestment of retained profits. Impaired domestic investment incentives have probably tended also to increase the amount of private domestic saving devoted to capital outflow. This combination of a reduction of foreign direct investment and an increase in Malaysian capital outflow—both brought about chiefly by the weakening of the inducement to invest in Malaysia—has contributed to the requirement for external borrowing. It is an ironical fact that although the actual decline in export earnings came later and was much smaller than was projected by the plan, this small and belated decline has provided the pretext for abandoning aggressive action on the public development program. Because of the plan's initial conservatism with respect to export earnings, implementation of the plan's public investment targets would actually require less foreign assistance loans than the plan called for. In my judgment, this does not argue for lower external borrowing but rather for a more ambitious investment program, public and private, than was planned, and a resulting higher growth rate of real income.

Increasing taxation and reducing public expenditure to make good a shortfall in external borrowing, while perhaps inescapable, would merely compound existing economic problems. These budgetary adjustments, besides directly lowering private incomes and employment, would also impair further the incentives to invest, thus further reducing foreign direct investment and directing domestic saving away from investment at home to capital outflow. Thus, there is a real danger that a continuing shortfall of external borrowing below the level required for realization of planned growth targets, by calling forth higher taxes and restraints on public expenditure, will bring about a serious reduction in private investment. Fiscal restraint and the adverse tendency of private investment may well induce a cumulative downward spiral of incomes and non-agricultural employment, for reasons which are widely understood. For reasons less fully recognized than they should be, the adverse tendency of private investment may also induce a serious deterioration of the balance of payments. Although domestic fiscal and monetary deflation usually improves the current account of the balance of payments by reducing demand for imports of goods and services, this effect may under some circumstances be nullified by deteriorating terms of trade. It is also likely, particularly in the situation and external environment which Malaysia faces today, that any net improvement in the current account of the balance of payments would be more than offset by a markedly unfavorable development of private capital movements. When a country's balance-of-payments difficulties are due to domestic inflation, deflation, if practicable, is an effective remedy. When domestic inflation is not present, deflationary measures to correct balance-of-payments difficulties frequently worsen instead of relieving the difficulties, since net favorable effects on the current account are overshadowed by adverse movements on capital account. The historical experience of other countries which depended heavily upon capital inflow to finance their economic growth indicates that the balance of payments was strong during phases of accelerated growth, owing to a rate of capital inflow which outran even the rapid growth of imports; on the other hand, periods of retarded growth have been characterized by balance-of-payments difficulties owing to the shrinkage of capital inflow. Malaysia faces today just this sort of situation, and retardation of growth is likely to worsen the balance of payments; the root cause of retardation is the shortfall in external borrowing.

Since steps to increase public saving cannot offset but can only worsen the domestic economic and external payments difficulties caused by the shortfall in external borrowing, it is necessary to inquire whether increased domestic borrowing to finance public investment can satisfactorily be used to fill the gap. Increased domestic borrowing would necessitate drawing upon foreign exchange holdings to provide the external means of payment which increased foreign borrowing automatically supplies. This is, of course, the fundamental difference between domestic and external borrowing. The Central Bank is understandably reluctant to allow any decrease in the extremely high ratio of foreign exchange reserves to currency issue during the present period of transition to an independent banknote currency system. A substantial decline in the reserve ratio before the viability of a new currency system is completely taken for granted by the public would not be without some danger.

The Central Bank's own reserves could be somewhat increased, however, by (1) inducing the commercial banks to reduce further their holdings of foreign exchange, (2) reducing further, perhaps to zero, the proportion of insurance company policy reserves which can be invested abroad, and (3) accelerating the liquidation of government agency holdings of sterling securities. Although some or all of these actions are probably desirable, their contribution to Central Bank reserves would not be great, and their implementation would take time.

Some improvement in the reserve ratio could probably be achieved by raising the inordinately low interest rate now paid on savings deposits at commercial banks. The contention that holders of currency cannot be induced to deposit some part of their idle currency holdings is difficult to accept. Moreover, payment of an abnormally low rate of interest on small savings seems inappropriate on grounds of equity. A shift from currency to savings deposits would increase the reserve ratio by reducing the outstanding currency against which reserves are required.

Although I have not sought to estimate the possible effect on the Central Bank's reserve position of this combination of measures, the effect would undoubtedly be modest. This implies that domestic borrowing can be used to only a small extent to meet the shortfall in external borrowing without causing a reduction in the reserve ratio. I venture the judgment that a gradual decrease in the extremely high reserve cover could be permitted even during the present period of transition without disturbing confidence in domestic money. Although an abrupt and substantial decline in reserves during the present transition period might have dangers, domestic borrowing can safely be used even at present to meet some part of the gap caused by the shortfall in external borrowing.

To summarize the results of this lengthy analysis, there is no satisfactory and adequate substitute for substantially increased external borrowing. Fiscal retrenchment through higher taxes and reduced public expenditures retards growth, weakens incentives for domestic investment, and creates the danger of mounting balance-of-payments difficulties and reserve losses through the effects of sluggishness in domestic investment in augmenting private capital outflow and inhibiting private inflow. If the resulting reserve loss impaired confidence in the currency, the difficulties would be gravely compounded. Substantially increased reliance upon domestic borrowing in an effort to overcome the present retardation of economic growth would deplete reserves and might impair confidence in the currency. If this impairment reached serious proportions, the efforts to accelerate growth through domestic borrowing would probably fail and flight of capital would be large. Because of Malaysia's exceptionally strong reserve position, I would consider increased reliance on domestic borrowing to be less dangerous than further substantial fiscal retrenchment. The main conclusion which follows from the preceding analysis, however, is that there is simply no adequate and safe substitute for substantially increased external borrowing. Singapore's financial strength continues to be matched by strong growth performance; Malaysia's present financial strength can be sustained only if its former strong growth performance is reestablished. Consequently, increased external borrowing is indispensable.

The major policy implication of the foregoing analysis is clear. An aggressive policy should replace the present somewhat hesitant policy with respect to obtaining and utilizing external loans. I am told that this hesitation is due in part to a feeling of uneasiness regarding the burdens and risks inherent in a growing external debt. This attitude seems to me particularly unjustified in Malaysia's case for a number of reasons.

First, the country's credit standing is exceptionally strong. On any comparative basis, its foreign exchange reserves are extremely high whether measured in relation to annual imports, to the level of exports, to the amplitude of fluctuation in export earnings, to GNP, or to domestic money supply. These are the main standards by which adequacy of reserves is measured, and in terms of each of these standards Malaysia ranks high in comparison with both underdeveloped countries and advanced industrial countries. On a similar basis of international comparison, its external debt and annual debt service burden are extremely low in relation both to export earnings and to GNP. The principal amount of external public debt is less than foreign exchange reserves. Malaysia's high credit standing is due also to its past record of strong growth and to its success in maintaining political stability within a multiracial context. This political success, in turn, has been due in part to good growth performance; retardation of growth might induce political tensions.

Second, the present high credit standing cannot be preserved by using it haltingly. If external debt grew at a rate barely sufficient to maintain feeble economic growth, the proportion of foreign investment represented by direct investment would be excessively high. The rate of profits on direct investment is much higher than the interest on foreign loans. The combined rate of return on total foreign investment would be closer to the profit rate than to the interest rate, and this composite rate of return would be much higher than the rate of interest earned by Malaysia on its external assets. If external debt grows at a rate barely sufficient to sustain feeble economic growth, the net burden represented by interest and profits accruing to foreigners in excess of interest received by Malaysia on foreign assets will continue to grow not only absolutely but at a more rapid rate than the growth of GNP. This growing burden in relation to GNP, if it persisted long enough, would produce a gradual deterioration in credit standing and would eventually make even limited external financing much more difficult to obtain. Moreover, feeble growth performance directly impairs credit standing and may also do so indirectly through adverse effects on political stability.

Third, growing external debt does not represent a growing burden, provided the proceeds of the debt are productively used. If investment, public and private, is not grossly misdirected, an appropriate proportion will flow into export earning and efficient import saving industry. Under these conditions Malaysia gains so long as the social rate of return from the additional investments made possible by foreign borrowing provides a margin above interest charges. It is just as true for borrowing nations as for borrowing business firms that the borrower is enriched when the uses to which he puts the loan proceeds yield a higher return than the interest costs. Rapidly growing firms frequently finance their growth partly by growing debt; this is true for nations also. There is nothing inherently unsound in the process, provided domestic investment is not badly misdirected, for example, through high tariffs or import quotas.

Fourth, Malaysia possesses not only surplus labor, but also surplus land and unused external borrowing capacity. The quality of its private entrepreneurship and its public administration are high. All the elements are present to permit a high rate of economic development and the rate of growth actually achieved depends decisively on the government's political decision regarding the rate at which it is willing to bring its surplus labor, idle land, and unused financing capacity into productive uses. If these resources are not wasted in idleness or misdirected into unproductive uses, the growth of real income and external debt servicing capacity will greatly exceed the growth in debt service requirements.

Fifth, although dependence on a continuing inflow of external borrowing necessarily exposes the economy to the dislocation which might result from a sudden cessation of credit facilities, this danger seems remote when account is taken of the IMF and other financing which can be brought into action if needed. Credit conditions are not likely to become more stringent in the future than they have been in 1966 and 1967. Moreover, Malaysia's economic success has depended in the past on willingness to accept the risks inherent in maintaining an open economy, and it is just as unwise to curtail external borrowing as to curtail external trade in order to avert risks. Variability of export earnings affects debt servicing capacity, but the export earnings required by present debt service are so small that there would be little reason to fear even a considerable rise in this ratio.

II Some Financial Problems in Malaysia's Development[2]

Malaysia's Long-Term Growth Potential

Economists who are called upon by foreign governments to evaluate their development plans frequently have the unpleasant task of pointing out that the projected growth targets which they have been asked to review are overambitious, owing to a failure to take adequate account of the economy's resource constraints or structural problems. In the case of the Malaysian economy, it is pleasant to find that this is emphatically not the case. Perhaps the most important observation which a visiting economist can make is that the underlying economic constraints which limit attainable rates of growth in other underdeveloped countries are either wholly absent or only feebly present in the economy of Malaysia. Among countries customarily classified as underdeveloped, there are, I believe, few, if any, which can emerge into the "economically advanced" classification more rapidly than Malaysia's underlying economic potential permits it to do. On a reasonable appraisal of Malaysia's present and potential resources, attainable rates of growth of per capita real income, both during the present plan period and over the next fifteen or twenty years, are very substantially higher than the targets projected in the present plan. If this judgment is correct, present targets are much too low; insufficiently ambitious planning should be as sedulously avoided as overambitious plans.

Like most other underdeveloped countries, Malaysia has a large reservoir of unemployed and underemployed labor. Unlike most of them, however, it also possesses both a substantial amount of virgin land, readily accessible and of potentially high productivity, and a large and underutilized capacity to obtain external finance for use in expanding its capital stock and accelerating growth. Besides exceptionally large foreign exchange reserves, its high credit standing enables it to borrow substantially abroad at relatively favorable interest rates; productive use of an increased volume of external borrowing could accelerate economic growth,

2. From a Memorandum to Malaysia's Economic Planning Unit, August 28, 1967.–Ed.

thus expanding both domestic saving and enlarging the availability of external finance in the future.

Taking account of the effects of vigorous growth on both the capacity to attract external finance and on domestic saving, it may be said that vigorous growth generates its own financing. Sluggish growth, on the other hand, creates financial constraints by reducing the availability of outside funds and increasing the share of domestic saving devoted to capital outflow. Sluggish growth can create or amplify balance-of-payments difficulties, while rapid growth can remove them. The decisive factor is the strength of the inducement to invest (public sector investment as well as private investment), not the saving ratio. And the attitude concerning new investment commitments depends greatly on current and recent growth experience. Vigorous growth breeds a strong inducement to invest.

The concern expressed in some quarters that Malaysia may be facing a long-run balance-of-payments problem is, in my judgment, unjustified, and not merely because of the possibilities of external borrowing. The sharp decline in rubber prices has been primarily the result of increased volume, brought about by improvements in technology which have expanded output and reduced costs. For the efficient producers, rubber remains distinctly profitable even at today's prices. The world demand for rubber, natural plus synthetic, will continue to grow, and I venture to guess that the price of natural rubber has reached or is approaching the point at which most producers of synthetic will no longer find it attractive to invest in new capacity. Although synthetic rubber will undoubtedly continue to be priced competitively with natural rubber, because synthetic producers will wish to keep existing capacity active even at low profits instead of incurring losses by shutting down, there is a good prospect that, with expansion of synthetic capacity slowing down, natural rubber at prices not far from present levels will capture an expanding share of the growing world market. The planned reduction in British military outlays in Malaysia deprives the balance of payments of a certain amount of external receipts, besides increasing Malaysia's own defense requirements. At a more basic level, however, the ending of Indonesia's "confrontation" policy, which led to the

British cutback, is favorable in its longer term implications for trade with Indonesia and for the balance of payments. Malaysia is an efficient producer of its newer export products, notably palm oil and lumber, and these products enjoy a growing external demand. In manufacturing, opportunities for efficient import substitution are present and will keep expanding as the size of the domestic market grows; in manufactured exports the scope for trade with other countries of Southeast Asia is likely to expand.

This favorable assessment of export and import substitution prospects assumes that the Malaysian Government continues its wise policy of relying primarily on measures other than high tariffs and import quota restrictions to promote new industries. The experience of other underdeveloped countries shows quite conclusively that high import barriers, whether imposed for balance-of-payments reasons or to help domestic manufacturers, have channeled new investment away from efficient and into inefficient lines. They have hampered export growth and favored inefficient over efficient import substitution. Thus they intensify, instead of relieving, balance-of-payments constraints upon economic growth. Since the Malaysian Government has, on the whole, avoided the gross errors in commercial policy which most underdeveloped countries have fallen into, and since its exporting and import substitution prospects are in other respects favorable, growth prospects are not hampered by a long-term structural "bottleneck" of the balance-of-payments variety.

Malaysia is also relatively free from another structural maladjustment which provides a major impediment to growth in a number of underdeveloped countries. In many countries, the level of urban wages, for a variety of reasons, has become grossly out of line with the underlying labor supply situation, thus seriously hampering the absorption of surplus labor into more productive activities. Some countries with highly remunerative export products—Venezuela, Chile, and Zambia, to name only a few examples—instead of using for general development purposes the capturable "rents" generated by the major export have allowed a considerable part of this potential resource to be dissipated into high wages for a small number of workers in the export industry. This wage has set a standard which other non-agricultural workers have tried to approach, and the final result has been to raise industrial costs to a point where even limited industrialization requires a mounting subsidy, usually extracted through levies, partly disguised, which weigh heavily upon the export and agricultural sectors. It appears that labor market distortions of this type, common to many underdeveloped countries, are not present in a severe form in Malaysia.

In addition to these impressive elements of strength, Malaysia possesses an efficient and well-developed economic infrastructure in transportation, communications, and power; a demonstrated capacity in the public sector to carry out development projects with effectiveness; and an abundance of entrepreneurial capacity in its private sector. It has maintained a good record of political stability in the context of a multi-racial society. Under these circumstances it would be a great misfortune if Malaysia, whether through inadequate recognition of its potential for growth, through inappropriate financial policies, or for other reasons, settled for a rate of growth of real income and a rate of improvement in the welfare of the poorest members of its population greatly below its capabilities and lower than that of a number of other underdeveloped countries whose underlying endowment of resources and markets is markedly less favorable. Without much more detailed analysis, it would be inappropriate to attempt to estimate a reasonable target, but I venture the guess that an annual rate of growth of per capita real income more than triple the present plan target is readily attainable through appropriate policies and a substantially enlarged development effort.

Need for Growth-Promoting Financial Policies

Actual economic performance during the first two years of the present plan has been rather disappointing. There has been a distinct retardation of growth, a shortfall of public investment below planned levels, and, it appears, a less buoyant investment climate in the private sector. Some officials are disposed to attribute this disappointing performance to some adverse external developments, notably the sharp drop in the price of rubber. Although not often cited, the increase in shipping and insurance rates with the closing of the Suez Canal has raised the c.i.f. cost of imports and added to the adverse effect on terms of trade of the drop in rubber prices.

It is most important, in managing an open economy, to distinguish clearly between the direct and inescapable consequences of adverse external events and the indirect consequences which flow from the actions taken by the monetary and fiscal authorities in responding to such events. Depending upon the nature of their response, the financial authorities can either amplify or compensate for adverse external developments. Although, owing to Malaysia's extraordinary financial strength, the scope for compensatory action was (and remains) exceptionally wide, the measures actually taken have served to amplify, instead of offsetting, the effects on the domestic economy of adverse external developments. Consequently, the rather sluggish economic performance which has been attributed to adverse external factors has been due primarily not to their direct effects, but rather to the actions taken by the Malaysian authorities in responding to external developments.

In putting forward this interpretation of present difficulties, it is not implied that compensatory fiscal and monetary policies could neutralize the adverse economic effects of sudden and catastrophic external events, nor could monetary and fiscal policies remove the need for painful adjustments if there emerged an unfavorable long-term trend in demand for Malaysia's exports. But the events of the past two years were neither catastrophic in immediate impact nor symptomatic of a basically unfavorable underlying trend in external markets. The Malaysian economy, because of its high degree of openness, is much exposed to a kaleidoscopic variety of short-term external influences, sometimes predominantly stimulating and sometimes restrictive in their immediate impact; but her financial resources for cushioning the unstabilizing effects of these influences are also abundant. Unless the monetary and fiscal authorities are prepared to put these resources to work by using modern techniques of financial policy, the economy will be subject to frequent periods of sluggishness and, doubtless, occasional inflationary overstimulation as well. What is more important is that the long-term trend of growth will be held substantially below the rate made possible by the underlying economic potential. If, on the other hand, techniques of growth-promoting monetary and fiscal management are developed and used judiciously, the achievement of high and fairly stable growth rates will soon create in the private sector a climate of expectations under which investment commitments in new or growing industries and in agriculture will be made in accelerating volume. *Without the support of fiscal and monetary policies, the concept of comprehensive development planning, in an economy as open as Malaysia's, loses most of its meaning, since plan implementation is continually subordinated to temporarily disturbing external factors.* Growth-promoting monetary and fiscal policies should not merely be used to cushion the effects of unstabilizing external developments, but should be designed to reach and then sustain the highest growth rate which the economy can achieve without inflationary overheating.

Problems of Financing

The suggestion that the Government should actively adopt growth-promoting fiscal and monetary policies, and should even increase its expansionary efforts when faced by temporarily adverse external developments affecting the balance of payments, will doubtless arouse many objections on financial grounds. It seems appropriate, therefore, to summarize my views on the problems involved.

First, the new monetary system which replaces the Currency Board and transfers the note issue function to the Central Bank is not less rigid in any essential respect than the former system. Reserves, although exceedingly large, are locked in. The statutory reserve requirement is 80 per cent, and those at the Central Bank with whom I talked expressed the view that during the present period of transition and for some time in the future it will be essential to maintain a ratio of over 100 per cent, lest public confidence in the currency be disturbed. . . .

If the high statutory reserve requirement and the Central Bank's attitude regarding the need for maintaining reserves above 100 per cent of note issue are adhered to, a loss of reserves to settle the international balance of payments requires an approximately equal contraction of currency. In order to bring about a reduction in currency circulation, a multiple contraction in total money supply and time deposits would be required, and the full contraction required can be brought about only by curtailing commercial bank loans and securities. The Central Bank must take restrictive action to force this deflation unless the slump in private demands for credit does the job alone. Unless the Central Bank is able and willing to increase its domestic assets as its foreign exchange holdings decline, it cannot pursue an expansionary monetary policy to facilitate increased government and private borrowing in the face of adverse external developments.

Although I believe that the Central Bank officials exaggerate the need for keeping reserves substantially above the statutory minimum, their leeway under existing statutes to pursue expansionary policies would be rather slight even if present attitudes were changed. No Central Bank wants its reserves to approach the legal minimum. Under present conditions monetary expansion is directly geared to growth in reserves. In time, the present statutory requirement should be substantially lowered and the restriction against Central Bank purchase of government securities removed. It is fortunately unnecessary to take this step today because of the potential availability of external finance. External finance, if aggressively called into use, can supply the flexibility needed for growth-promoting financial policy. It will perhaps be useful to comment briefly on the main sources of external finance.

A. FOREIGN DIRECT INVESTMENT

Foreign direct investment has a critically important role in Malaysia's economic development, primarily because of its valuable contribution of "know-how," technology, and organization in new industries potentially well adapted to Malaysia's endowment of resources and to its domestic and external markets. Its "rub-off," or training, benefits of imparting new skills and knowledge to Malaysians are of great value. Foreign direct investment is also an external source of capital, but in timing and magnitude its amount must depend on the pace at which an enlarged industrialization program can be organized and brought effectively into action; matters should not be complicated by attempting to regulate the pace of direct investment to conform to short-term fluctuations in external financial requirements. For this and other reasons, external borrowing must play the key financial role.

B. IMF FACILITIES

The IMF's compensatory financing facilities should be fully used, since the sharp decline in the price of rubber represents precisely the kind of situation this facility was created to meet. The Central Bank should also draw freely on the gold tranche of its regular IMF quota.

C. FINANCIAL RELATIONS WITH LONDON AND OTHER CENTERS

In theory, Malaysia's membership in the sterling area gives it unrestricted access to the short-term and long-term lending facilities of the London market. In practice, these facilities have become greatly restricted through ceilings on bank advances, surveillance of security issues, and a variety of other informal controls. Lending to the outer sterling area has been curbed not only by general credit stringency but by an extensive apparatus of informal controls. The preferred status which sterling area members enjoy in principle is no longer of much practical significance. Moreover, this situation is likely to continue. The long-run working out of Britain's payments problem seems destined to include both continuing gradual liquidation of existing overseas assets and limitations on new lending. The principal exceptions will be the more profitable of the direct investments, with sterling loans being limited to the amounts deemed necessary to induce present holders of sterling balances not to shift them to other centers. Rigid reserve requirements have kept the sterling balances of such countries as Nigeria, Singapore, and Malaysia at a high and rising level, but the long-run viability of this system is questionable unless London can provide adequate lending facilities.

Since Malaysia's banking connections are so largely with London, I believe that the limited capacity of London to lend has been mistaken for a limited ability of Malaysia to borrow. I am confident that Malaysia's capacity to obtain credit, long- or short-term, elsewhere, particularly New York, will prove to be substantial. Australia has found it necessary to draw heavily on the United States in order to obtain the amount of external financing needed to realize its potential for economic growth, and I believe that Malaysia faces the same problem. Ordinary bank credit lines, term loans, and long-term open market loans are an essential supplement to suppliers' credits and project loans.

Suppliers' Credits and Project Loans

Two points should be made here. First, the credits should be used to the full extent except in those cases where the nature of the tying requires the borrower to pay higher-than-competitive prices. Even in this case, their use may be justified if the terms of the loan are sufficiently favorable to offset the higher prices. Second, suppliers' credits and project loans cannot meet more than a part of Malaysia's borrowing requirements. In 1966 roughly half of Malaysia's net private savings provided financing for new domestic investment; the rest was presumably devoted to private remittances and capital outflow.

Thus, foreign capital inflow must not only cover the import balance on current account which strong growth will entail; it must also offset the outflow of Malaysian capital. Since growth in currency circulation and bank deposits is a necessary accompaniment of economic growth, even the increase in reserves which the present rigid system calls for represents a requirement for external finance.

The growth of direct investments should be geared to the need to import "know-how" as a highly valuable component of the industrialization program. The financing contribution is an incidental feature. This means that borrowing must play the major financing role. Suppliers' credits tied chiefly to importation of capital goods and project loans which cover direct foreign exchange costs plus only a small portion of local currency costs should be more fully and effectively used but cannot fill the financing gap. Local currency costs include payments for services, such as internal transportation, having a high import content. The local wage and profit incomes generated by local currency costs of projects are spent in part on imports, and of the saved portion of incomes a substantial portion flows abroad. In addition to using the gold tranche of the IMF quota and its compensatory financing facility, it is above all necessary to make increasing use of ordinary bank loans and open market borrowing abroad.

If the declining tendency of rubber prices continues during the next year, and if the Malaysian financial authorities follow their present course in responding to this tendency, the reduction in capital inflow and the increase in capital outflow may proceed to a point where emergency borrowing becomes necessary to meet a critical balance-of-payments situation. When the price of rubber finally recovers, the authorities for a time will doubtless persist in considering it necessary to practice severe restraint with respect to development outlays in order to repay emergency borrowing and to try to replenish reserves. Furthermore, if the pound should be devalued and if Malaysia, unwilling to accept the merely nominal bookkeeping loss on its sterling holdings which adherence to the present gold parity of its currency would entail, devalued its currency along with sterling, the unfavorable financial pressures would be intensified. Malaysia's domestic price level is largely determined by world prices and the exchange rate. The rise in price level accompanying and following devaluation of the Malaysian dollar would increase the demand of business firms and the public for money to transact even an unchanged volume of business at higher prices, but this demand could not be accommodated without a further decline in the reserve ratio or additional external borrowing. If the financial authorities remained reluctant to accept either of these alternatives, they would be led, unfortunately, to a further intensification of monetary restraint and fiscal retrenchment. For one or another of the above reasons, the near-term development may well turn out to be the emergence of a sizeable surplus on current account despite low rubber prices; an adverse balance of payments owing to developments in the capital account; and a marked retardation of growth, or absolute decline in real income, unless the Malaysian Government drastically changes its present financial policies.

III Comments on Previous Memoranda[3]

In the two memoranda to the Economic Planning Unit, emphasis was focused on those points which seemed to me to require special stress when addressing one's observations to Malaysian officials. There prevails here an insufficient recognition that, barring catastrophic domestic or international political developments, Malaysia's growth potential, for a considerable period ahead, is relatively free from the underlying constraints which limit the growth prospects of many underdeveloped countries. Overcautious planning, an excess of fiscal and financial orthodoxy, reluctance to permit idle land to be brought into productive use, or an unduly restrained or misdirected industrialization policy could hold the actual rate of growth substantially below levels rather readily attainable; since I was asked to give my attention to financial matters, my memoranda concentrated upon the first two of these inhibiting factors.

The existence of a considerable margin of unused external financing facilities and the need for a more aggressive policy of foreign borrowing are the specific points which chiefly need to be emphasized in Malaysia. It is quite clear that the Malaysian Government has been too slow in drawing upon project loans and suppliers' credits already granted; moreover, conversations with local bankers, including the local managers or representatives of two of the American banks, indicated that additional loans, apart from suppliers' credits and project loans, could be arranged without difficulty. Thus, Malaysia is not making adequate use of the funds which could be obtained even under present world financial conditions.

1. Effects on Malaysia of the International Monetary Situation

If I were reporting, however, to officials in Washington, I would stress that the recent retardation of Malaysia's growth, and the more serious retardation and payments difficulties which may well

3. Written as a private memorandum to William B. Gates, who was head of the Harvard Development Advisory Service group in Malaysia; dated September 1, 1967.—Ed.

be in prospect, are to a substantial extent the result of financial and other policies of the United States and British governments. It is expecting a great deal—perhaps too much—to suppose that the Malaysian Government, steeped in orthodox financial doctrine learned from British colonial civil servants, can be persuaded to experiment with an untried compensatory fiscal policy relying chiefly upon foreign borrowing, at a time of changeover of the domestic currency system, fears of sterling devaluation, extremely tight money in London, tight money in New York, informal U.S. and British payments controls from whose effects underdeveloped countries are by no means so fully exempted in practice as on paper they are supposed to be, and sharply shrinking foreign aid appropriations. Indeed, I found Malaysia an instructive case study of the injury inflicted on innocent bystanders by the measures, many of them both futile and pernicious, taken by the United States and Britain for balance-of-payments reasons. The ineffectualness and harmfulness of some of these measures are illustrated at a number of points by recent Malaysian developments. Indeed, as an American, I felt some private embarrassment in criticizing the Malaysian financial authorities for their undue anxiety regarding the balance of payments and for taking inappropriate and harmful measures as a result.

It is probable, in my view, that the Anglo-American decision respecting devaluation of sterling taken immediately after the Labor government came to power in Britain was decisive in establishing a firmly fixed pound-dollar rate; that the United States will continue to provide such further finance for future rescue operations as may be needed; and that Britain's resort to wage controls has made devaluation largely ineffective as a supplementary remedy. It is unlikely that British workers, having become resistant to further restraint on money wages, are sufficiently subject to money illusion to accept a real wage cut through devaluation.

Whether or not one accepts this conjecture, the region whose balance of payments should have been of concern to the United States and the British governments—to the extent that such concern was appropriate at all—is the extensive region which includes the United States, Great Britain, and the group of countries holding a major portion of their reserves in dollars or pounds and conducting most of their trade with the United States, Britain, and each other. It is the consolidated balance of payments of this region *vis-à-vis* the rest of the world which is of relevance. Intra-region payments developments are quite secondary. This region includes virtually all the non-socialist world except Continental Western Europe, the French Community, and South Vietnam, Cambodia, and Laos. Many of the measures of direct control taken by the United States to influence its balance of payments had their principal effect on the payments position of Great Britain and other countries of the dollar-pound areas, with resulting negative feedback on the United States balance of payments. Whether their final effect on the payments position of the dollar-pound region as a whole was slightly positive or slightly negative is difficult to determine, but it was surely small. Many of the British measures of direct control also had their predominant effect within the dollar-pound region, with little if any net effect on the whole region's payments position *vis-à-vis* Continental Western Europe. In the largely unintended tug-of-war between Britain and the United States, Britain may have gained some improvement on balance at the expense of the United States payments position, but since its gains were used to repay some of the emergency credits, very little was changed in the end.

Like the direct measures to control the balance of payments, the escalation of interest rates by the United States and Britain was largely an exercise in futility. Balance-of-payments considerations were a major reason in both countries for an undue emphasis on monetary rather than fiscal restraint. The consequences in the United States are well known; since an increase, not a reduction, in private investment in Great Britain is needed for eventual improvement of Britain's international competitive position, greater fiscal restraint would have had the advantage of freeing resources for private investment by reducing the public sector's net draft upon private saving, while with less severe monetary stringency, these freed resources would have been absorbed by increased private investment—with a smaller increase in unemployment and greater gain in productivity than has occurred. The effects of American and British tight money on the dollar-pound region's balance-of-payments position *vis-à-vis* Continental Western Europe was largely nullified until 1966 by an offsetting escalation of interest rates in some European countries. About the middle of 1966 credit stringency began to approach the danger point, and shortly thereafter there was a prudent if belated backing away, in several countries, from the extremes of monetary stringency.

Because of Malaysia's high degree of openness, in trade and in finance, that country conveniently illustrates some of the undesirable side effects of British and American policies. Malaysia's rigid monetary mechanism, under which sterling reserves, except in rather nominal amounts, can be freed for external payments purposes only by domestic deflation, is viable only if external borrowing is rather elastically available. Since neither Britain nor the United States desires to impose severe deflation on Malaysia, and since the United States is better able than Britain to provide financing, the final result is likely to be retardation of Malaysian growth, with some resulting reduction in imports (chiefly from the dollar-pound area), and some transfer of financing responsibility from London to New York.

Although in my memoranda I emphasized the effect of the weakening of the inducement to invest in Malaysia in increasing the outflow and curtailing the inflow of capital, the direction of causation has not been wholly one way. The possibility of sterling devaluation made flight of capital into Swiss francs or gold appear to some Malaysian owners of wealth a more attractive use of resources than investment in Malaysia. The British tax on income from overseas investments, probably supplemented by informal official suasion, encouraged offerings of British investments to local buyers in Malaysia, competing directly with the use of investible funds for new investment. Monetary stringency, through its effects on the financial positions of corporations investing abroad, has also operated to postpone foreign direct investment. Thus, the weakening of investment in Malaysia is to some extent a result, and not exclusively a cause, of the changed international capital flow. I believe, however, that the chief direction of causation was from domestic investment incentives to capital flows.

Finally, the sharpness of the decline in the price of rubber, which has impaired the inducement to invest, has doubtless been enhanced by industrial slowdown in most of the advanced countries, and especially by the slump in automobile production in the United States, Britain, and Western Europe—partly the aftermath of last year's excessively tight money. Sales of rubber from the United States stockpile on a declining market, although their effect was probably exaggerated by the Malaysian government, hardly helped. Lacking knowledge of the reason for this decision, one is inclined to assume that the sales were motivated by a combination of balance-of-payments and budgetary considerations. When account is taken of negative feedbacks, the net effect on the United States balance of payments was undoubtedly trivial. Whether the fiscal effects on the United States economy were anti-inflationary turns largely upon whether the rubber producers, whose loss of export earnings probably exceeded the amount which we secured from sales out of the stockpile, adjusted to this loss chiefly by reducing their imports or chiefly by external borrowing and drawing upon their reserves. If the first, the effect on the American economy would be anti-inflationary; if the second, spending is cut, the deflationary effect is direct; when imported commodities differ in their domestic economic effects from curtailment of the Government's domestic spending. When domestic spending is cut, the deflationary effect is direct; when imported materials are sold from the stockpile the effect is deflationary only if the reduction in United States imports is reflected back through a reduction in the imports of the producing countries. Although the above generalizations neglect a variety of complicating factors—for example, sales of natural rubber have an effect upon domestic producers of synthetic—they hold as a first approximation.

Viewed in the larger setting, Malaysia's recently disappointing economic performance and the more serious difficulties which may be in prospect are largely caused by external developments, even though the Malaysian government could do a great deal to offset their adverse effects. Of the unfavorable external influences, the most fundamental and pervasive have been the stresses and strains within the international monetary system, which have influenced especially capital movements, the demand for Malaysia's exports, and the incentive to invest.

Given the fact that the strained condition of the international monetary system has persisted for almost a decade, and still continues, one may well be inclined to ask whether the optimistic judgments expressed in my memoranda both regarding Malaysia's underlying balance-of-payments prospects and regarding the growing availability of external finance do not require modification to allow for the consequences of continuing strain in the international monetary system. My own view is that the condition of chronic strain which has afflicted the international monetary system since the restoration of convertibility of European currencies at the end of 1958 is slowly subsiding, not through comprehensive, deliberate action to bring it to an end but because the principal finance ministries and central banks are finding it increasingly wearying to sustain the mood of anxious preoccupation without which the condition of strain would soon disappear. If this judgment is overoptimistic, my optimistic appraisal of Malaysia's long-term potentialities requires modification, since attainable growth rates in economies so open as Malaysia's would surely be impaired by an indefinite continuation of strain in the international monetary system and the progressive elaboration of mercantilist controls by Britain and the United States in a ceaseless effort to defend the balance of payments.

2. *Development Planning and Neo-Classical Growth Models*

The standard techniques of macro-economic programming used by development planners to determine attainable growth targets, relying usually upon a saving bottleneck, a foreign exchange bottleneck, or an absorptive capacity bottleneck, are not of much use in setting growth targets when none of these constraints is present. I should have liked to use the Malaysian example as a means of indicating some major limitations of standard methods. These methods are of considerable use for countries such as India, but they are one-sided and partly misleading for a number of other underdeveloped countries and almost entirely misleading for countries such as Malaysia. I should have liked also to suggest some hypotheses regarding possible determinants of the attainable growth rate in cases of the Malaysian type. Finally, I should have liked to use the Malaysian case to indicate my reasons for believing that modern neo-classical growth models distort more than they illuminate the actual growth process.

12 *Inflation and Development: Brazil*[1]

This essay expounds some thoughts about inflation which I developed during a two-week visit to Brazil in the summer of 1966. Rather than expose my ignorance by saying much about the specific case of Brazil, I shall concentrate on some theoretical reflections about inflation applicable mainly to less-developed countries, but not all confined to them, and shall use Brazil as the principal example. The subject is a hoary one and my justification for setting these thoughts down is my view that most of the writings about inflation in Latin America skirt a real analysis of the central points. As a result of inadequate analysis, the anti-inflation or dis-inflation efforts there are to a large extent misdirected and likely to fail.

As one goes through the literature on the monetarist versus the structuralist views, the hardest thing to figure out is what the question is. It is like the game that certain "in" groups played a few years ago in which you give the answer and it is up to the other fellow to figure out what the question was. The best example is "The answer is 9-W." The question is, "Do you spell your name with a 'V,' Herr Wagner?"

1. Revision of a transcript of a talk given to the Economics staff of the Agency for International Development on May 1, 1967. First published as "Stabilization and Monetary Policy in Less Developed Countries," in Jesse W. Markham and Gustav F. Papanek (editors), *Industrial Organization and Economic Development, In Honor of E. S. Mason* (Houghton Mifflin, Boston, 1970), pp. 396-413. Reprinted by permission.—Ed.

The other thing that the controversy reminds me of is the observation of Frank Ramsey's that most debates follow the pattern of A's saying "I went to Granchester the other day," and B's saying, "No, I didn't." This is the same variety of discourse.

I want to begin with a simple theoretical construct of a neutral or nearly neutral inflationary path, using it to provide a basis for analyzing the effects of a particular inflationary process in a particular country.

"Neutral" Inflation

One can conceive of a neutral, or more accurately, a nearly neutral inflation. I will state later on why I use the qualification "nearly." By a "neutral" inflation I mean an inflationary process which has no effect on any real economic magnitudes—output, employment, composition of output and employment, and so on. It is possible to conceive of such an inflation. It is probably very difficult to realize it in practice.

Two sets of conditions would be necessary for the realization of this kind of neutral inflation. One is a set of subjective conditions and the other a set of objective conditions.

SUBJECTIVE CONDITIONS

These conditions relate to the state of expectations, and when you consider expectations in this context, three aspects are relevant.

1. First the question of the uniformity or diversity of the expectations of individual economic entities—firms and households—in the economy. Do individual firms and households expect approximately the same degree of inflation in the future? Do they have the same future inflationary path in mind, and if not, is the diversity of expectations great or small?

In an open economy the expectations of foreigners who are engaged in trade and financial operations with this economy are also relevant. An example of the importance of the expectations of foreigners is the European inflations after World War I and the accompanying exchange depreciation. In the early stages of these inflations there was a very widespread expectation that European currencies in due course would be restored to the pre–World War I parities. And I recall seeing estimates that in the early stages, Germany got about a billion dollars from ill-advised foreign speculators and foreign bull speculators in marks. This was a form of unintended private foreign aid.

2. The second aspect of expectations that is of importance is the precision or fuzziness of the expectations of each decision-making entity regarding future price-level behavior, or, to be a little more formal about it, whether the variance of expectations is high or low.

3. The third aspect is *ex ante* versus *ex post*. Suppose the expectations were uniform and each entity's state of expectation could be thought of as having a sort of mean value. Is this expectation vindicated by the result, or is the inflation greater or less than was foreseen? If the inflation has been generally underestimated or overestimated, there will be windfall gains and losses.

So far as the subjective conditions are concerned, the neutrality or near-neutrality of an inflation depends upon expectations being (a) highly uniform as among economic entities, (b) precise, i.e., held with low variance, and (c) vindicated in practice, with the expected path turning out to be the realized path.

Incidentally, why avoidance of inflation is a good thing is a question which many people do not bother to ask. A large part of the case for price-level stability is that, as a practical matter, it is rather hard to imagine that the subjective state of expectations that is required for neutrality could be fulfilled around a sharply rising price level. Thus the case for price-level stability is that it is probably a prerequisite for coalescence of expectations.

OBJECTIVE CONDITIONS

On the objective side, the condition for near-neutrality of inflation is that markets have to behave in such a way that prices equate supply and demand.

When you come to apply this notion to Latin American economies—indeed, to economies generally—you confront the fact that, with or without inflation, prices do not equate supply and demand in these countries, anyway. So a more expedient statement—although just what it means I do not know—of the objective condition is that the price distortions for near-neutrality of inflation should be no different from what they would be under price-level stability.

An illustration of what I have in mind when I state the objective condition in this way is that, with or without inflation, the level of urban real wages for common labor is often above that which clears the market. And, I suspect that the level of interest rates paid by borrowers is often below that which would clear the market without rationing if financial institutions were adequate to make credit accessible to all sectors of the economy. Under these circumstances, clearly, all price distortions cannot be blamed on inflation. That is why the objective condition for neutrality of inflation is fulfilled if the underpricing of finance and the overpricing of common labor in urban markets are merely no greater than they would be without inflation.

If both subjective and objective conditions are fulfilled, then inflation is nearly neutral. The reason for saying "nearly" is that there would still be two departures from neutrality. The first is that under the sort of equilibrium-inflation path that I have in mind, while holders of bank deposits would receive a nominal rate of interest at least high enough to offset the inflation, it is hard to see how interest could be paid to holders of currency. As a result, the distribution of money holdings between currency and bank deposits would be altered a little bit. The significance of that point is probably not very great.

The second departure from full neutrality is more important. The function of money as a unit of account under this kind of nearly neutral inflation would be seriously impaired. Children, in order to equip themselves for the economic decisions they have to make during their lives, would have to memorize a log table instead of a multiplication table. The point is that the key function of accounting is to measure gain and to separate recurrent gain or profit from non-recurrent capital gain. In accounting under neutral inflation, all the items would have to be dated and deflated and expressed in units of account having the purchasing power of a given date, and people would have to learn to think this way; they would have to penetrate the veil of money in order to make economic decisions. Although people accustomed to living in inflationary environments manage to do it quite well, even without memorizing log tables, this is a serious inconvenience. To the extent that accounting falls short of perfection the inflation will not be wholly neutral.

This is a rather long theoretical disquisition. The usefulness of this notion of a neutral inflation is that it gives some rigor and precision to the cliché that the harmful results of inflation are due to the distortions caused by inflation.

Distortions

What does the word "distortions" mean? "Distortions" means essentially departures from the two sets of subjective and objective conditions.

Apply this, for example, to the notion of forced saving. Forced saving occurs when wealth is transferred from those who would have consumed or used for non-productive capital flight a high proportion of what is being taken away from them to those who will use for these purposes a smaller proportion of this exaction which is being imposed on the rest of the community.

In Brazil it seems that the chances are very good that forced saving was quite substantial for a time during the 1950's. In the late 1950's and early 1960's, I suspect that forced saving, measured in real terms, declined markedly. There are a number of reasons. Probably the diversity of expectation among economic entities has been very greatly lessened and, as a result, there are fewer suckers. This is the principal reason why forced saving is much more difficult to extract through inflation.

There is a widespread notion that inflation lowers real wages. But in the case of a country like Brazil, or most of the South American countries, I do not see how one can possibly tell. There is not much money illusion left. In fact, there are rather good grounds for believing that the growth and strengthening of labor organizations in urban areas has been in part a product of inflation, and it is possible to argue that real wages are higher than they would have been without inflation. It is just as easy to argue the opposite, however. Everybody has very strong opinions about this, and nobody has evidence that is worth very much.

The significant transfers of wealth in Brazil are now not based upon diversity of expectation or money illusion or anything of this sort. They are based upon inequality of access to scarce resources. I have in mind particularly finance, credit, and foreign exchange.

One of the general points that I am trying to make is that there cannot be a general theory of the effects of inflation. The distortions, the departures from the equilibrium path, are of a different sort in different stages of inflation in a particular country, and there are also differences among countries. You can have a general theory of how to analyze the consequences of inflation, but not widely applicable generalizations about the consequences of inflation.

Now, so far as the price distortions are concerned, I propose to talk chiefly about two prices, or two sets of prices; one is interest rates, and the other is foreign exchange rates. I want to emphasize that other price distortions may also be associated with inflation. Quite often there is a lag in the upward adjustment of some prices, particularly in public utility rates and railroad rates; subsidies may be used to keep these prices down. Other things also may be subsidized, and you may have rent controls, but I think the most important prices are interest rates and foreign exchange rates.

So far as foreign exchange rates are concerned, currency overvaluation—that is, the underpricing of foreign exchange—is not inherent in inflationary situations. It is generally present, however, in South American inflations. One may perhaps also say it is inherent under inflationary conditions in members of the IMF that adhere to the Articles of Agreement, because under the Articles you are not supposed to devalue until after it is too late—that is a short summarization of IMF—and, of course, if you adhere to that rule under inflationary situations there will be a tendency toward chronic overvaluation of the domestic currency.

But in European inflations after World War I and in the later phases of the inflations in Europe during the 1920's, there was in a number of countries a tendency for the external depreciation of the currency to lead the domestic depreciation of the currency.

I said that inflation is advantageous to those who have the most favored access to scarce resources. If you are thinking about South America, this means the government. It also means large firms, especially firms that own banks, and to a large extent it means foreign firms. Foreign-owned firms are particularly favored borrowers, especially from foreign-owned banks but also from some of the domestically owned banks.

I said that the government enjoys favored access to resources. It certainly does in the sense of being able to borrow from the central bank, create money, and so on. When finance is underpriced, one may say it should be the goal of any rational economic entity which is trying to get ahead in the world to be a net debtor. It would seem that the government, when it can borrow from the central bank, is in the best position of all to make itself a net debtor.

It has been widely believed in Brazil and other South American countries that the government, with its control over the instruments of foreign exchange regulations and deficit finance, is singularly well equipped to mobilize the resources for a development program. In fact, however, much of the foreign exchange and capital controlled by the government is dissipated through indirect subsidies to buyers of commodities, such as petroleum products, which are favored by foreign exchange, import licensing, and tariff policies, and to users of public utilities, such as the railroads, whose chronic operating deficits are covered by government loans.[2] So although the government is favored by privileged

2. In addition to dissipating the resources it does control, the government is also constrained from enlarging its development program by a tax system whose weak administration and inelastic structure fail, especially under inflationary conditions, to maintain the government's share of national revenues. One curious phenomenon which illustrates how minor deficiencies of the tax system are amplified by inflation is the prevalence of open refusal to pay taxes. Under the traditional laws, direct taxes are assessed, and the assessment can be protested. Moreover, as long as a protest is kept alive, none of the tax liability must be paid. Of course, the lawyer's fee rises as inflation proceeds, but it is still worth dragging out the case until the legal costs equal the gain expected from the continuing reduction in real tax lia-

access to finance and control over foreign exchange, it is also burdened by public policies and private practices which greatly deplete the supply of government-controlled resources actually available for investment in a development program.

Finance and Credit

Let me now enumerate some of the financial features in Brazil as of the summer of 1966 that seem to me of key importance.

I gathered that banks were charging the equivalent of about 35 per cent per annum interest to borrowers on, typically, very short-term loans. No interest was paid to demand depositors, and a low interest rate was paid on time deposits. While I was there they were changing over to a system of paying somewhat higher interest rates. I think the rate on time deposits had been 4 per cent. They were adding a so-called monetary adjustment of around 8 per cent. But the volume of deposits eligible for such supplementary interest payments was narrowly restricted. They were very afraid that if they did not restrict these payments the system would be too popular. These higher rates were specifically for small savings and so on.

The demand for credit vastly exceeds the amounts that the banks lend at the 35 per cent interest rates, so that bank lending is very much a rationing process, not only when efforts are made to tighten credit, but even when the Brazilians are being loose about it. They are never truly loose except to certain favored borrowers and typically, even then, loans are very, very short-term.

Commercial banks lend only to urban borrowers. The Bank of Brazil is both the central bank and the main source of credit for agriculture—actually for very little more than agricultural marketing. In addition to the commercial banks and the Bank of Brazil, there are so-called finance companies which draw upon their time drafts, drawn upon business firms. Their lending rate in ef-

---

bility, then dropping the case and paying the by-now-negligible tax. The proliferation of practices of this sort, nourished by inflation, makes administration costly, reduces even further the elasticity of government revenues, and limits the government's ability to mobilize resources by the conventional means of taxation.

fect was about 70 per cent per annum, and they sold their paper —their lifetime certificates of deposit, if you will—in the form of bills of exchange, at yields of about 35 per cent per annum to the investor. The volume of such credit was equal to about 15 or 20 per cent of the outstanding amount of bank credit.

In addition to these forms of credit, there is a colossal amount of inter-firm credit, and this is important to keep in mind. The firms that can borrow from banks do so for one or two months and they sell on four- to six-month credit, so that this financing is all in the form of trade bills similar to the European method of financing, rather than accounts-receivable financing, but it amounts to the same thing. The typical large firm's balance sheet will include a certain amount of bank borrowing, and on the asset side very little cash and a volume of accounts receivable, which is—like the accounts payable—a high multiple of the amount of bank borrowing. It is interesting to trace out the effects of attempts to restrict bank credit.

A firm adjusts to restriction of its accustomed availability of bank credit, apart from whatever it does to inventory, by curtailing the amount of credit it will extend to its trade customers, by seeking to reduce its accounts receivable, and by delaying payment on its accounts payable. Bank credit is the narrow apex of the pyramid which supports a substantially multiplied volume of inter-firm credit, as well as consumer credit. If the authorities try to contract bank credit, a domino theory is applicable, because the leverage is very high.

If government steps on the credit brake, the demand for credit will not abate, even if the public believes that the rate of inflation will soon be retarded and hence revises its expectations in some subjective sense. The demand for credit increases for the same reason that the late Ivar Kreuger kept going deeper and deeper into the hole long after he knew that it was virtually impossible to get out of it.[3] He made his bankruptcy more and more utter.

3. Ivar Kreuger was the managing director of the Swedish Match Company after World War I. He arranged loans totaling more than £50 million to various European governments in exchange for monopoly rights. His operations expanded in the inflationary environment of the 1920's, but with the depression and financial contraction of the 1930's he resorted to increasingly complex and fraudulent financial activities, including falsifying balance sheets, setting up dummy companies, and

This effect reflects the very simple principle that if you must choose between committing suicide today or tomorrow, you prefer tomorrow over today. Even though there is only a very low probability that you can avert disaster, you prefer disaster later —if it is some sort of ultimate disaster—to disaster now. This preference operates very strongly when the amount of real wealth represented by financial intermediaries' credit is very, very small. Another effect might operate to increase the demand for credit even more. With funds exceptionally tight, those who still have unused borrowing power will borrow so that they will have sufficient funds in case they might need them later when credit is even tighter.

There is no long-term capital market except the long-term credit that may be provided by the government development bank. What is the obstacle to long-term lending and borrowing? One would suppose that if there is any diversity of long-term expectations, there would be a market for long-term loans. If I believe that the average annual rate of inflation over the next twenty years is going to be 20 per cent per annum and you believe it is going to be 30 per cent, why do I not lend you at, let us say, 25 per cent per annum? We both ought to be happy, given this state of expectation, so there ought to be a market. But there is not. The reason is that the diversity of expectations is really less than the uncertainty of each individual's expectations. That is, if my belief that inflation is going to proceed at the rate of 20 per cent really means that I believe it will be between zero and 40 per cent and your belief that it will be 30 per cent really means a range of 10 to 50 per cent and we are both risk-averters, then there is no interest rate at which a loan can take place. The lender wants to be assured against this high variance of his expectations, and so does the borrower. This is why long-term loan markets dry up.

Please note that the revival of long-term lending and borrowing is not an instantaneous result of a year of approximate or even complete stability of the price level. In most European countries

forging securities of various governments. When his initially high reputation came into question and Swedish banks refused him further credit unless they could investigate his affairs, he shot himself. His death in March 1932 and the collapse of his fraudulent operations ruined many investors.

today the appetite for life insurance or other long-term obligations fixed in domestic currency is rather low because it takes a long time to obliterate—I don't want to sound Jungian about it—historical memories. And all this depends upon attitudes about political stability, too.

In Brazil the failure to develop a long-term domestic capital market has been accompanied by the failure to develop a significant long-term market in dollars. A dollar market has not been completely prohibited and there are five-year export credits for the purchase of machinery and that sort of thing. But I think there is no inclination on the part of lenders—American private lenders, let us say—to lend dollars in this kind of environment. Even though the borrower is willing to sign the obligation, the government's willingness to release foreign exchange for this purpose is equally important. The lenders must be prepared to gamble on this willingness for five years or so. They will do so when the loan is tied to export sales, but they have no taste for simple long-term loans, although I am sure borrowers do.

There is another point to make about the financial situation. Although it would seem that commercial banking should be an enormously profitable business where no interest is paid on demand deposits and interest earned on loans is 35 and 40 per cent per annum, the payments mechanism has become so costly that the net profit may not be as great as these wide gross margins would lead one to suppose. Certainly the bankers allege—although I do not cite this as evidence—that their costs are so great that they could not afford to pay much interest to depositors. The reason is that the payments system is extremely costly. Banks do not pay interest on demand deposits, but on the other hand they do not impose service charges.

The currency situation also contributes to high costs. The largest denomination note is the local equivalent of a dollar or a dollar and a half and a great many notes in circulation have the purchasing power of a tiny fraction of a cent. One of the greatest absorbers of salaried labor is the activity of counting out money. It has to be counted in the retail shops and then it has to be counted again when it is sent to the bank, and so on. This, of course, is due to the fact—true in central banks the world over—

that the fellow who orders a new supply of bank notes has no foresight at all. He does not extrapolate the inflation. He orders little if any more than would be enough at today's price level. By the time the notes are delivered four months later, it is far too little. And these old notes keep circulating.

The combination of high costs and inconvenience in handling currency and the absence of service charges on checks means that everybody has bank accounts like American college students, with an average balance for the month of $15.00 and 150 checks for an average amount per check of 65 cents. The velocity of money is high; the total amount of money in real terms is very low. The banks open branches like mad in order to compete with each other in attracting deposits. It is an example of the standard case of monopolistic competition without barriers to entry, similar to having four gasoline stations on every corner, except that in Brazil they are bank branches. I emphasize this because it is an important practical obstacle to doing what I think ought to be done.

In short, my general impressions regarding Brazil were, first, that inflation was no longer very effective as a device to obtain forced saving. Second—and this is more important—inflation very greatly inhibits the development of a capital market. The amount of saving mobilized through financial intermediaries is very, very small.

Saving and Profits

In orthodox economics there are two notions about the capital market. In classical political economy, capital accumulation takes place through the reinvestment of profits, including what we call interest on the owner's capital. The equalization of profits, after allowance for risk, among alternative uses of capital was conceived of as being carried out by the little entrepreneur's shifting his own capital out of Business A where profits were lower into Business B where profits were higher. Since the capital was mostly working capital anyway and since he was small, the shift was easy to accomplish.

In this classical view, the saving was really done by the fellow who is expanding the capital used in his business, and therefore the rate of capital accumulation depended directly on the amount of profits. The competition in the system depended upon the mobility of the businessman as well as upon the mobility of his capital from one line of business to another. When you apply this to the modern world, even in underdeveloped countries where in the modern sector the average size of firms is large and a good deal of fixed capital is employed, if you do not have a capital market, a loan market, and you want capital accumulation—you have to have some kind of internal mechanism that assures the large firms growing profits. What I am really saying is that monopoly in these countries is important chiefly because they have no capital market. The absence of the capital market is a barrier to entry, except by foreign firms. The large firms that do exist derive their profits to a large extent from favored access to the underpriced and scarce resources, and their entrepreneurship is devoted mostly to increasing their share of the scarce resources. In this system, lacking any kind of competitive spur to efficiency, profits are bound to be much too easy.

The Failure of Traditional Policies

The disinflation policy in Brazil, as I observed it, seemed to me doomed to failure. It had three facets. One was reduction of the budgetary deficit. That is okay. The second was holding back on money wage increases, following the utterly irresponsible splurge of the predecessor of the military dictatorship. This was, at least for a time, appropriate. They may have tried to overdo it, but the imposition of such restraint is a normal part of what one would try to put into an anti-inflation package.

The third facet was credit control. The whole emphasis on the credit control side, so far as extension of bank credit to the private sector was concerned, was one of blowing hot and cold. In the latter part of 1965, while the fiscal and wage-rate control portions of the disinflation program were going forward, bank credit was allowed to expand at an exceptionally high rate. The officials gave some technical reasons for this which I will not go into. The credit expansion crept up on them accidentally because the Bank of Brazil finances some purchases of coffee under the price-stabilization arrangements, and they had to pay out more than they expected. That increased the credit base for the commercial banks. The officials were aware at the time of what was going on, but felt that the anti-inflation measures should be moderate, that they should dampen inflation gradually. As a result, during that period, they were doing only two of the three things they ought to do.

Then, in the first part of 1966, they were restricting credit expansion. They were able to get away with it because the previous splurge of credit was being absorbed into the system. But it was fairly clear by the time I left that they would soon take their foot off the brake. And the foreign advisors keep saying: "What's the matter, are you chicken?"

The simple fact is that a bank experiencing net withdrawals must, in the absence of a money market, resort to rediscounting to keep its doors open. No bank goes to the Bank of Brazil and says "I want to borrow, I want to rediscount in order to make some loans I would not otherwise have made." They always say "I have to rediscount because I have an adverse balance at the clearing house." The adverse balance at the clearing house may be a result of loans already made, but the Bank of Brazil is faced with the question whether it wants this bank to close its doors, just as the commercial banks, in dealing with their customers, have to confront the agonized groans of borrowers that they will be insolvent if the loans are not made to them. The significant fact that the authorities must face is that these groans are not bluffs. Unless one is prepared to trigger a chain reaction of financial and commercial insolvencies and bankruptcies embracing the whole economy, one cannot appreciably reduce the rate of expansion of bank credit. In the background is the inertia of inflationary expectations. Everybody who ever got his balance sheet into a shape appropriate to expectations of inflation at a given rate is very vulnerable to a substantial retardation of inflation below that rate.

And, as I pointed out in mentioning the Ivar Kreuger phenomenon, even if the government does make people think that inflation may slow down, the impact effect of doing so through credit restrictions is, if anything, to make demand for credit increase, not decrease.

An Alternative Proposal

One general conclusion to which these considerations lead me is that halting the inflation is the wrong goal, or the wrong immediate goal. The immediate goal should be to eliminate the major distortions arising from the inflation, to make the inflation more nearly neutral. If you succeed in doing that, you can probably swing gradually over to the target—which I regard as a secondary and more remote target—of dampening and perhaps finally terminating the inflation.

The essence of eliminating the major distortions is to make the holding of domestic financial assets attractive in the face of the inflationary expectations that prevail. More specifically, this involves two things. One is to raise the price of foreign exchange to a point where an increased number of its holders think it a good thing to sell. In other words, one must make repatriation of capital attractive, undervalue the domestic currency to induce capital repatriation.

You may say that this will cause an accumulation of gold or foreign exchange reserves, which is a waste of resources. I think that the correct way to meet that is to offset the undervaluation by a substantial reduction of import barriers so that the repatriated capital, instead of adding to gold reserves, adds chiefly to the supply of imported goods.

The other thing needed to make holding of domestic financial assets attractive is to raise interest rates sharply. By this I do not mean the interest rates charged to borrowers; I mean the interest rates paid to depositors and lenders by financial institutions. They should be raised so that the combination of the high interest rate paid to depositors and the high price of foreign exchange will increase greatly the demand for domestic bank deposits and other domestic financial assets. To state it in other terms, strong inducements should be provided to increase the domestic propensity to save in domestic financial form. This has been done in South Korea.

Such action will have some negative effects in the goods market. Automobiles and household appliances were being sold on installment credit at interest rates of 100 per cent per annum and above.

The people who were buying at these terms were buying not primarily because they prized a dishwasher or a Volkswagen this year rather than a year hence so much that it was worth 100 per cent per annum to have them this year. A large part of the demand for such consumer goods reflects their desire to accumulate wealth in this form and their expectation that prices and their money incomes are going to rise enough so that they are getting a better buy now than by paying cash, let us say, a year hence. If these expectations are disappointed or revised, there will be at least a transitional slump in the household appliance and automobile markets. But, at the same time, with adequate depreciation of the external value of the local currency, there will be an export stimulus with an increase in saving. You will have an expansion of the flow of real saving through the banking system and some industrial investment, so that the automobile companies can make some capital goods instead of durable consumer goods. I mention this to make clear that I am not saying that the adjustment will be painless. Rather, I think a policy that seeks not to restrict credit, but to increase the desire to save is almost the only kind of adjustment that can be made.

The *ex post* measure of success of the kind of financial stabilization measures that I have been talking about would be growth in the *real* volume of bank credit. The goal is not so much to retard the rise in the price level as it is to remove major distortions. A good *ex post* index of success would be a reduction in the velocity factor in the equation of exchange. This means that bank credit would increase faster than the price level goes up.

So far as concerns price stability as a long-range goal, I have two things to say about it. One, as I have already said, is that price stability is probably the only way to get expectations to coalesce fully. However, with unstable governments and all the other difficulties, even price stability for a couple of years would not be sufficient to achieve the ideal state of expectations. But, the second point is that one must not demand perfection in these matters. It is not necessary to achieve this ideal state; therefore I do not think price-level stability is very important. The chances are very good that you can change the state of expectations gradually toward expectations of smaller price increases, and that you can, rather painlessly, get down to lower rates of inflation and finally price-level stability. That is, provided you accept inflationary expectations as a fact of life and set as the initial goal just bringing prices, especially interest rates and the price of foreign exchange, into equilibrium with this state of expectations. That is 90 or 95 per cent of the problem. Then, after that, you play it by ear.

One result of removing or greatly reducing the distortions induced by currency overvaluation and import substitution would be to make the allocation of investment much more productive. The substitution of a loan market for the present classical pattern of capital accumulation means that you will have a much more competitive economy and that much more attention will be paid to efficiency and productivity.

Another result is that if countries like Brazil or Argentina or Chile could "put their houses in order" financially, in this sense, I see no reason why they should not be able to attract a great deal of foreign private loan capital—probably not long-term, but short- and intermediate-term.

I regard foreign loan capital as a much better buy, from the point of view of the developing countries, than foreign direct investment. Although foreign direct investment may be worth the 15 to 30 per cent per annum rate of return—where the effects of innovation, teaching of know-how, and so on are great enough—much of this foreign investment merely exploits the wholly inappropriate profit opportunities that the underdeveloped countries create by their import-substitution policies. To have foreign investors borrow at 7 per cent and invest at 18 per cent in an economy where prices have something to do with scarcity values, with true rates of transformation, is very beneficial. But direct investment that earns a return of 20 per cent in a manufacturing activity where the value added may well be negative and where the investment is profitable only because of distortions in the import structure is not such a good form of external capital inflow.

Do not misunderstand me. I am not attacking American corporations who take advantage of these artificial profit opportunities. It is the unwise policies of the underdeveloped countries that create them. Nevertheless, I am saying that very often such investment does not contribute much to real development.

Further Problems

Given that a rash of bankruptcies would follow if inflation were eliminated under the present conditions in Brazil—following my earlier analysis—how then could inflation ever be eliminated without an outbreak of bankruptcies? Expectations may coalesce at some high rate of inflation and a non-distortive equilibrium path may exist. In that case, how could a country move from one non-distortive equilibrium path with inflation to another with price stability and still avoid running into the bankruptcy problem?

If you accept that there is much inertia of inflationary expectations, then you would not want the actual behavior of the price level, the actual rise in the price level, to fall far short of expectations. What you want is gradually to change expectations and change the price level, too. But I would say, whatever the state of expectations may be—this has to do with the subjective conditions—it is desirable to have interest rates and a price of foreign exchange which more nearly clear the markets than the present ones do. With all the fuzziness, and undoubtedly also some diversity, of expectation, there is a level of interest rates and foreign exchange rates that will result in a markedly increased desire for domestic financial assets. I think that that is a desirable thing by itself.

The coalescence of expectations is a very gradual process, so far as the long-term loan market is concerned, and I would not expect a domestic long-term loan market to revive, to develop very fast in any event, whether the price level is rising or is stable for a few years. But I do think it is possible to get a sufficient coalescence of expectations to expand quite considerably the real amount of saving flowing into investment through short- and intermediate-term loans. The state of expectations is doubtless going to be very blurred for a long time, no matter what happens. In the existing situation, the desire of every economic entity is to be a net debtor. The closed-economy identities, of which we economists are so fond, tell us that everybody cannot be a net debtor, but everybody can try to be one. In the situation that has prevailed for some time, with negative real interest rates, anybody who has maintained a balance sheet which by our normal standards would seem financially prudent has long since ceased to have any economic importance. Having such a balance sheet is a sure way to go broke during conditions of inflation. A precondition to paving the way for a damping down of inflation is to get firms' and households' balance sheets in what we would consider more respectable shape.

With the enormous incentives to being a net debtor reduced or removed, one can imagine that balance sheets of economic entities will approach what we regard as financially prudent. If, at that time, the rate of inflation were to diminish we would not expect to find many Ivar Kreugers. The first step is to get prices, interest rates, and exchange rates into such a shape that being a net debtor is not so enormously attractive as it seems to be at present.

A difficult problem may be the feasibility of having banks pay high interest rates, given the fact that they have opened so many branches. I do not know enough about the size of their net profits to know how serious this problem is. I think it is probably serious and that, over time, many bank branches should be closed down. But if the approach I suggest works, their real volume of earning assets will substantially increase, so even though the net profit per unit is smaller, there will be a larger profit base, if you will. But I rather suspect that in the transition period the government may have to put some supplementary capital into the banks in order to ease them over the transition.

In South Korea, where the kind of program that I have been, in effect, recommending for South America was tried, there was the advantage that the banks were government-owned. And, for a time at least, they paid higher interest rates to depositors than they charged to borrowers. (In theory, you could go around to the loan window, borrow some money, and deposit it, and make a profit. I am told this was not a widespread practice because people knew ways to make greater profits without depositing the money.) Clearly, I do not think it necessary to go that far. But nevertheless, payment of high rates to depositors may present problems for banks.

I do not think any program can do anything about the subjective conditions quickly. You can do something about the objective conditions. But you cannot improve the objective conditions by being even tighter in your credit rationing. That, if anything, makes things worse rather than better.

After this description of my proposal, a relevant question might be, "Is this all you have to do?" No. I think you have to do other things to promote real capital formation. I think that this proposal will greatly increase the *real* amount of bank credit expansion and that short-term commercial loans will develop, but many other things are needed for the development of a capital market. I would say about most of these other things that in an environment where there is no private appetite to accumulate wealth in domestic financial forms, there is no opportunity to develop a capital market.

Alternative Policies

If you want to weigh alternative courses of action, I think my program should be considered against a revalorization-of-debts program, which operates on the same principle. That is, instead of trying to restrict credit, to carry out overnight a general revaluation of debts as a substitute for a chain reaction of bankruptcies—the kind of thing that was done in stabilizing the German mark after World War I and in Belgium and Germany after World War II. You announce and put it into effect over the weekend so it is in effect by Monday morning, and people's bank balances after the write-down are so low that they want to accumulate financial assets despite their inflationary expectations. It is another way of achieving the same ends. Although this is another possibility, I think it is likely to be very strongly resisted and therefore can hardly be taken seriously as a policy that these governments would be disposed to carry out.

The alternative of forced saving is pretty well excluded for the reasons I gave earlier. These countries cannot resume development by going back to inflation as a means of forced saving. To the extent that forced saving is a possibility, the part of it that goes into private profits is often used in capital flight. The propensity of the beneficiaries of forced saving to save out of their windfalls may be no greater than that of the people who are squeezed in this process. The part of forced saving that goes to the government does not yield much productive investment.

Domestic public saving, i.e., an excess of tax revenues over current operating expenses, is also pretty well excluded, not because taxes cannot be raised—many countries have raised tax revenues—but because most countries tend to expand public ostentation expenditures as fast as they can raise taxes, so that they are never going to have enough tax revenue left over for the productive investment that they need.

In short, I think both forced saving and public saving are pretty well excluded. All that is left to fall back on, it seems to me, is the capital market, and you cannot do much about this until after you have removed or substantially reduced the distortions I have talked about. When that has been done, it would be appropriate to have development banks that borrow short from the banking system and make some long-term loans. There is also a need for agricultural credit, and agricultural credit institutions. I think in the Brazilian case—and I suspect this will be true in many countries—these are the two things that are most needed.

There is a great deal of talk about developing domestic markets for equity securities. I think the importance of doing so is vastly exaggerated. It takes a very long time to establish habits of disclosure and the other things that are needed before a corporation really can be what we regard as a public corporation in the sense that outsiders have equity interests in them. In the United States, disclosure is sufficiently great so that outsiders think that they are not at so great a disadvantage as to be crazy if they own common stocks. In other countries, there is a long way to go before that state of confidence concerning equity securities is achieved, so I do not think that an effort in that direction has much practical importance. When I talk about a capital market, therefore, I am talking about a loan market.

Some Consequences of the Proposal

It is not at all clear to me that, with development of a loan market, financial intermediaries would have to charge higher interest rates. Although one cannot know in advance, my guess is that they might well be able to lower the interest rates charged to borrowers.

One must remember that some of the forms in which individuals accumulate wealth are very costly. For example, doctors keep five Volkswagens in the back yard because wealth is safer in the form of Volkswagens. But, of course, the Volkswagens depreciate. People build houses and take five to eight years to do it. As soon as they have a little surplus cash, they order another load of lumber and dump it on their property. The next time they have a little surplus cash, they hire a carpenter right away. They have to get the lumber embodied in that house. That is not a good form of wealth accumulation, but under present conditions it may be better than keeping wealth in the form of money. If the interest rate paid on bank deposits were, say, 25 per cent, however; and if appropriate service charges were made for the use of check payments; and if, at the same time, the foreign exchange rate were allowed to float, import barriers were reduced, and the foreign exchange value of the currency were forced down to a level that induced repatriation of capital, I feel quite sure that the combination of price pulls would increase the lending power of the banks a good deal. The banks might then find it appropriate to lower the interest rates charged on borrowing, although nothing that I have said is conclusive about which way such rates should change. The first thing, certainly, is to narrow gradually the spread between rates paid to lenders and rates charged to borrowers and then to see, with a narrow spread, which way you want interest rates to go.

If my proposal were enacted, there would be a major structural shift in the economy. Although the present desire to flee from money affects the demands not only for automobiles and TV sets but also for non-durable goods like textiles, I venture the guess that the effects on the consumer goods industries other than durable goods would be fairly small. I do not think that the flight-from-money component of the demand for these goods is very great in relation to the demand for them based on desire for consumption proper.

I also think that consumer stocks are not so big that the transition would be hard for other consumer goods industries. The exchange depreciation would create larger export opportunities. Even though accompanied by relaxation of import barriers, it would provide some protection, and while some industries producing import substitutes would be hurt, other industrial opportunities would be opened up by the exchange depreciation and by import liberalization. But there may have to be some financing to ease the transition. To make this possible you would have to put capital into the banks and you might also have to provide some other financing to ease the transition. If, for example, you expanded agricultural credit and increased the availability of credit to industry, the automobile industry could begin to make tractors and trucks instead of merely passenger cars, and other industries could also shift output to capital goods.

One cannot be sure that the proposed set of policies would work. The difficulties of transition under them may not be too great, however, and they are certainly much less than those of putting on the brakes a little and taking them off, which creates a kind of perpetual stagnation. I think you could not revive the Brazilian boom by going back to all-out inflation, and that you could not revive it by credit restriction. Maybe it could not be revived by my program, either, but I would say that of the three methods, mine is certainly the least unpromising.

If this proposal were undertaken along with import liberalization and exchange depreciation, a theoretically very difficult kind of dynamic problem would arise: How do expectations change and what further adjustments become necessary after the initial steps? An answer involves a dynamic model. I would rather administer the second steps than write about them; I think playing by ear is not so hard, but writing out the symphony before you play it is impossible. If the government's macro-targets are expansionary, they are more likely to be realized, or more nearly realized, by following these lines than by doing what governments are in fact doing. I admit that the dynamics of the proposal is hard. The value of this analysis is that it shows that dynamics is what is really involved.

III *INTERNATIONAL MONETARY REFORM*

13 *Capital Movements, Gold, and Balance of Payments*[1]

Although there are reasons for believing that the underlying trend of the balance of payments is toward improvement, this does not provide a sufficient basis for confident prediction that the deficit will be eliminated in the period 1963-65. Moreover, there are few measures that the government can take to reduce this deficit without jeopardizing more important objectives.

My chief recommendations for reducing the deficit, within the framework of the present international monetary arrangements, would be that the method of informed surveillance should be used with adequate firmness in order to reduce substantially the outflow of long-term capital through flotation (including private placements) of foreign security issues in the U.S. market, and that such surveillance should also be extended to bank lending to foreign borrowers. With respect to new security offerings, new

1. Presented as an individual view to a group of academic consultants to the United States Treasury, which met several times a year with the Secretary and other Treasury officials during the Kennedy Administration. Professor Seymour Harris, who was Senior Consultant to the Secretary of the Treasury and organizer of the group, was growing restless with Despres's frequent expression of the view that the United States should simply ignore its balance-of-payments deficit. He asked Despres to prepare a statement which assumed that *some* measures would be taken and to suggest what their nature should be. The statement was presented April 1, 1963.—Ed.

issues of Western European borrowers should be entirely excluded. In the case of Canadian, Australian, and Japanese borrowing, a less categorical policy should be followed, but some restraints can usefully be imposed.

Although part of the expansion of bank loans to foreign borrowers served to finance additional U.S. exports, the marked expansion in 1960 and 1961 was due primarily to other causes. It is not proposed that the Treasury or the Federal Reserve attempt detailed scrutiny of each foreign credit. It is suggested, rather, that banks be given guidelines with respect to foreign loans and credits, and that the monetary authorities keep closely in touch with the large commercial banks to assure general compliance with the guidelines and to permit consultations on any large or non-routine requests for credit. The purpose of informal surveillance of commercial bank foreign lending operations need not be to bring about absolute contraction or even to halt the further expansion of such loans. Its chief purpose would be to provide assurance against expansion of loans and credits on any scale approaching that of 1960 and 1961.

The United States is the only country in which official surveillance of private lending abroad has been the exception rather than the rule. Although surveillance would not be welcomed by the financial community, the willingness of the larger banks, insurance companies, and investment bankers to comply with controls can hardly be questioned, provided the monetary authorities are willing to apply them. Excessive claims should not be made regarding the effectiveness of surveillance of selected types of capital outflow, since when some channels are restricted, a part of the balance-of-payments gain will be lost through increased flow through other channels. Despite such qualifications, however, a significant net reduction in capital outflow can be achieved by this means.

It is not proposed that controls be applied to U.S. direct investment abroad. The average rate of return on direct investment is high, and the outflow of capital through new direct investment abroad could not long keep pace with the mounting dividend income on past investment. Some benefit to the balance of payments in the short run would result from curbing direct investment in Europe, but over a somewhat longer period this would be wiped out by the dividend income foregone.

Apart from the effort to limit private lending abroad through informal surveillance, most other measures for quickly improving the balance of payments, within the existing monetary framework, appear undesirable. In the case of the U.S. Government account, the substitution of domestic for foreign procurement has gone at least as far as is desirable, and balance-of-payments considerations ought to be wholly disregarded in reaching the basic decision on the size of the foreign aid program and the scale of U.S. military forces and bases abroad. Import restrictions would be an undesirable reversal of our trade liberalization policies and most proposals for special tax concessions to stimulate additional exports are of questionable desirability. Any further firming of short-term money rates should be avoided until the production and employment gap has been considerably narrowed through a strong upward movement in production and employment. It would be highly premature to tighten money in anticipation of the stimulus expected from tax reduction.

It is assumed that prepayment of foreign debts to the United States will continue and that U.S. Government medium-term borrowing abroad will be expanded as much as circumstances permit. Our reserves and other resources for meeting payments deficits or withdrawals of short-term balances remain great; given the willingness to use them, they are much more than sufficient to meet any pressure against the dollar which appears at all likely over the next few years. Looking ahead three to five years, there are reasons for optimism regarding our balance-of-payments position, and the improvement may come earlier than this. The principal danger is not that we shall be unable to meet balance-of-payments strains, but that through excessive concern over the immediate payments problem, we may be tempted to sacrifice national objectives of greater importance.

During the past thirteen years over $8 billion of gold has gone into non-monetary uses, of which, at a guess, two-thirds or three-fourths may have gone into speculative hoards. The rate of non-monetary absorption has been rising and has been about $1 billion annually during the past few years. Given the present climate of speculative attitudes, involving continuing doubts about the pound and the dollar but with a lessening of enthusiasm for some of the Continental European currencies, the possibility of a substantial increase in the rate of non-monetary absorption cannot be dismissed.

Under these circumstances, consideration should be given to changing the present links between monetary reserves and the outside market for gold. The specific measures are as follows:

a. The U.S. Government would announce that it will sell gold only to foreign central banks which agree to limit their sales to central banks and governments; i.e., no sales in the London or other bullion markets.

b. The U.S. Government would inform foreign central banks that it will buy gold, now or in the future, only from those monetary authorities which now agree to refrain from purchases on their own account in the open market.

c. In order to protect gold-mining interests, the London gold pool could enter into twenty-year contracts with free-world gold producers to purchase gradually diminishing quantities at $35.

d. The London gold pool would stand ready to purchase outside gold (i.e., dishoarded gold or Soviet gold) at $30 an ounce for an initial period of six months and at not over $25 an ounce thereafter. The profits from purchases below the monetary value would be turned over to the IMF or some other international organization.

These proposed measures would forestall any future loss of existing monetary gold into private hoards and might well precipitate substantial liquidation of private speculative holdings.

14 *A Proposal for Strengthening the Dollar*[1]

In defending the dollar, the Government has pursued two major lines of policy. First, it has sought to strengthen the balance of payments without gravely compromising other basic domestic or foreign policy objectives. Second, it has sought, through cooperation of European central banks and treasuries, to minimize the drain of gold from the United States by maintaining and expanding the use of the dollar as a reserve currency and by arranging supplementary financing devices for meeting speculative pressures and other strains. It was hoped that such cooperation would grow as the imbalance in international payments was corrected and that further expansion of reciprocal financing devices would provide the base from which a strengthened and durable international monetary framework would evolve.

The first line of policy has been highly successful in strengthening the balance of payments, and the cost in terms of other basic domestic and foreign policy objectives appears so far to have been tolerable. The United States competitive position in world markets has become exceedingly strong; the export surplus in

1. Research Center in Economic Growth, Stanford University, Memorandum No. 38, May 1965, mimeographed. A modified and condensed version appeared in *A New Approach to United States International Economic Policy,* Hearings before the Subcommittee on International Exchange and Payments of the Joint Economic Committee, 89th Congress, Second Session, September 9, 1966, pp. 39-42.—Ed.

goods and services is larger than even the most optimistic forecasters could have dared to predict a few years ago. More recently, the balance-of-payments problem has been concentrated in the capital account, but the new voluntary controls are proving initially effective in restricting the outflow of U.S. capital. As a result, our present balance-of-payments position is definitely one of strength, as is shown in detail in Walter Salant's recent testimony before the Senate Banking and Curency Committee.[2]

On this point, the officially designated "deficit"—unfortunately still used in the Government's balance-of-payments releases and therefore accepted by the public as the key indicator—is a barrier to understanding of the real position and a misleading guide to policy. Foreign investment and lending by the United States properly serve not merely to finance the current account surplus but also provide some additional dollars to permit foreign balances to grow. With a workable international monetary framework, a position of balance in United States international payments would be one in which capital outflow provides enough dollars to the rest of the world to supply nearly all the increase in foreign balances in the United States required to meet normal, year-to-year growth in foreign demands for liquid dollar funds occasioned by the expansion of the world economy and of international trade and finance. The officially designated "deficit" ignores this second source of foreign demand for dollars. It treats as a deficit any increase in short-term liabilities to foreigners not matched 100 per cent by additions to the U.S. gold and foreign exchange reserves. In effect, this concept denies the basic principle of banking and ignores a critically important aspect of this country's role as world banker and financial intermediary. Thus, the official concept is biased towards deficit, so that a state of balance or of moderate surplus in United States international accounts appears, under the official concept, as a "deficit." It would be conservative, I believe, to consider an officially designated "deficit" below two billion dollars as representing, properly

2. See *Balance of Payments—1955,* Hearings before a subcommittee of the Senate Committee on Banking and Currency, 89th Congress, First Session, on "The Continuing Deficits in Our Balance of Payments and the Resulting Outflow of Gold," Part 1; reprinted as "A New Look at the U.S. Balance of Payments," Brookings Institution Reprint 92 (1965).—Ed.

speaking, a position of surplus. Viewed in these terms, the position today is surely one of considerable surplus.

The present strong position does depend in part on the effectiveness of the new voluntary controls on U.S. private capital outflow. There is no reason to assume that these controls will suddenly and rapidly become ineffective, but voluntary controls do not wear well and erosion must be expected. The guideline controls are probably at their peak of effectiveness now. Moreover, the sharp rise in foreign short-term borrowing in late 1964 and early 1965 is now producing a temporary spurt in the backflow of repayments.

The second major line of policy—the appeal for central bank cooperation—has become ineffective. It did succeed until late 1964 in holding gold losses to a small figure, but this was accomplished at considerable cost. First, it left behind an overhang of reluctantly held foreign official balances. Second, this country's efforts to persuade European central banks to keep accumulating dollars as a gesture of international cooperation and its evident reluctance to incur gold losses also contributed to the unfavorable climate of attitudes regarding the dollar and stimulated the appetite of others for gold. The use of the dollar as a reserve currency, instead of its being regarded as a facility which the United States was willing to provide for the benefit of countries desiring to hold dollar reserves, came to be considered an arrangement which this country was striving to preserve for its own purposes. A bank which seeks to increase its deposits in this fashion inevitably arouses uneasiness in the minds of its depositors.

Recent events—the impasse in the discussions at the IMF meeting in Tokyo last September, De Gaulle's position on gold and substantial conversion of dollar balances into gold by European official holders—make it unmistakably clear that the United States has reached the end of the line in appealing for European central bank cooperation. The hope that by strengthening our balance of payments we would restore confidence in the dollar, increase the willingness of foreign central banks to hold dollar reserves, and create a favorable climate for enlarging the scope of international monetary cooperation has proved to be unrealizable. Although our balance of payments has become strong, gold losses have increased owing to substantial central bank conversions of dollars into gold. The balance of payments is strong but the dollar remains weak. This must seem paradoxical to those who have maintained that the dollar problem was a balance-of-payments problem and that as soon as this country's international payments were brought into balance all would be well.

The long-term objective which this country sought to achieve through central bank cooperation was to strengthen the international monetary mechanism by increased use of various forms of credit, on a firmly committed and dependable basis, and reduced use of gold in settlement of international payments. Since central bank cooperation has not succeeded in bringing this about, the Government should promptly adopt a new approach to achieve the needed strengthening of the system. This can be accomplished by measures which the United States can itself take to reduce the present attractiveness of gold and increase the dollar's attractiveness as an international asset. We can readily create a situation in which foreign central banks and governments will be required by immediate and obvious self-interest to participate in a strengthened monetary system.

In a fundamental sense, the dollar is not merely "as good as gold"; it is much better than gold. It is only the willingness of the United States to buy gold in unlimited amounts at $35 an ounce which keeps gold as good as the dollar. So long as we stand ready to convert gold into dollars without limit at $35 an ounce, the holding of gold becomes a safe and cheap method of insuring against—or profiting from—dollar devaluation. The convertibility of gold into dollars is universally taken for granted; it is the ability of the United States to keep converting dollars into gold which is questioned. Gold's special attraction, both to foreign central banks and monetary authorities and to private hoarders and speculators, depends upon this. If convertibility of gold into dollars were convincingly limited, gold would lose its attraction to central banks and to private hoarders and speculators. Dollars would become at once the preferred liquid asset.

It should be stressed that although the Government is completely committed to defending the dollar, it is not committed in comparable degree to the defense of gold.

The special and predominant position of the dollar as international money is not an artificial contrivance; it arises naturally and inevitably from the relative weight of the United States in the world economy and from this country's role in world finance and trade. A large part of the world trade, including trade between third countries as well as U.S. trade, is transacted in dollars. The United States is, by a wide margin, the world's chief international lender, and this country's very large net creditor position on both private and government account keeps growing year by year. During the past half century almost all foreign currencies have undergone successive depreciation against the dollar and the dollar has shown by far the smallest loss of purchasing power of any major currency.

Under these conditions, it should not be surprising that, despite the unfavorable climate of speculative attitudes regarding the dollar during recent years, private foreign demand for balances in the United States has continued to increase. From the end of 1960 to the end of 1964 these private balances increased from $7 billion to $10.6 billion. Although the U.S. Government apparently provided forward cover for a portion of these foreign-held dollars, the growth in world trade, in U.S. foreign trade, and in U.S. short-term and long-term lending abroad necessitated an increase in foreign holding of dollars for transactions purposes alone. Such growth is a normal feature of an expanding world economy. Owing to the unfavorable climate of speculative attitudes, private foreign balances in this country are undoubtedly at a subnormal level in relation to ordinary requirements. Although they would be temporarily reduced from their present level during a speculative dollar crisis, they could not readily be maintained at the reduced level for any sustained period.

In its origins, the use of the dollar as a reserve currency arose from causes broadly similar to those which have induced the growth of private foreign balances, and with a strengthened international monetary mechanism the dollar would be generally preferred to gold as an international reserve asset. It should not be assumed that, even under today's conditions, all foreign official balances here seek conversion into gold. A large part of the foreign trade of Canada, Japan, and Latin America is with the

United States and they depend heavily upon the United States for external financing, both long and short term. Countries such as these can be expected to hold a substantial fraction of their reserves in dollars. Nevertheless, the growing preference for gold as a reserve asset is undeniable.

Despite this preference, it is gold rather than the dollar whose use as international money is artificial and contrived. The resulting and quite unnecessary tyranny of gold is increasingly preventing the dollar from performing fully and effectively its appropriate role as international money. Further worsening of this situation will have highly adverse economic consequences, here as well as abroad. We were mistaken from the beginning in regarding the defense of the dollar as a balance-of-payments problem. As conventionally defined, a balance-of-payments deficit means nothing more nor less than an increase in foreign short-term liabilities without offsetting gold inflow. As was previously pointed out, annual "deficits" of perhaps two billion dollars would be normal under a healthily functioning international monetary system; less than this over a prolonged period would have undesirable deflationary effects on the world economy. Substantial swings in the balance of international payments extending over periods of several years should be expected, however, and it would be undesirable to eliminate them. "Deficits" of three or four billion dollars for a few years are trivial by any fundamentally meaningful criterion for an economy the size of the United States'; it is only in relation to gold that the deficits have not been trivial. In treating the problem as a balance-of-payments problem, we have not, in fact, been defending the dollar. Instead, we have been engaged in attempting to defend the contrived role of gold as international money at the expense of the dollar.

The real problem is and has been one of dethroning gold by building a strong international monetary mechanism resting on credit money rather than gold. Because of the dollar's inherently special position as a world currency, the United States can bring about this change through its own action without depending upon international agreement in advance. In principle, there are two methods of doing this. One method would be to discontinue selling gold at a fixed price. Although the dollar would initially depreciate, the unwillingness of other governments to experience an appreciation of their own currencies against the dollar would quickly induce them to buy and hold dollars as the only available means of halting such an appreciation and the dollar would then, by force of necessity, become the dominant form of international reserve money. This course of action, however, would violate our pledge to sell gold at $35 an ounce. The other method of subordinating gold to the dollar is to deprive gold of its present unlimited convertibility into dollars. This is the action which I recommend. The specific steps to carry out this recommended change are outlined below.

Announcement of future limitations on United States gold purchases would not immediately be convincing if made at a time when this country is losing gold. As a preparatory step, therefore, it is necessary to terminate the gold drain quickly by inducing prompt conversion into gold of that portion of dollar reserves which foreign central banks now contemplate liquidating. In order to expedite liquidation of this overhang, the Government should inform foreign governments and central banks that (1) we welcome the continued use of the dollar as a reserve currency by governments and central banks which have decided, as a matter of settled policy, that they wish to hold a reasonably stable fraction of their reserves in this form, but that (2) the United States balance-of-payments position has reached a point where the Government now invites immediate withdrawal of dollar reserves previously accumulated in excess of desired amounts. It should also be stated that "dollar bloc" countries, i.e., countries which hold the major portion of their reserves in dollars, and the sterling area would be exempted from capital movement controls except to the extent necessary to forestall substantial indirect leakage of U.S. capital to third countries. Finally, the interest equalization tax should also be lifted for all "dollar bloc" countries. Japan, for example, would be exempted from application of the tax.

This step would involve a substantial, once-and-for-all gold loss. It would be far less disturbing, however, and less likely to snowball, than the slow, prolonged drain which is now in process. An outsider lacks the confidential information on which to base an estimate of the size of the official withdrawals which the request for immediate conversions would induce. At a guess, however, the loss would be less than half of the $12 billion held here by foreign central banks and monetary authorities. Once the withdrawals have been completed, the strength of the present balance-of-payments position should be reflected in excess market demand for dollars and a tendency towards gold inflow.

Liquidation of the overhang of reluctantly held dollars would have been somewhat easier if Federal Reserve statutory reserve requirements, instead of merely being reduced, had been eliminated. However, both former Secretary Dillon and Chairman Martin stated that the reduction in requirements was designed to symbolize and underscore our willingness to regard the whole gold stock as available for international payments. Since the Federal Reserve has power to suspend reserve requirements, no major difficulty is presented in making sufficient gold available. Legislation to eliminate the requirements can afterwards be obtained.

If market reaction to the withdrawal of official funds should produce a wave of private speculation against the dollar, existing swap credits, IMF drawings, and our remaining gold holdings would be much more than sufficient to overcome any speculative attack. Moreover, present controls on U.S. capital outflow would limit the size and duration of a speculative attack by (1) curbing any possible domestic speculation against the dollar and (2) curbing foreign short selling by making it difficult for foreigners to borrow dollars. Private foreign balances in the United States are already low in relation to normal transactions needs and a considerable proportion are committed through forward sales; although private foreign balances could be reduced in the event of a speculative attack, the reduction would be temporary and limited. Thus, private speculation, if it occurred, would be manageable in amount and of brief duration.

The changes in gold-buying policy which I propose should be promulgated upon completion of the preparatory step are outlined in somewhat detailed and specific terms in the paragraphs which follow. It need hardly be added that some of these details are for illustrative purposes only.

1. The present 25 per cent gold reserve requirement against Federal Reserve notes should be repealed and it should be made more explicitly clear than at present that all the monetary gold which the United States holds would be used if necessary in defense of the dollar. Gold should be treated not as a last line of defense to be conserved and husbanded but as a readily available reserve to be employed alongside swap credits and forward exchange operations and IMF drawings and other newly developed financial devices. Although we have reiterated our determination not to devalue, continuation of the existing reserve requirements against Federal Reserve notes, together with U.S. zealousness to avoid gold losses whenever possible, has created a widespread impression that in the face of persistent gold losses the U.S. would resort to devaluation long before its $13 billion of monetary gold had been exhausted.[3]

It is widely accepted that if a devaluation of the dollar should occur, this would be accompanied or immediately followed by a general devaluation of other currencies. Consequently, devaluation of the dollar would do nothing to improve the competitive position of the U.S. in world markets, even if such an improvement were desired for balance-of-payments reasons. The chief effect of a devaluation of the dollar would be the change in the U.S. liquidity position through a writing up of the dollar value of monetary gold holdings. If a 50 per cent devaluation were undertaken with a 13 billion monetary gold stock, the new value of that stock would be $26 billion. This is the only advantage, if it be deemed an advantage, to be gained from dollar devaluation. (Since devaluation would greatly weaken the rest of the world's willingness to hold dollars and dollar claims, even this advantage would be illusory.) It should be noted that devaluation would be utterly pointless even in terms of the liquidity position of the U.S. if it were deferred until our gold holdings were exhausted, since with a monetary gold

3. "Devaluation" is used here in the sense of raising the dollar price of gold.—Ed.

stock of zero, there would be nothing to write up. A general devaluation of currencies at a time when U.S. gold reserves were exhausted would only increase the dollar fetching power of foreign gold holdings and of newly mined South African and Russian gold. Although exhaustion of the U.S. monetary gold stock would doubtless necessitate a suspension of gold payments, it would not necessitate devaluation, which is a very different thing, and would, in fact, render devaluation pointless, except as a means of providing massive windfalls to foreign monetary authorities and gold speculators and mining interests. It is well understood, of course, that the U.S., without gold of its own, would not find it attractive to supply such a windfall to others. Belief in the possibility of dollar devaluation rests squarely, therefore, on the assumption that there is some floor to United States gold reserves not far below present levels and that if this floor is reached, the United States would feel "forced" to devalue. This belief would be greatly weakened if convincing evidence were provided that there is no such floor. Elimination of Federal Reserve requirements against Federal Reserve notes, together with greater use of gold along with swap credits and other financing devices for day to day international payments purposes, would go far to destroy belief in the possibility of devaluation.

2. In addition, the United States should announce a new policy with respect to the purchase of gold. While continuing to stand ready to sell gold without limit at the statutory price of $35 an ounce, the U.S. should impose strict limitations upon the amount of gold which it stands ready to buy at this price and should substitute firm credit lines for the monetary gold rendered redundant by quota limitations on U.S. purchases. This proposal involves no change in the price at which we would stand ready to buy gold. However, it would end the unlimited convertibility of gold into dollars, and it would substitute credit for the monetary gold made redundant by the quota limitations.

Special limitations regarding gold purchases would be

made for underdeveloped countries, dollar reserve countries, and Great Britain. In the case of all other countries, the United States should declare its readiness to enter into a series of bilateral and reciprocal gold purchase plus credit agreements along the following lines:

i. The U.S. would stand ready to make net purchases of gold at $35 an ounce in an amount not exceeding one-third of the monetary gold held by the other party to the agreement at the time of announcement of the new U.S. gold buying policy. The other party would agree to sell gold to us only when necessary for balance-of-payments reasons. (The remaining two-thirds of the other country's gold reserves, together with such gold, if any, as might be subsequently acquired, would be ineligible for purchase by the U.S.)

ii. Reciprocally, the other country would stand ready to buy up to this amount of gold from the U.S. when necessary for balance-of-payments reasons.

iii. Firm reciprocal credit lines (swaps) permitting drawing without specified maturity and covered by an exchange value guarantee would be established in amounts equal to twice the reciprocal commitments with respect to gold purchase. It would be mutually agreed that drawings under these credits would go hand in hand with gold sales in the ratio of two units of credit utilization to one of gold sales. Under such an agreement, a country wishing to obtain, say, $150 million for international payments purposes would sell 50 million of gold to the U.S. and draw 100 million under its credit line. Thus, access to dollars through gold and credit combined would remain unimpaired, credit replacing the gold rendered unusable by U.S. purchase limitations.

In the case of countries holding the major portion of their reserves in the form of dollars (e.g., Japan, Canada) and of all underdeveloped countries, it seems appropriate to make eligible for purchase by the United States at $35 an ounce all gold reserves held by the monetary authorities of these countries on the date of announcement of the new gold policy. Swap credits would then be unnecessary. Any gold subsequently acquired by these countries would be ineligible for purchase by the United States.

Great Britain's position as a financial and reserve currency center justifies special arrangements. The U.S. should propose a reciprocal gold-plus-credit agreement similar in form to the reciprocal agreements outlined above, but making British gold eligible for purchase by the United States in an amount equal to the full British central gold reserve on the date of announcement of the new gold purchase policy. Britain would, in turn, stand ready to purchase an equal amount of gold from the U.S. and gold transactions would be meshed with drawings under swap credits in the ratio of 1 to 2.

Measures would also have to be taken with respect to the IMF in order (1) to assure that gold ineligible for direct sale to the United States did not reach us indirectly through the IMF as intermediary, (2) to assure the convertibility into dollars of existing IMF gold holdings, and (3) to prevent the IMF from becoming a dumping ground for gold ineligible for sale to us. These are matters of technical detail which raise no insuperable difficulties.

The steps outlined above surely would result in a marked shift in asset preferences from gold to dollars and would remove the elements of weakness which impair the effective operation of the existing system by preventing the United States from performing its appropriate banking function. A dollar reserve system would be established free of the critical weaknesses of the existing system.

The proposal outlined above should not be considered a rigid blueprint. It is undoubtedly susceptible of modifications and improvements. More important, its adoption or even its serious consideration in U.S. official quarters would require a radical change in prevailing official doctrine regarding the dollar's relationship to gold and the applicability to a world financial center of traditional notions of balance-of-payments equilibrium. So long as present doctrines are adhered to and so long as solutions are sought by attempting to negotiate multilateral agreements for supplementary reserve assets which do not give recognition to the inherent asymmetry between the position of a financial center and that of its clients, there is little reason to expect much improvement in the condition of contained crisis which has prevailed during the sixties. Thus, a radical change in the prevailing doctrine is needed. With such a change, the task of devising appropriate measures to end the crisis and provide an international monetary environment favorable to growth and development, and to commercial and financial liberalization, would be a simple task. It could be accomplished either by steps of the type outlined above or by other measures having equivalent effect.

The result would be the establishment, in effect, of a world dollar standard under which loan finance, short and long term, would be available to borrowers with credit standing at the market rates (with aid to underdeveloped countries at concessional terms). United States monetary policy, and the resulting level of interest rates, would have to be determined in full consultation with foreign governments and appropriate international agencies in order to provide financing terms consistent with world economic growth and stability. Purely domestic stabilization policy would then rely largely upon fiscal instruments, unless the requirements of both domestic and international stabilization coincided in pointing to a need for greater monetary expansion or restraint.

The measures proposed above, if adopted, will yield, I believe, a number of highly valuable results. Confidence in the dollar will be fully restored and undesirable constraints on United States domestic and foreign policies will be removed. A strong and durable international monetary mechanism will be established, using dollar balances as the preferred form of central bank reserves and of private international liquidity. This will be a dollar-reserve system without the critical weaknesses of the present system. The central role of the United States as banker and financial intermediary and the general preference for dollars as a store of liquidity will enable interest rates in the United States to be maintained well below European rates. Voluntary controls on U.S. capital outflow, the interest equalization tax, the tying of foreign aid, and the Government's "Buy American" program will cease to be necessary and can be ended. The reciprocal credit with Britain which I have proposed should secure the pound's link to the dollar and give time for working through present difficulties.

Admittedly, the program which I have proposed is somewhat bold. Although it will, of course, be hotly opposed as both Utopian and evil by those on whom gold casts a mystical spell, nevertheless the monetary history of the past several centuries may be epitomized as the progressive substitution of credit money for commodity money and these proposals would represent a further step along this path.

If this program is judged to have merit, it can and should be carried into effect quickly so that it may be completed before the British credit comes up for further renewal. If General de Gaulle, by posing the issue with absolute starkness, precipitates a fundamental reconstruction of the international monetary system substituting the dollar for gold as the preferred reserve asset, we will owe him our thanks. Whether or not a program of action along the lines which I have proposed is put into effect, there can now be little doubt that the crisis of the international monetary system which we have been experiencing for the past half dozen years will culminate in the dethronement of gold and its replacement by the dollar. The only question is whether this transition will be effected deliberately, or by the compulsion of events and with considerable injury to the free-world economy. This country's international financial position gives it the power to decide whether to carry out the transition deliberately or await the compulsion of events.

Under a strengthened international monetary system based on the dollar, the financial power of the United States will be greatly increased. It will be exceedingly important at this stage that we refrain to the greatest extent possible from using this power unilaterally, and that we develop, through the IMF and OECD, settled habits of multilateral policy consultation and determination.

General de Gaulle's effort to use international monetary policy as a major instrument of power politics is almost laughable. In their effectiveness the weapons at his disposal are on a par with his independent nuclear deterrent. His use of the monetary weapon can injure the French economy and the free-world economy for a time, but it cannot succeed in its intended objective of downgrading the position of the dollar. On the contrary, it is hastening the predominance of the dollar. If international cooperation in monetary matters had been possible, the present crisis of the international monetary system might have been solved through agreement to establish a multilateral system leaning less heavily upon the dollar. French intransigence, however, has been a major factor foreclosing this outcome, and there are now no remaining alternatives to a world dollar standard. It will then become necessary for this country to operate the system in such a fashion as gradually to subdue the feelings of frustration which this outcome will cause in some quarters abroad.

This interpretation of the present international monetary confrontation as one in which the French Government is unwittingly defending the dollar while the United States Government is unwittingly defending gold will perhaps be dismissed as carrying paradox to the point of absurdity. But the crisis of the international monetary system has generated many such paradoxes. While the United States Government has felt it necessary, in its efforts to restore confidence in the dollar, to keep asserting its unequivocal commitment to the dollar's defense, it is also generally acknowledged that the dollar could not be successfully devalued against foreign currencies even if this country so desired, because other governments simply would not tolerate the resulting appreciation of their currencies against the dollar. Must one therefore conclude that the dollar's present external value is at the same time difficult to maintain and impossible to change?

It is paradoxical that the country whose currency has shown the greatest strength during recent years is one which has been running a larger import balance in goods and services, in relation to its gross national product, than most underdeveloped countries receiving foreign aid; it has been borrowing short not merely to lend long but also to finance current imports, and it has continued to experience gold inflow despite efforts to retard the further growth of its short-term foreign liabilities by such measures as non-payment of interest on foreign deposits. The country is Switzerland.

In the later years of the Marshall Plan the United States balance of payments was in a position of so-called deficit and Western Europe in surplus. European voices were not raised to point out that this country was merely giving back what it was borrowing at short term nor to demand that aid should be cut. It is ironic, although not surprising, that such demands are being made when the aid is going to underdeveloped countries. The implication is that foreign official holders of dollars should be given veto power over United States policies. Although the United States would reject any such explicit demand, mistaken preoccupation with the balance of payments has been one factor leading us to restrict aid and curtail its real amount through tying.

It is paradoxical that not only laymen but also many economists regard a steadily widening gap between this country's short-term foreign liabilities and its gold holdings as "a bad thing," as if the principle of fractional reserve banking were unheard of, while they also acknowledge that if the gap stops widening, through elimination of the United States deficit, deflationary strains which would finally become unendurable would be imposed on the world economy. Must we conclude that a United States deficit is both bad and essential to a healthy world economy?

This catalogue of current paradoxes could be boringly expanded. It is strange that just as we have slowly emancipated ourselves from irrational preconceptions about fiscal deficits, we have come under the spell of irrationalities about balance-of-payments "deficits." All the paradoxes cited above, and many others, are resolved once it is recognized that the United States performs an essential banking and deposit-creation role for the rest of the world, that the existing international monetary system is inhibiting effective performance of this role, and that the problem can be solved not by abandoning the role—i.e., eliminating the "deficit"—but only by modifying the system. Looking beyond the present crisis of the system, it is not the international role of the dollar but the role of gold which is in jeopardy. The course of action which I have recommended would, if successful, preserve for gold a limited role in settling international payments. Thus the recommendation, if seemingly bold, would be conservative in final result.

Supplementary Comments (1965)

The proposal presented above provides a means of putting into effect John Williams' key-currency approach of a generation ago. If the Government had accepted this approach at that time instead of the White Plan, we would surely have avoided the difficulties which have beset us since 1959, and the British, freed of recurrent sterling crises, might have been able to share more adequately in Western Europe's vigorous economic growth. Finally, the financing needs of the rest of the world might have been met with less dependence on U.S. Government aid.

The means which I propose for transforming the present vulnerable gold-exchange standard into a truly strong dollar-sterling standard is a change in United States gold-buying policy. Under my proposal, the amount of gold which we would stand ready to buy at $35 an ounce would be limited, in general, to one-third of the present foreign official holdings, with an offsetting introduction of credit to complement gold as a source of dollars, in the ratio of two of credit to one of gold. Apart from favored treatment accorded to the limited amount of gold held by less-developed countries and dollar bloc countries, the only other exception to the one-third limitation would be Britain, the purpose of this exception being to underwrite securely the pound-dollar peg. The proposal amounts to a partial demonetization of gold, and although gold would continue to be used in strictly rationed amounts at its present monetary value in settling international payments, its free market price would fall. Incidentally, we should offer to enter into the same reciprocal gold-plus-credit arrangements with the U.S.S.R. and Eastern Europe as with Western European countries.

The announcement of such a change in gold-buying policy

would not have carried conviction while the dollar was weak. The dollar's only remaining source of weakness, however, is the overhang of reluctantly held balances in the hands of European central banks, and we should invite the remaining reluctant official holders to convert into gold before we adopt the new gold-plus-credit formula. The preparatory step would underscore our own confidence in the dollar's underlying strength, and the subsequent announcement of restrictions on gold purchases would produce a dramatic and lasting shift in present, perverse asset preferences, moving them away from gold to dollars and pounds. The reserve currency system would cease to be, as it has been, a system good only for "fair weather."

The international monetary system can be strengthened only by building upon the present system and correcting its weaknesses —not by tearing it down in favor of some abstract blueprint. The Triffinites and the Rueffites are at one in desiring to eliminate the weaknesses of the present gold-exchange standard by abolishing it. The Triffinites are naive in believing that European central banks, which are reluctant to keep accumulating dollars instead of gold, will be satisfied by any scheme which proposes to fund their existing liquid dollar claims into long-term obligations and which asks them to accept further accretions to reserves in the form of book credits with the IMF.

The Rueffites are dangerously naive in another respect. They believe that if they could succeed in demoting the international financial role of the United States—and of Britain—to a level comparable to that of France and the other EEC countries, the result would be beneficial to France and Continental Western Europe. Nothing could be more completely wrong. The cost in terms of reduced earnings of New York and London banks would be slight indeed in comparison with the much greater cost in terms of blockage of European trade which would be produced by the withdrawal of the essential financing facilities which these centers provide. For the United States, the loss of bank earnings would be a small thing; for Continental Western Europe, the loss of the dollar financing facilities would be a disaster. Europe is getting only a foretaste of this today, through our voluntary capital controls.

It is an impressive fact that the EEC has made virtually no progress in financial "harmonization," in integration of capital markets, or in the development of arrangements for mutual financial support to bridge the payments difficulties of individual members, and that even the modest recommendations made by its Secretariat remain unheeded. Moreover, apart from the Dutch banks, whose resources are limited in relation to the total requirements, the prevailing banking traditions and practices in Continental Western Europe are primarily domestically oriented and fail to furnish the financing facilities which foreign trade requires.

This gap in Europe's financial structure used to be filled by sterling and sterling credits before World War II. Since the restoration of convertibility at the end of 1958, the dollar has largely replaced sterling in performing this role. The increasing transactions needs for dollars resulting from use of dollars as the unit of account, medium of exchange, and standard of deferred payment in intra-European trade and finance, and in Europe's transactions with the outside world, goes far to explain the substantial growth in private foreign balances in the United States and the even more striking growth of Euro-dollars deposits in the face of a predominantly unfavorable climate of speculative attitudes regarding the dollar. Moreover, it is impressive that after the interest equalization tax was announced, most new security issues by European borrowers for sale to other Europeans were denominated in dollars and that New York investment banks were asked to participate prominently in the underwriting. Last of all, the unreflecting haste with which the European Payments Union was dropped simultaneously with the restoration of current account convertibility at the end of 1958 is evidence of the absence, in Continental Western Europe, of the kind of banking and financial tradition upon which a viable international system must rest. It was indeed fortunate for the initial success of the EEC that it was launched at a time when all its members enjoyed substantial payments "surpluses," thanks to the United States "deficit."

If France and Continental Western Europe find distasteful the condition of financial dependence implicit in present arrangements—and such an attitude is understandable—the solution, surely, is not the self-destructive course of forcing us to withdraw the financing facilities upon which they so heavily depend and which they have, until recently, taken for granted. It is, rather, to transform their own financial institutions, markets, and practices so that the role of financial intermediary formerly performed largely through sterling and now chiefly through the dollar can be more largely performed by themselves. But I have the impression that only a few members of the European financial community perceive this, and even after it becomes more widely perceived the necessary transformation of institutions and habits will still be a long, slow process. Meanwhile, Western Europe's own interests will be best served if they reconcile themselves to continued use of dollars and sterling and stop talking about "reciprocity."

It is now clear that the necessary strengthening of the international monetary system cannot be achieved merely by patient and tactful negotiation with European central banks. These negotiations did produce the critically important result of containing speculative dollar crises and they greatly helped to hold down the gold drain, but the new financing devices which have been developed will not automatically evolve into a longer range reconstruction of the system.

The reason why these arrangements cannot, in my view, be quickly enlarged and developed into a flexible international monetary mechanism is the persistence in the minds of European central bankers of an orthodox but obsolete view about the way a fixed-exchange-rate system must work. I am disposed to place the blame for the persistence of this outworn orthodoxy on the economists, rather than on the central bankers themselves. According to the orthodox theory of the gold standard, the balance of payments in goods and services must adjust to the capital movement, if equilibrium is to be maintained. Although, when disequilibrium appears, the provision of some financing by surplus countries is admitted to be permissible to facilitate transition to a new equilibrium, such financing, it is held, must be in very limited amounts and must be short term, lest compensatory financing degenerate into a device for merely perpetuating the disequilibrium by delaying needed adjustments.

The traditional theory fails to take into account some of the essential functions performed by international capital movements; as a corollary, it implicitly denies the special need for, and the requirement for, effective operation of a world financial center. I refer, of course, to Britain before World War I, Britain and the United States in the interwar years, and predominantly the United States since World War II. Capital outflow from the financial center serves not merely to transfer real resources to other countries by financing the financial center's current account surplus but also serves to supply liquid balances to the rest of the world in the growing amounts needed for the healthy expansion of world trade. It is this second function which is ignored in orthodox theory and by European central bankers. The flow of capital between the financial center and the rest of the world is a two-way flow—a large outflow of capital in the form of direct investment, long-term loans, and short-term credits and a smaller inflow chiefly through foreign accumulation of liquid balances and marketable securities.

It is quite wrong to say that under an adequately functioning reserve-currency standard the supply of liquidity to the rest of the world would depend upon the size of the "deficit" in the balance of payments of the financial center. The opposite would be the case. Until the imposition of the voluntary controls, the size of the United States "deficit" depended upon the rest of the world's demand for additional liquidity, since subject only to the limits set by the financial market's estimate of the borrower's creditworthiness and his future debt-servicing capacity, other countries had had access to a flexible source of liquidity adjustable to their needs and preferences.

The only trouble is that the workability of such a system depends upon the willingness of the rest of the world to regard liquid claims against the financial center as, for all practical purposes, the best form of liquidity. Gold may remain symbolically in the background so long as, in practice, it is not preferred. Recent difficulties have been due to the fact that this essential state of practical preferences has not prevailed, especially among Continental European central banks. It is foolish to assert that a reserve-currency system is unfair because it exempts the reserve center from the balance-of-payments discipline which other countries must accept; more important is the fact that while other countries are able to borrow from the reserve center in amounts limited only by their general credit standing and estimated debt-servicing capacity, the reserve center can negotiate credits abroad only with the greatest difficulty—since a banker is not supposed to seek loans from his clients. Thus, the lack of reciprocity in the reserve-currency system works both ways. The discipline to which other countries are subject is not what is postulated by orthodox gold standard theory because it is nullified by ample access to external finance from the reserve center; the only discipline is that of credit standing. The reserve center's access to external finance has a different basis; it can only with difficulty exceed the rest of the world's desire to accumulate liquid claims against the reserve center. Consequently, when gold takes the place of the reserve currency as the most desired form of liquidity, this pressure, mistermed discipline, becomes not only excessive but finally intolerable. With the system headed for breakdown, the financial center, to avert this climax, must restrict its activities as banker and financial intermediary, as we have now done through the interest equalization tax and voluntary controls on capital outflow. These controls provide the opportunity for basic strengthening of the system. If the opportunity is not seized, and if, instead, present controls are retained or made compulsory, they will be found to have gravely injurious economic consequences for other countries.

The voluntary capital controls represent a temporary effort to limit capital outflow to the financing of real transfer through the current account surplus and to suppress the fulfillment of the second function—the provision of the liquid assets needed by a growing economy. Given the unwillingness of European central banks to accept additional liquidity in financial form, we had little choice, although it is regrettable that the consequences of this choking off of needed growth in liquidity are being inflicted on innocent bystanders, such as Japan and Australia.

My pessimism regarding the possibility of solving the problem through negotiations with European central banks and finance ministries is due to my belief that the principles of gold standard orthodoxy are too deeply rooted in their minds to be quickly dislodged. I believe that this adherence to a theory which is not only obsolete today, but did not work even in the nineteenth-century heyday of the gold standard (really, a sterling standard), is the main stumbling block to international agreement. This is the chief obstacle, rather than either any mystical, irrational yearning for gold or power politics. In the case of Spain, and possibly the French monetary authorities in some degree, gold may have a somewhat irrational appeal, but this is scarcely true for the financial authorities in other countries. Moreover, political considerations, although they have cut both ways, have operated, on balance, to give official support to the dollar. Most European central banks have kept more of their reserves in dollars, and have provided larger credit facilities than they would have done if guided strictly by orthodox European central banking doctrine. They have done so partly for reasons of political friendship and partly to help avert or contain crises.

If this judgment is correct, negotiation to achieve substantial improvements seems unpromising, and action of the general type which I have proposed is the only method of reconstructing in the near future a workable reserve-currency system. If carried out, this proposal will enable us both to meet the financial needs of other countries and to relieve ourselves of the strains and difficulties with which we have had to cope for half a dozen years.

15 *Toward the Demonetization of Gold*[1]

Mr. DESPRES. I would like to make some general comments about where we stand today and what it seems to me that the problems are. I would describe the whole period since 1959 as a period of contained international monetary crisis, and this is ironical in many ways. The franc was devalued and stabilized in 1958, and at the end of 1958 the advanced countries of the free world achieved general current account convertibility. This was a kind of a culmination of one of the long-term objectives of American foreign economic policy, to establish a world in which you would have liberalized multilateral trade without restriction on international payments, so that it didn't matter whether people wanted to spend their vacations at home or abroad, and whether you were using foreign exchange or domestic currency. It was supposed to be a world free from intense balance-of-payments preoccupations.

The ironical part of it is that this kind of culmination resulted in what amounts to a quasi-mercantilist world, in which countries

1. *A New Approach to United States International Economic Policy,* Hearings before the Subcommittee on International Exchange and Payments of the Joint Economic Committee, 89th Congress, Second Session, September 9, 1966, pp. 10-14, 28-33, 35-38.—Ed.

are taking measures for balance-of-payments reasons, to get a "favorable balance of payments," to restrain out-payments in one way or another, to encourage in-payments, and so on.

The reason I say "quasi-mercantilist" is that we have sought, despite payments difficulties, to push forward with some of the commercial policy objectives of long standing, such as the Kennedy Round. At the same time, we have taken a lot of measures of a mercantilist variety for the sake of husbanding foreign exchange, such as tying aid and the Government's substitution of domestic for foreign military procurement.

The situation has been one of contained crisis. I do not share the fears of some of my colleagues at the table about a forced devaluation of the dollar. Until General de Gaulle's statement—was it in the latter part of 1964, I think it was—I think one can say that there was a general consensus among the advanced industrial countries that the crisis would be contained; that whenever a panic run developed, some emergency devices would be brought into play to prevent things from getting utterly out of hand, to prevent a blowup. And although France is no longer a member of this consensus, and has made it very clear that they do not desire to forestall a blowup—nevertheless, the consensus remains very strong, I think, among the other countries concerned, and when the spokesmen of the Federal Reserve Bank of New York and former Under Secretary of the Treasury Robert Roosa talk about the highly sophisticated techniques that have been developed for intervening in the exchange market and for mutual support and so on, and laud themselves and their colleagues abroad on the efficient methods of cooperation that have been developed, there is this much truth to it.

For the purpose of forestalling an undesired breakdown of the system, the methods, although in part informal, are I think very good, very reliable, and I would say that the lack of French cooperation alone is not potent enough to eliminate this consensus, to weaken the system decisively. So that I don't fear a breakdown or a forced devaluation.

What I think is wrong about the present situation is that it not only provides a pretty good guarantee against things coming to a head, it also provides a very good guarantee that a situation of chronic, low-grade, contained crisis will be sustained indefinitely into the future.

Now one thing that might be asked, although we never do, is what is wrong with this permanent state of stress and strain? After all, the world has got along since the end of 1958 in this state of semi-crisis or contained crisis. I think that what is wrong with it is that it contains two important long-run dangers:

1. The long-run danger which hasn't become starkly evident as yet is of a serious retardation of Western world economic growth.

2. I describe the situation as quasi-mercantilist. I think the long-run tendency is for it to become more and more mercantilist, that it is incompatible with liberalized trading arrangements.

If there is to be aid to underdeveloped countries, it is going to be on a reduced scale, and there will be a strong tendency—our own tied aid is an example—for a kind of a partitioning of the free world into economic or economic-political blocs, with financial and economic intercourse fairly open within the blocs, but with serious barriers between blocs. And I think this kind of a world is bad, not only economically, but in terms of our political objectives.

Now, how do we get out of the trap? I would like to think that our slow progress is due to the fact that these matters have been left to negotiation among technicians, and that the negotiations among heads of government might be more effective.

But I don't think that this gets at the root of the problem. The root of the problem, it seems to me, is intellectual, and there is an oft-quoted passage toward the end of Keynes's "General Theory" which now I can't quote. The ideas of economists, both when they are right and when they are wrong, have far greater effect on the way the world is run than is commonly appreciated. Practical men who believe themselves to be quite exempt from intellectual influence are usually the slaves of some academic scribblers of a few years back.

I think we are in that kind of a situation here. The essential doctrine which is accepted by central banks, ministries of finance, and governments, comes, of course, from economists, and I think that the doctrine is out of tune with the realities of the economic world in which we live, and that until this gets fixed up, there is not much chance of progress.

Moreover, I would say this: that the ideas that I think are wrong are held at least as strongly in the United States as anywhere else. All that would be required to put things right would be for the American Government, for American experts, to change their view of the problem.

The problem is, in other words, to a large extent of the self-fulfilling-prophecy variety. It exists in our minds, and it would go away if we thought more realistically about how the international economy actually works and must work.

Now that thesis requires some elaboration, and maybe I ought to stop and let some other people talk.

Chairman Reuss. Unless there is objection from some quarter, I would say do tell what are these intellectual devices which are preventing the new Jerusalem.

Mr. Despres. The main point I would say is this. The view of balance-of-payments matters, which you will find in almost any official document or in much of the economic writing that you pick up, is a view that derives from David Hume, the Scotch philosopher of the eighteenth century, who assumed a world in which everybody used the metallic currency, and in which there was no international lending or borrowing, and in which, therefore, all countries were equal in the sense that each faced the same kind of balance-of-payments problem. There was symmetry in international economic relationships in this sense.

We do not have that kind of a world. We have a world in which the United States exercises a predominant economic and financial role. On the economic side we are, and have been for several years, the only substantial net provider of real resources. I mean by this, current account surplus to the rest of the world.

France provides, in relation to her economic size, a sizable amount to the French community abroad, but it is still true that we are the only country with a large export surplus in goods and services, and this is the measure of the real resource contribution. We are, moreover, the world's financial center. The dollar is not just a domestic currency. It is a world currency, and for deep-seated reasons having to do with the advantages which are provided by size, the structure of finance, whether domestic or international, is hierarchical in organization, and the United States is at the apex. American lending and investment abroad performs two purposes.

It performs the purpose of transfering real resources, which the conventional wisdom acknowledges, and it performs the second purpose of providing financial assets to the rest of the world of types which other countries desire, and taking financial claims of types which other countries desire us to take—this process of financial mediation being an essential part of the flow of saving into investment, not only internationally, but let us say within foreign countries.

The needed expansion of German oil refinery capacity, for example, is facilitated by the acquisition of German refinery companies by Texaco, because Germans are willing to take Texaco stock and are not as willing to take the securities of a German oil refining company. This kind of trade in financial claims occurs quite generally and pervasively.

With a properly functioning international capital market the countries other than the financial center that have good credit standing have no need for additional reserves. Subject only to credit standing, the international ebb and flow of capital frees them of any balance-of-payments problem, as conventionally defined. Their only problem would be to stay within the comfortably wide limits imposed by credit standing. The attempts of all schemes for improving international liquidity to find some universal formula based on the principle of symmetry are beside the point. There is no inadequacy of liquidity so far as other countries with good credit standing are concerned.

Contrast with this the position of the financial center. I would like to call attention to the fact that just a few years ago the U.S. Treasury had great difficulty in borrowing abroad, with the special issues of Roosa bonds, amounts less than we were simultaneously providing to India and Pakistan by way of AID. Now the unwillingness of foreign governments and central banks to buy themselves or to authorize the marketing in their countries of U.S. Treasury obligations was not due to the fact that they thought these were poor securities or that American credit worthiness was inadequate. It was due to the fact that they thought there was something deep-seatedly wrong in sparing us the necessity of losing gold.

Now this is where I say a bad doctrine is the cause of the difficulty. It is widely thought that the shift into gold—incidentally, this isn't a French monopoly, the Germans, I think, have converted more dollars into gold than the French have. They have simply done it in a more discreet fashion. This desire for gold rather than dollars is not due first and foremost to fears on the part of foreign central banks that the dollar will be devalued. It is due first and foremost to the fact that the economics that they have been taught says that to relieve us of the pressures which gold loss would entail would be somehow wrong. It is the attitude of the central banks which accounts, in turn, for the private speculative demand for gold, and it is our own very great timidity and fear about losing gold, the intensity of our preoccupation with this problem, which has also bolstered and strengthened this attitude.

Now what I am really saying is this: things will not be changed essentially by international negotiations. There may be some token accomplishments in the way of international liquidity arrangements of little practical importance, but things will not be changed essentially and the present, contained crisis won't be ended until the reserve asset preferences of foreign central banks are radically altered.

The United States has this problem entirely within its control. It is not a matter of international negotiations. The United States doesn't even have to do any of the things that I proposed in the spring of 1965. It merely has to change its mind by recognizing the fact that in the present-day world, gold derives value from the fact that it is convertible into dollars. It must lose its intense anxiety about losing gold. It would be highly useful, incidentally, if, instead of merely abolishing the reserve requirement against member bank reserves, we abolished the gold reserve requirement against Federal Reserve notes also, as a token of our willingness to lose gold.

If our obvious pain in undergoing gold loss disappeared, the whole situation, I think, would be utterly transformed. We could have a functioning international capital market, and without a functioning international capital market, the chances in the long run of maintaining anything approaching liberalized trade are almost nil.

I would say also that with the exception of a few economists like Dr. Mundell, the whole approach to this balance-of-payments problem is to treat it as a problem of the adjustment of the current account, of the trade account. In a world functioning with open international capital markets, a large part of the adjustment consists of international capital movements accommodating to changes in trade balances, so that most countries other than the reserve center are not under what is conventionally thought of as balance-of-payments constraint. They are under another kind of constraint, the constraint only of credit standing.

They do not encounter balance-of-payments difficulties until their ability to import capital from abroad is impaired. The U.S. position is truly unique, since we are the banker. We are the only country which cannot borrow on the basis of credit standing, and I would say that the reason we can't is because economists, central bankers, governments, are under the spell of this David Hume myth. I admire Hume but I am just opposed to applying eighteenth-century economics to the twentieth century.

. . .

Chairman Reuss. Mr. Despres?

Mr. Despres. I feel I have sown more confusion than light, if one can sow light. Let me say what kind of an international monetary and financial environment I would like to see first and then say something about the present situation.

I would like to see an international monetary and financial environment in which the movement of capital between countries is substantially unrestricted, and I think this to be necessary for liberalized trade.

I don't think that close balance in the current account can be achieved in the modern world, or should be achieved in the modern world, and that accommodating capital movements have to play an important role as they would play under a system of freedom of international capital movements.

Under such a system, we would be the world financial center.

As the world financial center, it would be our job to base our monetary policy, interest rates, and all the rest, not on the domestic stabilization requirements, primarily, but first and foremost on what we concluded, in consultation with other countries—and I stress this because I have been called a jingoist—what we concluded to be appropriate, conducive to stable, non-inflationary world economic growth.

This would mean that not only we, but other countries, would have to rely much more heavily for domestic stabilization purposes on fiscal policy, basing our monetary policy on international considerations, in the light of the world role of the dollar and of the U.S. financial markets.

Let me say this: that I think the importance of the financial role of the United States is not merely that it provides liquidity, and I think a great deal of confusion arises from the fact that people say the U.S. deficit has generated liquidity, as it has. That is only one-half of the picture, however, and if you think of the United States as a bank, the liquidity that it provides to other countries is on the liability side of the U.S. bank's balance sheet.

On the asset side are the loans and investments that we make in our role as financial intermediary. Now, if the deficit in our balance of payments were removed, the significance of that removal would be not merely that this source of liquidity was removed, but equally important—I would say, indeed, more important—is that this source of lending, financing on the asset side, was removed, and from this point of view, none of the proposals for finding some international arrangement to substitute for the U.S. deficit make any contact with the problem, because the problem is not just to provide the liquidity.

These international arrangements—whether a Triffin plan or CRU (Composite Reserve Unit), or something else—would not acquire the types of assets that U.S. lending and investing are acquiring, would not meet the financial needs which American financing activity is meeting. Moreover, using rigid formulas for growth of liquidity, they are undesirably inflexible and in this respect inferior to the informal Basle arrangements.

So that I would say that all the proposals for dealing with what is called the international liquidity problem are at least 50 per cent irrelevant. I am not saying they are harmful, but they would not obviate the need for a U.S. deficit from the point of view of a healthy world economy.

Now starting from where we are, the sacrifice which this would call for from us is a substantial sacrifice with respect to the use of monetary policy for domestic purposes, and actually I would say it would also require this sacrifice from other countries.

The Germans, pursuing highly expansionary fiscal policies, have sought through monetary policy, and without much success, to curb their inflation. Their first allegation was that monetary policy was ineffective because when they raised interest rates, it attracted funds from abroad. So that the Germans wanted the United States to pursue a tight money policy, in order to assist them in fighting their domestic inflation.

Now, I don't think just fighting a German and Dutch inflation is the correct role for American monetary policy either, but the interesting thing is that as we have tightened in this country, interest rates in Germany have gone up even more, money has got tighter, but the inflation seems to proceed. What I am really saying is although within a range monetary and fiscal policy can be thought of as alternative domestic stabilization devices, this is only true within a range.

We have found that in the United States tight money is not a good offset to an excessively expansionary fiscal policy, so that we wouldn't have been surrendering too much.

Now, I don't view the present situation without alarm or without concern. As I said, I don't think devaluation of the dollar is likely to be forced upon us, because I think there is that degree of international cooperation, despite the French.

I do think that the breakdown of the international capital market is bad news. I think the prognosis for trade restriction, for reduced aid, for deciding all these matters like foreign aid, military dispositions, not on their merits but on a very bad criterion, the balance-of-payments criterion, I feel all these tendencies are going to grow.

This is the thing that I do view with great and long-standing concern, and the thing that concerns me most is that I know of no proposal, among those currently circulating, which, if adopted, would meet the essential problem. So I am really much more concerned than other people.

I deplore the fact that the international negotiations among technicians haven't gotten anywhere, or have gotten a very little distance, but I regret even more that if any of the proposals that have been made had been adopted, it still wouldn't have met the problem, and the real point is that—as in the case of the multilateral nuclear force idea—the pretense of a non-existent equality under which an attempt is made to frame proposals to conduct negotiations, when in fact there is a profound lack of symmetry in the situation of the negotiators—the attempt to maintain a facade of equality makes the whole thing not only of zero productivity, but I would say counterproductive.

The only solution, it seems to me, is for the United States to understand its role and to act. And I think that action is of two sorts.

We can act to destroy this foreign central bank appetite for gold ourselves, but I think it is equally important to act to give them an important share, through OECD perhaps, in the determination of U.S. monetary policy so far as it affects the world level of interest rates.

Chairman REUSS. Who is the "them"?

Mr. DESPRES. The other members of OECD.

Chairman REUSS. Yes; not the foreign central bankers, but the governments.

Mr. DESPRES. This I regard as not the crucial question, although I would answer "Yes" to you. My feelings are that it would be better to have the governments do this than the foreign central bankers.

Chairman REUSS. Mr. Ellsworth?

Representative ELLSWORTH. Is it true, is it an accurate characterization of what you are saying to us, to say that you feel that the United States ought to quit worrying about having a deficit in its balance of payments, and that in fact, it ought to have a deficit in its balance of payments because of the fact that that permits these direct investments on the part of the United States all around the world, and that if the United States could change its mind and could view having a deficit in its balance of payments year after year as a positive good, that then there wouldn't be any necessity to create this artificial asset which these negotiations are revolving around? Is that what you are saying?

Mr. DESPRES. Yes; I am saying that. I am saying that not only American direct investment abroad, but American international lending—

Representative ELLSWORTH. Yes.

Mr. DESPRES. On quite a flexible basis—

Representative ELLSWORTH. Yes.

Mr. DESPRES (continuing). Is important, and that the international arrangements would not substitute for the American lending and investing. It would not be a sufficient substitute.

Representative ELLSWORTH. You are saying that really this concern about creating a new artificial asset, so people would have something else than dollars, sterling, or gold, to put in their reserves, is really another way of just papering over what you regard as a very serious situation, and that ideally we shouldn't be worried about creating this new artificial asset.

What we should be doing is worrying about changing everybody's attitude, ours and everybody else's, toward the role of the United States in the financial world as it exists today. Is that what you are saying?

Mr. DESPRES. That is correct, and I think that if we changed our attitude about gold, other countries would change their attitude about gold.

Representative ELLSWORTH. I understand.

Mr. DESPRES. Fundamentally, I regard the dollar as the most desired, inherently the internationally most desired form of asset, and that gold is valued because we stand ready to buy it. Just as used to be the case for the price of wheat before wheat got in short supply, we are propping gold.

Representative ELLSWORTH. Let me ask a question to clarify something in my own mind. Would you explain to me or attempt to, so that even I can understand it, what exactly is the direct link between our having a deficit in our balance of payments on the one hand, and on the other hand our ability to engage in this financial intermediation function that you have talked about as a direct investor and as a lender.

Mr. DESPRES. Yes.

Representative ELLSWORTH. In other words, why is it necessary for us to have a balance-of-payments deficit in order for us to perform that function?

Mr. DESPRES. The United States typically has a surplus on current account, net exports of goods and services. If our lending and investing abroad precisely equaled the surplus on current account, then one could say that the function of the lending and investing was exclusively to effect real transfer of goods and services to other countries and one could call this, if one wanted, a position of balance.

What I am really saying is this: that American lending and investing abroad performs two functions. One, it finances real transfer of goods and services. Two, it is a trade in financial assets. It enables foreign countries to get financial claims of the type that they desire, while we provide financing to permit investments that go forward abroad. We not only export a part of our savings to the rest of the world but our financial markets help other countries to mobilize their savings for investment use.

Now this excess American lending and investing—in excess of real transfer—we choose to call a deficit. By so doing, we are in effect asserting that this role of financial intermediation, this role as banker, is not a valid role for a country to play.

What I am saying is that this isn't a deficit. The financial intermediation role is a valid role. Indeed, it is an essential role to a liberalized free-world economy, and it falls to the United States because we stand at the apex of the world financial pyramid. Our role cannot be multilateralized just as our nuclear role cannot be multilateralized.

You see, the definition of a deficit, the traditional definition, the Department of Commerce definition, is that the deficit is the amount of liquid financial claims that other countries acquire from the United States as the result of our financial intermediation role, as a result of our lending and investing in excess of real transfer.

What I am really saying is that if we stopped doing this, we would leave a hole in the world's financial mechanism which would not be filled by any of these international monetary arrangements, and what is called a deficit, I am saying, should not be considered a state of disequilibrium. On the contrary, it is necessary to a healthy equilibrium.

Now the problem that I think concerns Dr. Mundell is this. If the United States is freed from constraints with respect to international lending and investing in excess of real transfer, which is what financial intermediation is, what is to keep us from doing either one of two things: one, easing up on credit extension and putting the world into an inflationary boom or, two, tightening up on credit and therefore imposing a severe depression on the rest of the world?

The first of these we have never done. The second of these we did do in the late 1920's. American tight money imposed for alleged domestic reasons, in 1928-29, hurt the rest of the world long before it hurt us, and imposed a depression on the rest of the world.

My answer to this is that we should commit ourselves to adopt a monetary policy geared to what seems to be reasonable from the point of view of stable world economic growth, and forgo the use of monetary policy, just to curb our private domestic boom or to provide extra domestic stimulus in a recession, and we should do this in consultation with the rest of the world, I mean arrive at our monetary policy in consultation with the major foreign countries.

Now, this is distinctly an American solution, and a true internationalist would say he would rather have a supranational central bank. I would rather have a supranational central bank, too, but I am stressing I would not rather have an international central bank, which is a very different thing.

I am also saying, I guess, that if you did have a central bank, the central bank would not only have to create liquidity, but it would have to be willing to acquire the kinds of assets that American lenders and investors acquire and that central banks usually don't touch, in order to replace the American deficit. It would also have to manage flexibly and not by rigid formula.

You know, I really think I have been talking in kind of classroom world federalist terms about this problem. I think that the world isn't ready for a true supranational solution, and I think that the very good second best is to recognize the existing organic structure of world finance, and to adopt a setup which accommodates to what exists, instead of maintaining or seeking to maintain this pretense of equality.

Chairman REUSS. Why don't you settle for an international central bank of the sort which seems to be our Treasury's current negotiating position, plus a sweeping out of the intellectual cobwebs, if they are cobwebs, of people in governments generally on quasi-mercantilism, which you would describe as getting rid of the idea that there is something evil with lending long and borrowing short to do it, "ex-Humeing" the world in short? If we did all that, why wouldn't you be very happy?

Mr. DESPRES. Well, I don't regard that as—you didn't ask me this question—as a very likely outcome. You may not regard what I propose as a very likely outcome either. But the thing I had in mind is this.

I think a U.S. deficit ought to be a normal and a current feature of a healthfully growing world economy operating under liberalized trade.

Therefore, the International Central Bank or whatever other arrangements would have to keep providing reserves to us; we would be the client in the sense of the borrower or the recipient of owned reserves. I think this would be very hard to sell, and I think that—

Chairman REUSS. The compromise I was suggesting to you was one in which we would be able to continue to run deficits caused by our lending long and borrowing short, with the cheery acquiescence of the new enlightened central bankers of the world, but the need for long-term liquidity, quite a different thing, could be met by a Joe Fowler [Secretary of the Treasury] type international central bank. Why wouldn't that give you an answer on both questions?

Mr. DESPRES. That is all right. I don't see any separate long-term need for liquidity, apart from the need for financing appropriate payments deficits, but yes, that would be all right, would be my answer.

I would be reasonably happy if that were the outcome, but I don't see it as the outcome, because of the principle of symmetry or equality, from which all these problems are approached.

. . .

(The following materials were subsequently supplied by Chairman Reuss for inclusion in the record:)

MITGLIED DES DIREKTORIUMS DER DEUTSCHEN BUNDESBANK,
Frankfurt, September 14, 1966.

Mr. HENRY S. REUSS,
Member, House of Representatives,
Capitol Hill, Washington, D.C.

DEAR MR. REUSS: I read in the New York Times of September 10, that Professor Despres has made the following statement before a Congressional Sub-committee:

"I think the West Germans have converted more dollars into gold than the French. They simply did it in a more discreet fashion."

This statement is factually completely wrong. As I assume that the Sub-committee was the one presided over by you, I send you enclosed a copy of a letter which I have sent to Professor Despres on the subject.

With best personal regards,

Yours sincerely,

OTMAR EMMINGER.

MITGLIED DES DIREKTORIUMS DER DEUTSCHEN BUNDESBANK,
Frankfurt, September 14, 1966.

Professor EMILE DESPRES,
Stanford University,
Stanford, California.

DEAR PROFESSOR DESPRES: I just read in the New York Times that at a panel session with a Senate-House Economic Subcommittee you made the following statement:

"I think the West Germans have converted more dollars into

gold than the French. They simply did it in a more discreet fashion."

May I point out that this statement has no foundation in the facts.

During the 4½ years from 1962 to August 1966, the German authorities have only converted 25 million dollars into gold with the US Treasury, in the sense in which the French authorities convert a large part of their dollar accruals by tendering them to the US Treasury for conversion into gold.

It is true that the German gold reserves have increased, during the period from 1962 through August 1966, by altogether 633 million dollars (as against more than $3 billion in the case of France!). But most of the increases in the German reserve came about not through conversions with the US, but either through gold sales of the IMF in connection with support operations for the pound, or through the gold distribution to members of the "Gold Pool," that is out of the net surplus of newly mined (and Russian) gold accruing on the London gold market.

These facts are illustrated in the following table:

Gold holdings of the Deutsche Bundesbank—Changes from 1962 to August 1966

(Million $)

	1962	1963	1964	1965	1966 JANUARY TO AUGUST	1962 TO AUGUST 1966
U.S. gold sales	....	....	+225	....	....	+225
IMF gold sales	....	....	+93	+132	....	+225
German gold subscription to IMF	....	....	....	....	−103	−103
Transactions with London gold pool and other diverse sources	+15	+164	+87	+30	−10	+286
Total net change	+15	+164	+405	+162	−113	+633

This table needs a few comments:

1. The item "US gold sales," as it appears in the US Treasury gold statistics, includes a special transaction in 1964, which in reality was a triangular transaction between Italy, the US and Germany. During the Italian foreign exchange crisis in the spring of 1964 (when a special support operation for the Italian lira was

mounted, with the participation of the US and of the German Bundesbank), it was agreed that the Italian authorities would pay $200 million in gold to the German authorities; for technical reasons this gold went first to the US Treasury and from there to the Bundesbank. Thus, you find in the US Treasury statistics a purchase of $200 million of gold from Italy and a simultaneous sale to Germany of the same amount.

2. The gold sales by the IMF were part and parcel of the two special support operations for the pound by the "General Arrangements to Borrow" (Group of Ten). While the "Ten" put up altogether $903 million in credits to the IMF as a means of partially refinancing the IMF loans to the UK, they also sold some of their currencies to the IMF for this same purpose against gold. The Bundesbank which contributed the largest part to the credits under the G.A.B., also got a proportionately large share of these IMF gold sales.

3. As to the London Gold Pool, the contribution and receipts of the participating central banks follow an agreed schedule.

While it is true that we have welcomed these various accruals of gold to our reserves, as they have brought the proportion of gold to total reserves more nearly to the intended magnitude, we have carefully avoided large-scale conversions at the expense of the US Treasury, in order not to "upset the apple-cart" at an untoward moment. We have fully explained this reserve policy of ours, including our considerations of international solidarity and cooperation, in the last two Annual Reports of the Bundesbank.

I do not want, however, to be misunderstood. All the foregoing considerations do not imply that we would not believe it to be justified, under normal circumstances, to convert any surplus dollars which may accrue to us beyond the limits which we consider proper. If the dollar has such a universal attraction as a reserve currency, this is due, at least in part, to the fact that the US authorities stand ready to convert it into gold for any legitimate monetary purposes.

With my best regards,

(signed) OTMAR EMMINGER.

(Mr. Despres's response to the foregoing follows:)

OCTOBER 3, 1966.

DR. OTMAR EMMINGER,
Mitglied des Direktoriums der Deutschen Bundesbank,
Frankfurt (Main), Germany.

DEAR DR. EMMINGER: I wish to acknowledge with thanks your letter of September 14. The interpretation which you placed upon my statement is alone sufficient to indicate that the statement needs clarification and elaboration, which I welcome the opportunity to provide.

Changes in German and French official reserves from the end of 1960 to the end of 1964, and from the end of 1964 to July 31, 1966, are given in Table 1 below. In Table 2, the percentage composition of German and French official reserves at each of these

TABLE 1 Changes in Official Reserves

(In millions of dollars)

	END OF 1960 TO END OF 1964	END OF 1964 TO JULY 1966	1960 TO JULY 1966
Germany:			
Gold	+1277	+54	+1331
IMF reserve position	+604	+305	+909
Foreign exchange	−1031	−582	−1613
Total	+850	−223	+627
France:			
Gold	+2088	+1388	+3476
IMF reserve position	+417	+311	+728
Foreign exchange	+947	−526	+421
Total	+3452	+1173	+4625

TABLE 2 Percentage Composition of Reserves

	DEC. 31, 1960		DEC. 31, 1964		JULY 31, 1966	
	GERMANY	FRANCE	GERMANY	FRANCE	GERMANY	FRANCE
Gold	42	72	54	65	56	75
IMF reserve position	5	9	11	11	17	13
Foreign exchange	53	19	35	24	27	12
Total	100	100	100	100	100	100

three dates is shown. These tables are derived from the figures on official reserves published in the September 1966 issue of the IMF's *International Monetary Statistics.*

Some of the significant points reflected in these tables are the following:

1. Total French reserves increased very substantially, while total German reserves showed only a moderate net increase during the period from the end of 1960 to the end of July 1966. This is ascribable to differences in the balance-of-payments positions of the two countries.

2. German official holdings of foreign exchange were steadily drawn down during the five-and-a-half-year period. French official holdings increased $0.9 billion from the end of 1960 to the end of 1964, and were drawn down $0.5 billion in the subsequent nineteen months. The decrease in French official holdings of foreign exchange in the latter period was slightly smaller than the reduction of German official holdings. The German decrease made possible a further increase in IMF and gold reserves in the face of a small payments deficit.

3. Taking the five-and-a-half-year period as a whole, the gain in French holdings of gold and IMF reserves has been ascribable primarily to the balance-of-payments surplus; the foreign exchange portion of French reserves has at all times been rather small and only a small part of the gain in gold and IMF reserves is attributable to a change in the relative share of the foreign exchange component. The foreign exchange component increased from 19 per cent at the end of 1960 to 24 per cent at the end of 1964; reflecting the change in French policy regarding international monetary matters, this ratio has subsequently been reduced to 12 per cent.

4. The increase in German holdings of gold and IMF reserves over the five-and-a-half-year period chiefly reflects a steady shift in the composition of German official reserves, and is due only secondarily to a net surplus in the balance of payments. The foreign exchange component has been steadily reduced from slightly over one-half at the end of 1960 to slightly over one-fourth at the end of July 1966.

In your letter to me of September 14, you have stressed that

German gold acquisitions have not been effected through purchases from the United States Treasury. I find it difficult to detect the significance of this point. Since the United States stands ready to sell gold to foreign central banks and monetary authorities on demand, it follows that when the demand for gold of foreign monetary authorities exceeds the supplies forthcoming from net production, the IMF or Russian or Chinese sales, the difference is made up by withdrawals from the U.S. monetary gold stock. It makes little difference whether a particular country decides to buy its gold from the United States or from some other source. The significant decisions of foreign central banks and monetary authorities are their decisions with respect to the composition of their reserves.

In stating that "the West Germans have converted more dollars into gold than the French," of course I did not mean to imply that Germany's total acquisition of gold had been greater than that of France. The German balance of payments position since 1961 would barely have permitted this even if all foreign exchange holdings had been converted into gold. I did mean to indicate that the increase in gold holdings brought about by drawing down holdings of foreign exchange (chiefly dollars, one presumes) had been greater in the case of Germany than in the case of France.

Your letter made me aware that the statement from my testimony which the New York Times selected for quotation was subject to possible misinterpretation, which I hope this elaboration will eliminate. Let me add that the intention underlying these two sentences was not to criticize German policy with respect to reserves. My intention was to prevent undue importance from being given to the recent change in French policies. I believe there is a tendency in many quarters to exaggerate the importance of the change in French policy on international monetary matters in jeopardizing stability of the international monetary system. Even before the change in policy France had continually held a relatively high fraction of its reserves in the form of gold. Moreover, the French payments surplus is unlikely to continue indefinitely at its present level. International cooperation, even without French participation, is strong and flexible enough to meet any additional pressures resulting from French actions. Consequently,

I regard the present system, because of international cooperation, as relatively invulnerable—at least so long as a moderate deficit persists in the United States balance of payments. It is not the vulnerability of the present system but its adverse effect in reducing aid to the underdeveloped world, complicating and perhaps impairing collective defense arrangements, and in hindering the international mobility of goods and capital which is the overriding problem today. The system is breeding a revived mercantilism and its apparent durability is not a source of much satisfaction to me. I regret that international cooperation, while strong enough to secure the system against crisis and breakdown, is not strong enough to reform it in a fashion conducive to free-world growth, development, and economic integration.

With cordial regards,

Yours sincerely,

EMILE DESPRES.

16 *International Financial Intermediation*[1]

I

The danger of a breakdown of the international monetary system, as it has evolved during the 1960's, is, in my judgment, exceedingly slight. In this somewhat limited sense, the system is far more resilient than is commonly believed, and fears of its imminent collapse seem quite misplaced.

The resiliency of the system is due to the deeply rooted consensus among the central banks and finance ministries of all the major countries except France regarding the necessity of preserving it and their willingness to provide such financing as may be needed to prevent strains and crises from getting utterly out of hand. The informal arrangements among central banks for mutual financial assistance have been adequately institutionalized, and their strength is not measured by the size of the publicly announced swap credits and other financial aids; when an emergency has arisen, the financial resources previously committed have been speedily supplemented to the extent needed to overcome the crisis, and this type of cooperation can be expected in the future. Moreover, central banks, whatever preferences they

1. Joint Committee Print, *Contingency Planning for U.S. International Monetary Policy,* Statement by Private Economists, submitted to the Subcommittee on International Exchange and Payments of the Joint Economic Committee, 89th Congress, Second Session, 1966, pp. 23-29.—Ed.

may entertain concerning the composition of their gold and foreign exchange reserves, recognize the need for limiting their rate of gold accumulation to amounts which the system can endure without breakdown.

Finally, a devaluation or upward revaluation of a major currency—which, if it occurred, might trigger a chain reaction of speculative capital flows—seems wholly unlikely. The large inflows of speculative capital to Germany and the Netherlands which followed the upward revaluation of the mark and the guilder in 1961 utterly discredited this device, in the minds of central bankers and financial officials, as a remedy for domestic inflation and balance-of-payments surplus, and this experiment is not likely to be repeated by other countries—despite its popularity in economics textbooks. The leadership role of the United States in mobilizing large-scale financial support to defend the pound during its successive crises of recent years has eliminated devaluation without U.S. consent as a practical policy option for the British Government so long as the United States remains willing to mobilize the further financial support which may be required in any future sterling crisis. The United States, in turn, fearing that the withdrawals which it would experience following a devaluation of sterling would exceed its contribution of resources needed to forestall devaluation, would rather finance defense of sterling than consent to its devaluation. Consequently, the present parity of the pound seems to be quite secure, and the wage freeze in Britain combined with rising costs among her industrial competitors gives promise of performing effectively the function which devaluation might otherwise have performed. The underlying deficiencies of Britain's competitive position cannot be directly remedied by wage freeze or devaluation; they arise in large part from the fact that during the 1950's Britain did not enjoy the burst of industrial investment which American aid made possible for Continental European countries. In Britain's case, American aid, instead of being used for large-scale investment in industrial expansion and modernization, served chiefly to finance capital export and overseas military commitments. The progressive retrenchment which is taking place in foreign lending and in military commitments is likely to provide the margin of resources for higher industrial investment, and the inducement to undertake such investment may be forthcoming after the full effects of the wage freeze have been felt in export markets and British monetary policy has become less severely deflationary.

Prior to 1965 France had participated hesitantly in the international monetary consensus and the French financial contributions had been modest; consequently, the change to explicit non-participation early in 1965 was not a major shift in policy. The conversion of French reserves into gold, apart from moderate working balances, appears to have been completed, and the era of large surpluses in France's balance of payments seems to be at an end. Under present conditions France is likely soon to be faced with the choice of accepting a payments deficit and a gold drain as the price for continuing her moderately expansionary fiscal and monetary policies or undergoing a retardation of growth brought about by tighter money to defend her reserves. In any event, French non-participation in the international monetary consensus does not critically impair the effectiveness of the consensus.

The outlook for the U.S. balance of payments is such that we may soon be entering a period during which we find ourselves accumulating rather than losing reserves. Despite outpayments resulting from the military involvement in Vietnam and a decreasing export surplus, the balance of payments in 1966 has shown a small surplus under the Bernstein definition and only a moderate deficit under the liquidity definition. This has been due to very substantial short-term borrowing abroad by New York banks and short- and long-term borrowing abroad by American corporations and their foreign subsidiaries. Extremely tight money plus official suasion and voluntary controls were responsible for this wholly abnormal movement of capital, and as monetary conditions become less tight repayment of short-term borrowings of American banks and corporations is to be expected as financing reverts to more normal patterns. Although the 1966 showing must be judged a temporary abnormality, there are other reasons for expecting a shift in the international payments relationships between the United States and Continental Western Europe.

Industrial capital formation and economic growth are slackening and profit margins are narrowing abroad. Under these conditions, expenditures of European subsidiaries of American corporations for new plant facilities and the acquisition of existing firms should diminish. More basically, retardation of European growth means, despite creeping inflation, a diminution in the excess of their business and personal demands for additions to liquid assets over the amounts which their domestic financial institutions are prepared to supply. This excess demand for financial intermediation, which, under unrestricted conditions, would normally be met by external finance provided largely by the American money and capital markets, is what we have mistakenly regarded as a deficit in the U.S. balance of payments. Consequently, the shrinkage of the European demand for U.S. financial intermediation which is likely to be brought about by retardation of growth abroad may be expected for a time to move the U.S. balance of payments toward what we mistakenly regard as balance.

This analysis leads to two general conclusions. First, widespread fears that we are headed toward crisis and breakdown of the international monetary system are, in my judgment, misplaced. Second, and somewhat more speculatively, the decline in the U.S. gold reserves may be checked for a time as the result of retardation of growth and lowering of interest rates abroad. (Even if this forecast is borne out by future events, it will remain desirable to abolish the statutory reserve requirement of 25 per cent against Federal Reserve notes in order to underscore that, in any future emergency, our gold holdings would be fully available for international payments purposes.) In general, therefore, we can continue to muddle through, but whether we should be satisfied to do so is an entirely different matter.

II

The grave danger inherent in existing international monetary arrangements is not that they are likely to break down but that they may endure for a long time, with highly damaging economic and political consequences.

The restoration of current account convertibility by the principal European countries at the end of 1958, following devaluation and stabilization of the French franc, brought to a conclusion the postwar reconstruction of international economic and financial relations. Import quotas had been eliminated or greatly relaxed, currencies had been stabilized, and a relatively liberal system of multilateral trade without restriction on international payments for commercial purposes was established. This fulfilled a long-standing objective of American foreign economic policy, which rested on the postulate that a regime of non-discrimination (apart from customs unions and free trade areas) and convertibility would not only serve the direct economic interests of the United States but would be broadly conducive to healthy economic and political development of the non-Communist world.

It is ironical that the whole period since the restoration of convertibility has been one of contained crisis and intense balance-of-payments preoccupations. Existing international monetary arrangements not only provide protection against an acute crisis leading to breakdown but also assure continuation of a low-grade contained crisis lasting indefinitely into the future. This is their basic defect. The long-run dangers inherent in this situation are substantial retardation of economic growth of both the industrially advanced and the low-income countries, and an increasingly mercantilist tendency in economic policies. Second only to the U.S. military involvement in Vietnam, balance-of-payments preoccupations have exerted a widely pervasive and undesirable constraining influence on both foreign and domestic policy. Even if the gold outflow is halted for a time, anxious preoccupation with the balance of payments will continue to weigh heavily upon major foreign policy and domestic economic policy decisions since, in the climate of attitudes which has now become entrenched, we shall continue to regard our liquidity position as delicate, maintaining that our position as world banker will not permit us to relax our guard. The present international monetary system is defective not because it is likely to collapse but because of the harmfulness of the financially restrictive and mercantilist measures which are applied to defend the system.

III

The main source of present difficulties is the inflated world demand for gold. The substantial private speculative accumulation of gold, motivated chiefly by the desire to profit from an anticipated devaluation of the dollar and other currencies, has been derivative in nature. The basis for these speculative anticipations and the originating source of the inflated total demand for gold has been the evident preference of most Western European central banks for gold rather than dollars as a reserve medium. Although fears of dollar devaluation may have played a part, the preference for gold is not due primarily to this cause.

In the special case of France, political factors have undoubtedly played a part in demands for gold; since the nineteenth century French governments have regarded all forms of foreign lending, whether private or official, as an instrument of foreign policy to be used for political purposes. In the case of other European countries, however, it does not appear that political considerations have been a factor.

The main source of European desires to limit accumulation of official reserves in the form of dollars is the heritage of obsolete theories regarding the way in which an international monetary system based on fixed exchange rates should function. According to traditional doctrine, which is still professed by many economists and generally accepted by central bank and financial officials, it would interfere with the proper working of a fixed exchange standard if the United States were relieved of the pressures and the discipline which a strained liquidity position entails. Consequently, although demands for gold have been limited by the general desire not to subject the international monetary mechanism to intolerable strain, within this limit demands for gold have been maintained at a sufficient level to keep pressure on the United States to balance its payments. Our evident anxiety in the face of gold losses has made this not too difficult a task.

The trouble is that the orthodox theory simply does not conform to the economic realities of the present-day world. My reasons for this view were stated in hearings before the Subcommittee on International Exchange and Payments on September 9, 1966 (see Paper 15 of the present volume), and I also submitted a proposal for shifting prevailing asset preferences from gold to dollars through certain steps which would result in a partial demonetization of gold (see Paper 14 of the present volume). It seems unnecessary to repeat these views and this proposal here. A few supplementary observations are given below.

IV

Under a regime of fixed exchange rates, generally low tariffs, and convertible currencies, and an unrestricted international market for loan capital, quite substantial upward or downward fluctuations in aggregate domestic demand for goods and services can be accommodated without serious inflationary or deflationary consequences. In an open economy of this sort, a growth in domestic demand which outpaces the growth of output is largely compensated by shifts in the external trade balance, thus minimizing the domestic inflationary consequences which excess demand in a closed economy, or an economy in which imports competitive with domestic production are restricted by high tariffs or quotas, would produce. In an open economy the inflow of goods responds sensitively and limits the rise in prices. Provided the country enjoys good credit standing, the shift in the trade balance can be financed by attracting foreign capital through a moderate rise in interest rates.

This capital inflow not only permits domestic investment to outrun domestic saving by financing increased imports; the gross capital inflow serves also to meet a part of the growing demand for liquid assets which accompanies economic expansion. Within a stable external environment this process of rising capital inflow can continue so long as the general growth of productivity, including appropriate expansion of efficient export earning and import substitution activities, is sufficient to give no grounds for questioning the country's ability to service its rising external debt. It should be noted that in this typical case, the balance of payments moves into surplus through buoyant growth of demand, since the external financing meets some of the growing demand for liquid financial assets as well as for goods and services.

By the same token, a retardation in domestic demand relative to output will shift the trade balance toward net exports, lower interest rates, reduce capital inflow, and move the balance of payments toward reduced surplus as domestic banks and other intermediaries meet a larger share of the diminished growth in demand for liquid assets.

The foregoing simplified analysis has been put forward to illustrate the accommodating role of international capital movements which traditional doctrine largely ignores. With a properly functioning international capital market countries with good credit standing need owned reserves only in amounts sufficient to assure prospective lenders of their credit worthiness. Subject only to credit standing, the international ebb and flow of capital frees them of any balance-of-payments discipline as this is conventionally defined. The accommodating role of capital movements permits flexible adaptation of the current account to changing domestic economic circumstances.

A properly functioning international capital market cannot be sustained, however, if gold is demanded on a large scale in exchange for the liquid claims which its financial intermediation generates. Such demands result in restriction of capital outflow, tight money, or both. The balance-of-payments discipline imposed on the financial center thus reacts back upon the clients.

It is important to note the close interrelationship which must exist between the international mobility of goods and of loan capital. If goods movements are restricted by high tariffs and quotas, shifts in the trade balance cannot do much to mitigate domestic inflationary or deflationary tendencies. Under these circumstances, a high degree of international mobility of loan capital would be undesirable since it would complicate the task of the central bank in attempting to curb inflation or deflation by monetary policy.

By the same token, it is hard under present-day conditions to conceive of a regime of low tariffs integrating national markets for goods into a world market without a parallel international mobility of loan capital. Although much of the theory of international trade assumes a close balancing of imports and exports, it is conspicuously evident that countries with limited credit standing almost invariably rely heavily on import controls to balance their international payments. If the primary cause of impaired credit standing is inflation and currency overvaluation, as in several Latin American countries, a major benefit of financial stabilization would be to facilitate import liberalization and attract private loan capital.

V

A fundamental and insufficiently discussed issue is whether to encourage or limit severely the international mobility of untied loan capital. Severe limitation goes hand in hand with increasing restriction of trade. The likely outcome would be a division of the world economy into rather insulated economic blocs within each of which goods movements and financial movements would be relatively free. This seems to me highly undesirable, but it should be recognized that the other alternative involves major problems. It needs to be complemented by further reduction of tariff barriers lest the mobility of loan capital between the United States and Europe outrun the mobility of goods.

It is widely recognized that centralized economic planning of the Soviet type has been biased toward self-sufficiency, since planning of international trade raises special complications and involves some loss of control. It is now becoming evident that the aggregative type of national economic planning through monetary and fiscal policy which is generally practiced in the mixed private-enterprise economies of the non-Communist world introduces some desire for insulation of capital markets in order to avoid impairing the usefulness of monetary policy for domestic stabilization. International mobility of loan capital limits the scope for national differences in open market interest rates. The United States, as the financial center, would determine through its monetary policy the level of interest rates around which interest rates elsewhere would have to cluster.

Decisions on U.S. monetary policy would have to be made in collaboration with other members of the Group of Ten on the basis of general requirements of free-world economic stability. The remaining task of achieving strictly domestic economic stabilization would be left chiefly to fiscal policy in each country, although special controls over residential mortgage rates and agricultural credit, as well as tax incentives to industrial investment, would still be instruments of domestic stabilization. The dangers of undue reliance on monetary policy as a domestic stabilization device have recently become apparent, however, both in the United States and several other countries, and it is evident that a shift in policy mix is desirable on other grounds.

17 *The Dollar and World Liquidity: a Minority View*[1]

The consensus in Europe and the United States on the United States balance of payments and world liquidity runs about like this:

1. Abundant liquidity has been provided since World War II less by newly mined gold than by the increase in liquid dollar assets generated by U.S. balance-of-payments deficits.

2. These deficits are no longer available as a generator of liquidity because the accumulation of dollars has gone so far that it has undermined confidence in the dollar.

3. To halt the present creeping decline in liquidity through central-bank conversions of dollars into gold, and to forestall headlong flight from the dollar, it is necessary above all else to correct the United States deficit.

4. When the deficit has been corrected, the growth of world reserves may, or probably will, become inadequate. Hence there is a need for planning new means of adding to world reserves—along the lines suggested by Triffin, Bernstein, Roosa, Stamp, Giscard, and others.[2]

1. Written with Charles P. Kindleberger and Walter S. Salant. Brookings Institution Reprint 115 (1966). This article, with several sentences omitted, originally appeared in *The Economist* (London), February 5, 1966.—Ed.

2. For one of many good discussions of the proposals by Triffin, Bernstein and Stamp, as well as others not mentioned above, see *Plans for Reform of the Inter-*

So much is widely agreed. There is a difference in tactics between those who would correct the U.S. balance of payments by raising interest rates—bankers on both sides of the ocean and European central bankers—and those in the United States who would correct it, if necessary, by capital restrictions, so that tight money in the United States may be avoided while labor and other resources are still idle. There is also a difference of emphasis between the Continentals, who urge adjustment (proposition 3 above), and the Anglo-Saxons, who stress the need for more liquidity (proposition 4). British voices urge more liquidity now, rather than in the future. But with these exceptions, the lines of analysis converge.

Four Counter-Propositions

There is room, however, for a minority view which would oppose this agreement with a sharply differing analysis. In outline, it asserts the following counter-propositions:

1. While the United States has provided the world with liquid dollar assets in the postwar period by capital outflow and aid exceeding its current account surplus, in most years this excess has not reflected a deficit in a sense representing disequilibrium. The outflow of U.S. capital and aid has filled not one but two needs. First, it has supplied goods and services to the rest of the world. But secondly, to the extent that its loans to foreigners are offset by foreigners putting their own money into liquid dollar assets, the U.S. has not overinvested but has supplied financial intermediary services. The "deficit" has reflected largely the second process, in which the United States has been lending, mostly at long

---

national Monetary System by Fritz Machlup, Special Paper in International Economics No. 3, revised March 1964 (International Finance Section, Department of Economics, Princeton University). See also *World Monetary Reform: Plans and Issues,* edited by Herbert Grubel (Stanford University Press, Stanford, 1963). For Robert V. Roosa's present views, see his *Monetary Reform for the World Economy* (for Council on Foreign Relations by Harper and Row, New York and Evanston, 1965). An English translation of the suggestions by M. Valéry Giscard d'Estaing, made when he was Minister of Finance and Economic Affairs of France, may be found in various speeches published under the title *Statements Made by M. Valéry Giscard d'Estaing on International Monetary Problems,* Collection Ouvertures Economiques (L'Economie, Paris, 1965).

and intermediate term, and borrowing short. This financial intermediation, in turn, performs two functions: it supplies loans and investment funds to foreign enterprises which have to pay more domestically to borrow long-term money and which cannot get the amounts they want at any price; and it supplies liquidity to foreign asset-holders, who receive less for placing their short-term deposits at home. Essentially, this is a trade in liquidity, which is profitable to both sides. Differences in their liquidity preferences (i.e., in their willingness to hold their financial assets in long-term rather than in quickly encashable forms and to have short-term rather than long-term liabilities outstanding against them) create differing margins between short-term and long-term interest rates. This in turn creates scope for trade in financial assets, just as differing comparative costs create the scope for mutually profitable trade in goods. This trade in financial assets has been an important ingredient of economic growth outside the United States.

2. Such lack of confidence in the dollar as now exists has been generated by the attitudes of government officials, central bankers, academic economists, and journalists, and reflects their failure to understand the implications of this intermediary function. Despite some contagion from these sources, the private market retains confidence in the dollar, as increases in private holdings of liquid dollar assets show. Private speculation in gold is simply the result of the known attitudes and actions of governmental officials and central bankers.

3. With capital markets unrestricted, attempts to correct the "deficit" by ordinary macro-economic weapons are likely to fail. It may be possible to expand the current surplus at first by deflation of United States income and prices relative to those of Europe; but gross financial capital flows will still exceed real transfer of goods and services (i.e., involve financial intermediation, lending long-term funds to Europe in exchange for short-term deposits) so long as capital formation remains high in Europe. A moderate rise of interest rates in the United States will have only a small effect on the net capital outflow. A drastic rise might cut the net outflow substantially, but only by tightening money in *Europe* enough to stop economic growth; and this would cut

America's current account surplus. Correcting the United States deficit by taxes and other controls on capital, which is being attempted on both sides of the Atlantic, is likely either to fail, or to succeed by impeding international capital flows so much as to cut European investment and growth.

4. While it is desirable to supplement gold with an internationally created reserve asset, the conventional analysis leading to this remedy concentrates excessively on a country's external liquidity; it takes insufficient account of the demands of savers for internal liquidity and of borrowers in the same country for long-term funds. The international private capital market, properly understood, provides both external liquidity to a country, and the kinds of assets and liabilities that private savers and borrowers want and cannot get at home. Most plans to create an international reserve asset, however, are addressed only to external liquidity problems which in many cases, and especially in Europe today, are the less important issue.

With agreement between the United States and Europe—but without it if necessary—it would be possible to develop a monetary system which provided the external liquidity that is needed and also recognized the role of international financial intermediation in world economic growth.

Europe Needs Dollars

Analytical support and elaboration of this minority view is presented in numbered sections, conforming to the propositions advanced above as an alternative to the consensus.

1. The idea that the balance of payments of a country is in disequilibrium if it is in deficit on the liquidity (U.S. Department of Commerce) definition is not appropriate to a country with a large and open capital market that is performing the function of a financial intermediary. Banks and other financial intermediaries, unlike traders, are paid to give up liquidity. The United States is no more in deficit when it lends long and borrows short than is a bank when it makes a loan and enters a deposit on its books.

Financial intermediation is an important function in a monetary economy. Savers want liquid assets; borrowers investing in fixed capital expansion are happier with funded rather than quick liabilities. Insofar as the gap is not bridged, capital formation is held down. Europeans borrow from the United States, and Americans are willing to pay higher prices for European assets than European investors will, partly because capital is more readily available in the United States than in Europe, but mainly because liquidity preference in Europe is higher and because capital markets in Europe are much less well organized, more monopolistically controlled, and just plain smaller than in the United States. With unrestricted capital markets, the European savers who want cash and the borrowers who prefer to extend their liabilities into the future can both be satisfied when the United States capital market lends long and borrows short and when it accepts smaller margins between its rates for borrowing short and lending short. European borrowers of good credit standing will seek to borrow in New York (or in the Euro-dollar market, which is a mere extension of New York) when rates of interest are lower on dollar loans than on loans in European currencies, or when the amounts required are greater than their domestic capital markets can provide. But when interferences prevent foreign intermediaries from bridging the gap, and when domestic private intermediaries cannot bridge it while the public authorities will not, borrowing possibilities are cut, and investment and growth are cut with it.

The effects are not confined to Europe, or even to the advanced countries. Slower European growth means lower demand for primary products imported from the less-developed countries. Preoccupation of the United States, Britain, and now Germany with their balances of payments dims the outlook for foreign aid and worsens the climate for trade liberalization. And the American capital controls are bound to reduce the access of less-developed countries to private capital and bond loans in the United States—and indirectly in Europe.

2. It may be objected that no bank can keep lending if its depositors are unwilling to hold its liabilities. True. But savings can never be put to productive use if the owners of wealth are unwilling to hold financial assets and insist on what they consider a more "ultimate" means of payment. If the bank is sound, the trouble comes from the depositors' irrationality. The remedy

is to have a lender of last resort to cope with the effects of their attitudes or, better, to educate them or, if neither is possible, to make the alternative asset (which, against the dollar, is gold) less attractive or less available. To prevent the bank from pursuing unsound policies—if it really tends to do so—it is not necessary to allow a run on it. The depositors can have their say in less destructive ways, e.g., through participating in the management of the bank of last resort or through agreement on the scale of the financial intermediation.

The nervousness of monetary authorities and academic economists is a consequence of the way they define a deficit and the connotations they attach to it. No bank could survive in such an analytical world. If financial authorities calculated a balance of payments for New York vis-à-vis the interior of the United States, they would find it in serious "deficit," since short-term claims of the rest of the country on New York mount each year. If they applied their present view of international finance, they would impose restrictions on New York's bank loans to the interior and on its purchases of new bond and stock issues. Similarly, the balance of payments of the U.S. financial sector consists almost entirely of above-the-line disbursements and therefore nearly equal "deficits." Between 1947 and 1964 the liquid liabilities (demand and time deposits) of member banks of the Federal Reserve System alone increased from $110 billion to $238 billion. This increase of $128 billion, or 116 per cent, was not matched by an equal absolute or even proportionate increase in cash reserves. Indeed, these reserves increased only $1.6 billion, or 8 per cent. Yet nobody regards this cumulated "deficit" of over $126 billion as cause for alarm.

The private market has not been alarmed about the international position of the dollar in relation to other currencies or the liquidity of the United States. Although there has been private speculation in gold against the dollar, it has been induced largely by reluctance of some central banks to accumulate dollars. The dollar is the world's standard of value; the Euro-dollar market dominates capital markets in Europe; and the foreign dollar bond market has easily outdistanced the unit-of-account bond and the European "parallel bond." As one looks at sterling and the major

Continental currencies, it is hard to imagine any one of them stronger than the dollar today, five years from now, or twenty years hence. Admittedly, short-term destabilizing speculation against the dollar is possible, largely as a consequence of errors of official and speculative judgment. It can be contained, however, by gold outflows and support from other central banks, or by allowing the dollar to find its own level in world exchange markets, buttressed by the combination of high productivity and responsible fiscal and monetary policy in the United States. In the longer run, as now in the short, the dollar is strong, not weak.

3. Since the U.S. "deficit" is the result of liquidity exchanges or financial intermediation, it will persist as long as capital movement is free, European capital markets remain narrower and less competitive than that of the United States, liquidity preferences differ between the United States and Europe, and capital formation in Western Europe remains vigorous. In these circumstances, an effort to adjust the current account to the capital outflow is futile. The deficit can be best attacked by perfecting and eventually integrating European capital markets and moderating the European asset-holder's insistence on liquidity, understandable though the latter may be after half a century of wars, inflations, and capital levies.

An attempt to halt the capital outflow by raising interest rates in the United States either would have little effect over any prolonged period or else would cripple European growth. With European capital markets joined to New York by substantial movements of short-term funds and bonds, the rate structure in the world as a whole will be set by the major financial center, in this instance New York. Interest-rate changes in the outlying centers will have an impact on capital flows to them. Higher interest rates in New York will raise rates in the world as a whole.

The effort is now being made to "correct the deficit" by restricting capital movements. Success in this effort is dubious, however, for two reasons.

Money Is Fungible

In the first place, money is fungible. Costless to store and to transport, it is the easiest commodity to arbitrage in time and in space. Discriminating capital restrictions are only partly effective, as the United States is currently learning. Some funds that are prevented from going directly to Europe will reach there by way of the less-developed countries or via the favored few countries like Canada and Japan, which are accorded access to the New York financial market because they depend upon it for capital and for liquidity. These leaks in the dam will increase as time passes, and the present system of discriminatory controls will become unworkable in the long run. The United States will have to choose between abandoning the whole effort or plugging the leaks. Plugging the leaks, in turn, means that it must either get the countries in whose favor it discriminates to impose their own restrictions or withdraw the preferences it now gives them. Accordingly, the choices in the long run are between no restrictions, restrictions on all outflows, and establishment of what is in effect a dollar bloc, or a dollar-sterling bloc, within which funds move freely but which applies uniform controls against movements to all non-bloc countries.

In the second place, it is not enough to restrain the outflow of United States-owned capital. As Germany and Switzerland have found, to keep United States funds at home widens the spreads between short-term and long-term rates in Europe and also the spreads between the short-term rates at which European financial intermediaries borrow and lend, and so encourages repatriation of European capital already in the United States. For Europe, this effectively offsets restrictions on capital inflows. "Home is where they have to take you in." It would be possible for the United States to block the outflow of foreign capital—possible but contrary to tradition. If this door is left open, the $57 billion of foreign capital in the United States permit substantial net capital outflows, even without an outflow of U.S. capital. Although it would require powerful forces indeed to induce foreign holders to dispose of most of their American investments, they might dispose of enough to permit the "deficit" to continue for a long time.

4. Capital restrictions to correct the deficit, even if feasible, would still leave unanswered a fundamental question. Is it wise to destroy an efficient system of providing internal and external liquidity—the international capital market—and substitute for it

one or another contrived device of limited flexibility for creating additions to international reserve assets alone? In the crisis of 1963, Italy borrowed $1.6 billion in the Euro-dollar market; under the Bernstein plan it would have had access to less than one-tenth of the incremental created liquidity of, say, $1 billion a year, perhaps $75 million in one year—a derisible amount. It would be the stuff of tragedy for the world's authorities laboriously to obtain agreement on a planned method of providing international reserve assets if that method, through analytical error, unwittingly destroyed an important source of liquid funds for European savers and of loans for European borrowers, and a flexible instrument for the international provision of liquidity. Moreover, agreement on a way of creating additional international reserve assets will not necessarily end the danger that foreigners under the influence of conventional analysis, will want to convert dollars into gold whenever they see what they consider a "deficit."

But, it will be objected, the fears of the European authorities about the dollar are facts of life, and the United States must adjust to them. Several points may be made by way of comment.

Europe Squeezes Itself

In the first place, the European authorities must be learning how much international trade in financial claims means to their economies, now that it has been reduced. Europe has discovered that liquidity in the form of large international reserves bears no necessary relationship to ability to supply savers with liquid assets or industrial borrowers with long-term funds in countries where financial intermediation is inadequately performed and which are cut off from the world capital market. Financial authorities in Italy, France, and even Germany have lately been trying to moderate the high interest rates which reflect strong domestic liquidity preference and the wide margins between the rates at which their intermediaries borrow and lend, as well as (in the case of Germany) their own policies. Having scant success in getting households, banks, or private intermediaries to buy long-term securities, these authorities are increasingly entering the market themselves. Investment is declining: in Germany with long-term interest rates touching 8 per cent for the best borrowers, in Italy despite Bank of Italy purchases of industrial securities, and in France where government bonds are issued to provide capital to a limited list of industrial investors. It is ironic that United States firms seem able to borrow in Europe more easily than European firms, as they continue investing in Europe while abiding by their Government's program of voluntary capital restraint. Given their liquid capital strength in the United States, they have no objection to borrowing short, and command a preferred status when they choose to borrow long. But their operations in Europe put pressure on European long-term rates and enhance the incentive of other European borrowers and United States lenders to evade the restrictions.

Europe's own capital markets cannot equal that of the United States in breadth, liquidity, and competitiveness in the foreseeable future. Europe must therefore choose between an open international capital market, using fiscal policy to impose any needed restraints, and use of monetary restraint with an insulated capital market. The second alternative involves serious dangers. Without substantial European government lending to industry, which is unlikely, the terms on which long-term money would be available may cause industrial stagnation.

The first choice is the more constructive one, but it can work only if its implications are understood in both Europe and the United States. The United States, too, has failed to appreciate the role of New York in the world monetary system and has acquiesced in the Continental view of the U.S. payments position. It must be recognized that trading in financial assets with the United States means a United States "deficit"; United States capital provides not only goods and services, but liquid assets to Europe, which means European acquisition of dollars. Moreover, the amount of dollars that private savers in Europe will want to acquire for transactions and as a partial offset to debts in dollars, and for other purposes, will increase. This increase in privately held dollars will involve a rising trend in the United States deficit on the Department of Commerce definition, though no deficit on the Bernstein Committee definition.

But that is not all. The new liquid saving in Europe which is matched by European borrowing in the United States is not likely to be held largely in dollars, and certainly will not be held entirely so. Savers typically want liquidity in their own currencies, and so do banks. If household and commercial banks want to hold liquid assets at home rather than securities or liquid assets in dollars, the counterpart of foreign borrowing by industry must be held by the central bank of their country in dollars, or converted into gold. This implies a deficit for the United States even on the Bernstein Committee definition.

Whether householders and banks want to hold dollars or their own national currencies, the effect is the same: both alternatives now frighten the United States as well as Europe. They should not. And they would not if it were recognized that financial intermediation implies a decline in the liquidity of the intermediary as much when the intermediation is being performed in another country as when it is being performed domestically. An annual growth in Europe's dollar-holdings averaging, perhaps, $1½ to $2 billion a year or perhaps more for a long time is normal expansion for a bank the size of the United States with a fast-growing world as its body of customers. To the extent that European capital markets achieve greater breadth, liquidity, and competitiveness, the rates of increase in these dollar holdings consistent with given rates of world economic growth would of course be lower than when these markets have their present deficiencies. But whatever rate of growth in these dollar holdings is needed, the point is that they not only provide external liquidity to other countries, but are a necessary counterpart of the intermediation which provides liquidity to Europe's savers and financial institutions. Recognition of this fact would end central bank conversions of dollars into gold, the resulting creeping decline of official reserves, and the disruption of capital flows to which it has led.

It must be admitted that free private capital markets are sometimes destabilizing. When they are, the correct response is determined governmental counter-action to support the currency that is under pressure until the crisis has been weathered. Walter Bagehot's dictum of 1870 still stands: in a crisis, discount freely. Owned reserves cannot provide for these eventualities, as International Monetary Fund (IMF) experience amply demonstrates.

Amounts agreed in advance are almost certain to be too little, and they tip the hand of the authorities to the speculators. The rule is discount freely, and tidy up afterwards, transferring outstanding liabilities to the IMF, the General Arrangements to Borrow, or even into funded government-to-government debts such as were used to wind up the European Payments Union. Owned reserves or readily available discounting privileges on the scale needed to guard against these crises of confidence would be inflationary in periods of calm.

Let the Gold Go

Mutual recognition of the role of dollar holdings would provide the most desirable solution, but if, nevertheless, Europe unwisely chooses to convert dollars into gold, the United States could restore a reserve-currency system, even without European cooperation in reinterpreting deficits and lifting capital restrictions. The decision would call for cool heads in the United States. The real problem is to build a strong international monetary mechanism resting on credit, with gold occupying, at most, a subordinate position. Because the dollar is in a special position as a world currency, the United States can bring about this change through its own action. Several ways in which it can do so have been proposed, including widening the margin around parity at which it buys and sells gold, reducing the price at which it buys gold, and otherwise depriving gold of its present unlimited convertibility into dollars. The United States would have to allow its gold stock to run down as low as European monetary authorities chose to take it. If they took it all, which is unlikely, the United States would have no alternative but to allow the dollar to depreciate until the capital flow came to a halt, or, much more likely, until the European countries decided to stop the depreciation by holding the dollars they were unwilling to hold before. If this outcome constituted a serious possibility, it seems evident that European countries would cease conversion of dollars into gold well short of the last few billions.

This strategy has been characterized by *The Economist* as the "new nationalism" in the United States. It can reasonably be interpreted, however, as internationalism. It would enable the United States to preserve the international capital market and thereby protect the rate of world economic growth, even without European cooperation.

While United States-European cooperation in maintaining the international capital market is the preferable route, it requires recognizing that an effective, smoothly functioning international capital market is itself an instrument of world economic growth, not a nuisance which can be disposed of and the function of which can be transferred to new or extended intergovernmental institutions, and it requires abandoning on both sides of the Atlantic the view that a U.S. deficit, whether on the Department of Commerce or the Bernstein Committee definition, is not compatible with equilibrium. Abandonment of this view, in turn, requires facing up to the fact that the economic analysis of the textbooks—derived from the writing and the world of David Hume and modified only by trimmings—is no longer adequate in a world that is increasingly moving (apart from government interferences) toward an integrated capital and money market. In these circumstances, the main requirement of international monetary reform is to preserve and improve the efficiency of the private capital market while building protection against its performing in a destabilizing fashion.

The majority view has been gaining strength since 1958, when Triffin first asserted that the dollar and the world were in trouble. Between 1958 and 1965 world output and trade virtually doubled, the United States dollar recovered from a slight overvaluation, and the gold hoarders have forgone large earnings and capital gains. Having been wrong in 1958 on the near-term position, the consensus may be more wrong today, when its diagnosis and prognosis are being followed. But this time the generally accepted analysis can lead to a brake on European growth. Its error may be expensive, not only for Europe but for the whole world.

18 *Gold–Where To From Here?*[1]

This memorandum presents some views concerning (1) a few of the problems of international monetary structure following the "gold pool" communique of March 17, 1968, and the Stockholm agreement, and (2) the question of U.S. policy toward the balance of payments.

The International Monetary System

The gold pool communique is a major turning point in the evolution of the international monetary system, although its full implications, and its results, will be realized only gradually. To an outside observer, two major factors seemed to provide the basis for the agreements reached at the meeting of March 16-17. In the first place, the common desire to preserve fixed exchange rates among the major currencies was exceedingly strong, and it had become quite evident, as a result of the positions taken by the United States representatives at earlier meetings, that the United States would not devalue in relation to gold under any conceivable circumstances. If the worse came to the worst, gold payments would simply be suspended and other countries would be faced

1. Statement prepared for a meeting of academic consultants to the Board of Governors of the Federal Reserve System, April 25, 1968.—Ed.

with the stark choice of allowing their currencies to appreciate or accepting dollars. If stability of rates was to be maintained, the burden would fall on countries other than the United States and their leverage in influencing American policies would be weakened. By halting the gold drain into private speculative holdings while the United States still held about one-fourth of the world's monetary gold, some role for gold in the international monetary system might be preserved, and additional time could be gained for reaching agreement on mutually acceptable methods of international settlement.

Second, it became clear to the Europeans, as a result of the Administration's proposals to tax tourism, its consideration of import surcharges and export rebates, and lively Congressional interest in import quotas, that a continued gold crisis could launch a new wave of protectionism, reversing the progress towards trade liberalization which had culminated in the Kennedy Round. The supply of relatively mild measures of direct control over the balance of payments had been nearly exhausted, and any further direct measures were likely to have drastic and unwelcome consequences.

The gold pool communique seems to involve an implicit recognition on all sides that the linchpin of the system is not the dollar's special tie to gold but the common desire of the governments and monetary authorities of the major countries to preserve stability of exchange rates. If this interpretation is correct, the climate for negotiating further needed reform of the international payments system has become more favorable.

It will be necessary over the coming months to put the new policies stated in the gold pool communique fully into effect. The effective establishment of a two-tiered market for gold involves a number of problems, not all of which are merely technical. The full operation of a two-tiered system depends upon preventing any substantial leakage of gold in either direction between monetary stocks and the outside market. With respect to leakage into the outside market, the communique is unambiguous both in terminating sales by the gold pool members themselves and in discouraging selling by other central banks. Although there is no immediate reason to expect substantial sales in the private market by other central banks, it would be desirable, as rapidly as circumstances permit, to secure the formal assent of other central banks to this policy.

With respect to purchases by monetary authorities if the outside price of gold should fall to the neighborhood of $35, the communique states a view but not the explicit decision which that view implies. It would be desirable to make that decision explicitly when it becomes practicable to do so. Failure to do so explicitly may have reflected less than complete agreement on this point among the members of the former gold pool. Moreover, several of the provisions of the IMF Articles of Agreement require amendment or reinterpretation if the future possibility of leakage of gold from the outside market into monetary holdings is to be effectively foreclosed.

A matter of greater immediate importance relates to the implementation of the agreement "to cooperate even more closely than in the past to minimize flows of funds contributing to instability in the exchange markets, and to offset as necessary any such flows that may arise." Since the 1961 upward revaluation of the mark and guilder and its aftermath, there has until recently been little speculation against the dollar vis-à-vis foreign currencies. Those who expected dollar devaluation foresaw a general devaluation of currencies against gold which would leave exchange rates unaltered. In recent months, however, the idea has taken hold that the dollar is fundamentally overvalued and the mark fundamentally undervalued, and that this will lead to realignment of the exchange rate. Whatever one may think of the validity of this view, it has constituted a speculative factor of substantial magnitude and the possibility exists that speculation on a change in the mark-dollar rate will continue to mount. Substantial purchases of forward dollars by the Bundesbank, together with the general measures in effect in Germany to curb the inflow of foreign funds, have served to offset these speculative pressures; if speculation mounts, the scale of official intervention required to hold the present exchange rate may have to be substantially increased. Since speculation did succeed in toppling sterling despite massive official support, it is now doubly difficult to convince the market that adequate resources are now committed to offset even very large movements of "hot money." It would be useful, in this connection, if instead of waiting until speculation becomes hectic, an announcement could be made in advance of the size of the additional commitments which have been made in accordance with the policy stated in the gold pool communique.

The Balance-of-Payments Question

The preceding paragraphs have enumerated some specific problems which arise in implementing the general policies stated in the gold pool communique. The underlying assumption was that the commitment to maintain stable rates among the major currencies is very firm, and that gold will play a relatively small role in international settlements. This still leaves open the possibility that direct balance-of-payments measures, both controls and taxes or subsidies, will be extended further, but there appears to be considerable awareness of the substantial disadvantages of proceeding further along these lines. If flexible rates and further use of direct controls are definitely rejected, it may not be excessively optimistic to believe that governments and central banks will increasingly accept the necessity to effect international settlements through transfer of financial assets on a sufficient scale to make the system work despite the lack of an adjustment mechanism.

In appraising this possibility, three possible courses of development must be considered. (1) If the United States can maintain fairly stable growth while avoiding a sustained rate of inflation which the other advanced industrial countries find unacceptably high, other countries may increasingly acquiesce in accumulating financial claims in a variety of forms to the extent required for settlement of international payments at stable exchange rates. (2) If the American economy undergoes prolonged deflation, which seems unlikely, other countries might turn to devaluation or depreciation as a means of cushioning the effects on their economies of American deflation. (3) If the United States undergoes sustained inflation at an unacceptably high rate, other countries may come to prefer appreciation against the dollar rather than accept the combination of larger-than-desired export surpluses and domestic inflation which the American inflation would impose upon them at stable exchange rates. Subject to the major qualifications stated in (2) and (3) above, it is my view that the U.S. balance of payments will tend increasingly to take care of itself if the international monetary system is so revised as to take into account the legitimate, indeed necessary, financial role of the United States in world economic growth.

This does not mean that a U.S. balance-of-payments deficit would necessarily be a permanent feature of the world economic environment. Much depends upon the evolution of the Euro-dollar market, the pace of integration of European capital markets, and largely unpredictable changes in asset preferences both in the U.S. and abroad. The United States, by reason of its financial size, will continue to serve, however, as the central money and capital market. Its backstopping role in relation to other financial markets is not accidental nor easily altered. The smooth performance of this role requires a willingness on the part of other monetary authorities to acquire such amounts of external financial assets as may be necessary. These need not be dollar assets. The claims can be direct or indirect (e.g., intermediated by the IMF) and could be denominated in dollars, dollars with exchange guarantee, or foreign currencies.

If the evolution of the international monetary system does proceed along this path, inequalities between the U.S. current account balance and autonomous capital movements will be settled by accommodating transfers of financial assets, in a fashion which somewhat resembles the process of domestic interregional settlement. In such a framework, the concept of balance-of-payments equilibrium and, with it, the distinction between financing and adjustment lose meaning.

It will doubtless be objected that this is wildly overoptimistic and that no such open-ended readiness to accept settlement in financial assets is in sight. If, however, acquisition of financial claims is preferred by governments and monetary authorities to any alternative options (appreciation, inflation, or controls), this is sufficient to assure the workability of the system. The limits within which accommodating movements of financial assets can be utilized in international settlements have been substantially extended, and this seems to me to point the direction of future evolution.

This evolutionary process, however, will involve a great deal of pulling and hauling, which performs an essential role in converting mere consultation on monetary and fiscal policy into an effective method of reciprocal suasion.

If stability of exchange rates is to be preserved, today's central problem is the confidence problem. It is a common belief that the restoration of confidence in the dollar depends simply and directly on a substantial reduction of the U.S. deficit. This belief is erroneous. The relation between the state of confidence and the size of the deficit is tenuous and complex.

A few examples may illustrate the point. The British balance-of-payments deficit, using the British definition, which approximates the "basic balance" concept, declined from £731 million in 1964 to £238 million in 1965, £176 million in 1966, and turned into a surplus of £175 million in the first half of 1967. Despite this improvement, the Middle East crisis and the dock strike were sufficient to topple the pound. This illustrates strikingly the failure of substantial improvement in the balance of payments to bolster the demand for sterling.

To take a much older example, the United States lost over $700 million of gold, or one-seventh of its gold stock, in the six weeks following Britain's suspension of gold payments in September 1931 and suffered further substantial gold losses in the spring of 1932, although at both times and throughout the world depression of the thirties the U.S. balance of payments was heavily in surplus. These gold losses were due to flights from the dollar by both official and private holders.

Again, Switzerland in the early 1960's ran a large current account deficit and also increased its long-term investment abroad. Yet the demand for Swiss francs was so strong that the increase in Switzerland's short-term foreign liabilities not only financed the deficit but provided large additions to gold reserves.

In the case of a country which is an international banking and financial center, changes in the amount of liquid balances which the world desires to hold in its currency can overwhelm balance-of-payments influences in producing strength or weakness in the currency. Moreover, for such countries there is no simple and direct relation between the state of confidence, as reflected in the demand for liquid balances, and the balance of payments. Constant reiteration of the proposition that the state of the balance of payments determines the strength or weakness of the dollar has doubtless created a somewhat closer connection than would otherwise exist. Balance-of-payments statistics have become headline news. It is, nevertheless, of importance to make the distinction, because some policies or developments having only small balance-of-payments effects might have a substantial effect in strengthening the dollar, while other measures, although reducing the deficit, would probably increase pressure against the dollar.

The general belief that progress towards de-escalation or settlement in Vietnam would strengthen the dollar seems to me wholly valid. This would be due primarily, however, to the effect on confidence and only slightly to the direct balance-of-payments effect. The balance-of-payments item representing offshore expenditures due to the Vietnam war is estimated at about $1.5 billion for 1967. A substantial part of this expenditure flows back to the United States in increased expenditures for American exports by Thailand, Korea, Japan, the Philippines, and Taiwan. Consequently, the net balance-of-payments effect is smaller than is commonly supposed.

The effect of a tax increase on the confidence factor, and therefore on the demand for dollars, would undoubtedly be substantial. Its balance-of-payments effect, however, would be rather modest. At a very rough estimate, an $8 billion tax increase might increase the current account surplus by something like $400 million. This is due fundamentally to the size of the U.S. economy in relation to the world economy. Because of the low marginal ratio of goods and services imports to GNP, a decrease of 2 per cent in growth of GNP might reduce imports by something like $800 million, but since U.S. imports, although small in relation to GNP, are a large fraction of total world trade, a substantial part of the reduction in imports would be offset by decreased export sales. One implication of this is that the application of stop-go policies, whatever their justification in the case of countries with high foreign trade ratios, is futile for the United States.

To press deflationary measures beyond the point which is judged desirable for domestic stabilization reasons would have only slight balance-of-payments effects in comparison with its costs in employment and output. Nor would excessive deflationary zeal in fiscal policy be likely to improve the state of confidence in the dollar, since such policies would undoubtedly be regarded as politically unsustainable.

In contrast to deflationary fiscal measures, severely tight money can have large effects in reducing the balance-of-payments deficit, as the 1966 experience showed. The effect on confidence, however, is quite another matter. The balance-of-payments improvement is correctly regarded as temporary and abnormal. Moreover, tight money is likely to impose severe pressure on such currencies as the pound, the Canadian dollar, and the yen, and evidence of weakness in these currencies, calling for official support operations through sales of U.S. dollars, will weaken the dollar by calling into question the stability of the existing exchange rate structure.

To the extent that the dollar's strength or weakness is influenced by the balance-of-payments position, it is the combined balance of payments of the dollar-pound area rather than the U.S. balance of payments alone which is chiefly relevant.

INDEX

Index

Agriculture, 65, 79, 81, 89, 265; *see also* individual countries; Primary products
Argentina, 11, 17, 52
Asset preferences, 224, 230, 241, 245, 260-64, 268-70, 274-76, 280-84
Australia, 11, 176

Bagehot, Walter, 276
Balance of payments, 28-55, 59, 63, 70-75, 180, 232-44, 258-71, 275-78, 282-85; *see also* individual countries
Bank of England, 4, 5, 8, 9, 75
Bernstein, E. M., 259, 275, 276, 278
Brazil, 190-206; agriculture, 204-6; banking system, 194-98, 202, 206; bankruptcy, 201-3; capital, 195-98, 200-206; controls, 190, 196; currency, 198, 200, 205; development, 190-91, 200-203; distortions, 198-99, 204; exchange rate, 205-6; forced savings, 188, 195, 203-4; foreign exchange, 190-91, 194, 198, 200-201, 205; imports, 198, 200, 205-6; inflation, 184, 192, 195-203, 206; interest rates, 191-92, 198, 200-205; investment, 199-204; monetary policy, 195, 197, 199, 203; prices, 196, 199-202; saving, 195, 198-99, 203-4; taxes, 191; wages, 196
Bretton Woods Agreement, 45ff.; *see also* International Monetary Fund; International Bank for Reconstruction & Development
Burgess, Randolph, xi

Capital flows, 30-31, 46, 48, 59, 61, 68, 71-75, 82, 182, 232-33, 240-42, 256-59, 263-68, 272-73, 281-82
Capital shortage, 43, 263, 269-70
Clark, Colin, 57
Comparative advantage, 61, 69, 76-77, 79

Currency, convertibility, 38, 72, 74, 183, 231, 236, 260, 263; valuation, 38, 75-76, 93, 98, 189, 219, 261, 264, 278, 280-81, 284; *see also* Devaluation; Dollar; Foreign exchange
Customs union, *see* Free trade; European Common Market

Deflation, 44, 47-49, 54, 71, 75, 218, 248, 263-64
De Gaulle, Charles, 215, 226, 227, 237
Demonetization of gold, *see* Gold
Despres, E., 9, 76, 80, 81, 82, 83, 84, 99, 209, 236, 239, 242, 245, 246, 247, 249, 250, 253, 256
Devaluation, 9, 37-38, 48-50, 54, 85, 189, 258, 282; *see also* Dollar; Sterling
Dollar, "bloc," xvi, 180-81, 219, 229, 273, 286; confidence, 215, 217, 221, 225, 227, 230-32, 271-72, 280-81, 284-86; conversions into gold, 216, 219-24, 251-53, 276-77; devaluation, 216, 220-21, 227, 237, 241, 244, 262, 277, 279, 281; international role, 68, 180, 213-20, 223-26, 228-29, 231, 235, 246, 253, 262, 267, 271, 276-77, 283; "shortage," 30, 67, 70-73, 83, 84, 85; standard, 225, 229
Dual-economy, 55-56

Economic blocs, 227, 238, 245, 265; *see also* European Common Market; Free trade
Economic Commission for Europe, 33, 35, 51
Economic growth, 62-63, 150, 183, 225, 229, 234, 238, 243, 248-49, 256, 259, 260-63, 268-74, 278, 282-83; *see also* European Common Market; Less developed countries
Education, 90, 97
Ellsworth, P. T., 245, 246, 247
Emminger, Otmar, 250, 253
Equilibrium, 45, 50, 52, 54-55, 57-59; international, 45, 48, 70-71, 75, 267
Euro-dollars, 231, 270-71, 274, 283
European Common Market (Economic Community), xvi; 60-85, 230-31, 235
European Payments Union, 231, 277
European Recovery Program (ERP), 29-32, 35, 43
Exchange rates, 6, 13, 23-24, 38, 46, 49-50, 58, 185-86, 189, 280-82, 284, 286; *see also* Currency; Foreign exchange; individual countries
External finance, 37, 55, 59, 260, 263; *see also* Foreign aid

Factor disequilibrium, 54ff.
Factor inputs, 52, 55-56, 59, 81, 95, 187-88
Financial intermediation, international, 193, 233-34, 240, 242, 248-50, 259, 263-64, 268-72, 274-76, 283-84; *see also* United States, financial intermediation
Fiscal policy, 45, 244, 263, 265, 275, 284
Fixed exchange rates, 179, 232, 262-63, 279
Foreign aid, 91-93, 228, 238, 256, 270

Foreign exchange, 46, 51, 85, 236-37, 258, 263; *see also* Currency
Foreign investment, controls, 3; *see* individual countries
France, 5, 8, 9, 16, 20, 63, 215, 226-27, 236-237, 253-55, 259-60, 262
Free trade, 45, 58, 61, 65-67, 73, 261, 265

General Agreement on Tariffs & Trade (GATT), 73, 82, 85-86
Germany, xii, 3, 13-27, 54, 186, 244, 250-55, 281
Gold, 3, 6, 9, 12, 175, 177, 212, 216, 218, 223, 227, 241, 246, 251-52, 261-64, 271-72, 277, 280; demonetization, viii, xv, 220-25, 236-56, 279-80; hoarding, 5, 211-12, 216, 278; international role, 29, 35, 216-18, 221, 229, 233, 252, 255, 258, 262, 277, 279, 282, 284; pool, 251, 279-82; speculation, 222, 261-62, 268, 271, 280; standard, 6, 7, 26, 58, 229-30, 232, 234-35
Great Britain, 3-9, 16, 34-35, 48, 66, 75, 78, 148, 158, 175, 179-81, 224, 231, 258-59; balance of payments, 4, 7, 35, 75, 175, 180, 183, 284; *see also* Sterling
Group of Ten, 252, 265
Growth effect, 63-65, 77-79

Haberler, Gottfried, 53, 56
Harrod, R. F., 49, 51
Hitler, Adolph, 13, 24
Hume, David, 239, 242, 278

Import barriers, 46, 50-52, 62, 64-66, 70, 72, 78, 80
Import substitution, 34, 41, 263
Income distribution, 52, 57-59, 188-89; inequality, 94-98
India, 11, 36-37, 95, 145, 183
Inflation, 50, 71, 75, 84, 93, 184-90, 193, 248, 258, 260, 263-64, 272, 276, 282-83; *see also* individual countries
Interest rates, 54, 181, 187, 189, 193, 245, 260, 263, 265, 267-68, 270, 272, 274-75
International Bank for Reconstruction & Development (IBRD), 74, 154, 160, 161
International capital markets, 240-44, 263-78, 283
International Clearing Union, xiii
International Monetary Fund (IMF), xiii, 75, 139, 167, 175, 177, 189, 212, 215, 220-21, 223, 227, 230, 251-55, 276-77, 281, 283
International monetary system, 182-83, 213-18, 220-36, 239-44, 257-67, 274-84; *see also* Currency; Dollar; Gold
Italy, 14, 54, 251, 275

Kennedy, John F., xiv
Kennedy Round, 237, 280
Key-currency approach, xvi, 229
Keynes, J. M., xiii, 46, 47, 102, 105, 238
Kindleberger, C. P., 45, 266
Kreuger, Ivar, 192, 197, 202

Less developed countries, 89-206; *see also* Brazil; Pakistan; Malaysia
Liquidity, 263-70, 284-85

Malaysia, 154-83; balance of payments, 154-63, 169-78, 182-83; budget, 157, 162, 165, 182; capital, 158-63, 168-69, 174-77; Central Bank, 158, 164, 173-75; controls, 160-61, 167; finance, 154-55, 160-69, 174-83; fiscal policy, 177-79; foreign exchange, 162-69, 174, 176, 182; growth, 163-68, 170-78; inflation, 163, 172-73, 182; investment, 155-56, 159-63, 166-70, 174-75; monetary policy, 165, 172-77, 181; planning, 156-57, 161, 168, 171, 173, 178; reserves, 154, 158-59, 164-66, 173-76, 181-82; trade, 159, 167, 172-76
Manoilesco, M., 56-57
Manufactures, 39-42, 55, 61, 65
Marshall Plan, xiv, 66, 83, 92, 228
Monetary policy, 72, 182, 184, 188-89, 264, 265, 275, 281, 284
Monopoly, 52, 58, 62-63, 145
Morgenthau, Henry, xiii
Mundell, R., 242, 248

NATO, 74, 84

Orcutt, Guy, 46
Organization for European Economic Cooperation (OEEC), 33, 39-43, 65-66, 72

Pakistan, 99-153; agriculture, 104-5, 133, 135, 142, 151; balance of payments, 107-8, 119-20; banking system, 100, 128-132; capital, 110-16, 119-20, 133-37, 140-44; controls, 103, 117, 133-39, 145, 147, 151-52; devaluation, 115-16, 141; development expenditures, 102, 106-10, 112, 114-15, 120, 123-26, 142, 151-52; Development Plan, 99-100, 102-3, 105-8, 111, 115, 118, 121-27, 138, 143-44, 151-53; foreign aid, 105, 108, 113, 116, 119-20, 123, 125; foreign exchange, 99-100, 102, 104-5, 107-8, 113, 116, 119-20, 123, 135-36, 139-41; import substitution, 100, 120; imports, 116-17, 119-20, 133, 141; income distribution, 103, 123, 136, 140-42, 147, 151; inflation, 103-4, 122-24, 130-32, 143-44; investment, 110-12, 125-26, 130, 143, 151; national income, 103, 111-13, 115-18, 152; Planning Board, 99, 114, 133, 136-39; Plan period, 109-11, 115-16, 118-19, price level, 102-4, 116-17, 141-44; price system, 133, 136-38, 141, 144; reserves, 108, 113-15, 122, 139; resource allocation, 126, 134, 136, 138-40, 142-44, 152; savings, 101-2, 107-18, 120-23, 129-32; tax system, 102-3, 138-40, 142-44, 147; terms of trade, 104, 113, 141-42; unemployment, 152-53; village aid, 110-11, 126
Planning, 51, 53, 59, 183, 265; *see also* individual countries
Population growth, 89-90, 92, 95
Price distortions, 133-46
Price system, 50-56, 94, 186-87
Primary products, 31, 34, 37, 40-42, 49, 56, 68, 78-79, 270
Protection, 38, 41, 56, 65, 69-70, 73, 79; *see also* Tariffs

Quereshi, Moen, 99, 106

Reichsbank, 14, 15, 16, 17, 26
Reichsmark, 17-22
Reserves, international, 240, 249, 255, 274; *see also* Dollar; Gold; Liquidity
Ricardo, David, 105
Robertson, Dennis, xv
Roosa, R., 237, 240, 266, 267
Rueff, J., 230

Salant, W., ix, xvi, 214, 266
Schacht, Hjalmar, 16, 26
Schlesinger, Arthur, Jr., xiv
South Korea, 47, 198, 202
Sterling, 9-12, 35-36, 164, 175, 229, 235, 258, 281; devaluation of, 177, 179, 181, 258, 281; *see also* Great Britain
Structural disequilibrium, 55ff.
Swap credits, 220-223, 226, 257
Switzerland, 3, 14, 16, 20, 227-28, 284

Tariffs, 38, 43, 64, 67, 73, 78, 263-65; *see also* individual countries; Protection
Technology, 40, 55, 62-63, 71, 77; transfer, 91, 95
Terms of trade, import/export, 33, 35-38, 48; agricultural/industrial, 48, 56-58; Western Europe, 40, 42, 44, 51, 55; *see also* individual countries
Trade, discrimination, 38, 48, 51, 54, 64, 66-67; gains from, 47, 57-59, 268; liberalization, 66, 70-76, 236, 238, 242, 244, 247, 249, 261, 264, 270, 280
Treaty of Rome, 60, 67, 69, 73, 79, 81-82
Triffin, R., 230, 243, 266, 278
Tripartite Monetary Agreement, 5, 6, 9, 75
Two-tier system, viii, 280

Unemployment, 45-49, 54-57, 68; disguised, 57; structural, 55
United States, agriculture, 69-71, 79-83; balance of payments, 67-68, 83-86, 179-183, 209-28, 243-49, 259-69, 271-80, 283-86; financial intermediation, 214-15, 224-26, 228, 230, 232, 239-43, 246-49, 267-69, 282-83; foreign aid, 29-37, 43, 55, 58, 89, 92, 105, 228-29; foreign trade, 67-69, 268-69, 285; gold drain, 213, 215, 219-21, 260-62, 280; inflation, 84, 282-83; interest rates, 225-26, 243, 265, 268, 272; reserves, 211-12, 214, 220-22, 259-60, 271; Treasury, 209, 210, 240, 250, 252; *see also* Capital flows; Currency; Dollar; Gold

Wages, real, 187, 188; *see also* Factor inputs
White, Harry, xiii, 229
Welfare state, 146-50
Williams, John, xvi, 228-29